The Language of Inquiry

THE PUBLISHER GRATEFULLY ACKNOWLEDGES THE

CONTRIBUTION PROVIDED BY THE GENERAL ENDOWMENT

FUND, WHICH IS SUPPORTED BY THE ASSOCIATES OF

THE UNIVERSITY OF CALIFORNIA PRESS

The Language of Inquiry

Lyn Hejinian

UNIVERSITY OF CALIFORNIA PRESS

Berkeley   Los Angeles   London

University of California Press
Berkeley and Los Angeles, California
University of California Press, Ltd.
London, England

Library of Congress Cataloging-in-Publication Data
Hejinian, Lyn.
    The language of inquiry / Lyn Hejinian.
        p.   cm.
    Includes bibliographical references and index.
    ISBN 0-520-21699-7 (cloth : alk. paper)—
    ISBN 0-520-21700-4 (pbk. : alk. paper)
        1. Hejinian, Lyn—Aesthetics.   2. Poetics.   I. Title.
    PS3558.E4735 L36 2000
    814'.54—dc21

                                    00-037776

09 08 07 06 05 04 03 02 01 00
10 9 8 7 6 5 4 3 2 1

TO

Finnian Ochs Hurtado

AND TO

THE MEMORY OF

Chaffee Earl Hall Jr.

CONTENTS

INTRODUCTION

In putting together this collection of essays, I have been aware of the fact that they will be read as poetics rather than poetry. But it would be a mistake to regard the poetics represented here as a discourse for which poetry is merely exemplary, one for which poetry stands at a distance, objectified and under scrutiny. Rather, these essays assume poetry as the dynamic process through which poetics, itself a dynamic process, is carried out. The two practices are mutually constitutive and they are reciprocally transformative. It is at least in part for this reason that poetry has its capacity for poetics, for self-reflexivity, for speaking about itself; it is by virtue of this that poetry can turn language upon itself and thus exceed its own limits.

Language is nothing but meanings, and meanings are nothing but a flow of contexts. Such contexts rarely coalesce into images, rarely come to terms. They are transitions, transmutations, the endless radiating of denotation into relation.

Poetry, to use William James's phrase, "is in the transitions as much as in the terms connected."[1] This is not to say that poetry is about transitions but that "aboutness" (in poetry, but, I would argue, also in life) is transitional, transitory; indeed, poetry (and perhaps life) calls conventional notions of "aboutness" into question.

Not all poets have an interest in poetics, and those who do hold very diverse notions of what such an interest might involve, what its scope and concerns might be, how much and what type of territory it might survey. For my own part, in reading over these essays, I realize that I have tended to cast *poetics* into the role of articulating how and why a poet works, elaborating her reasoning and reasons. *Poetics*, in this respect, seems as much a philosophical realm as a literary one. But it is a pragmatic realm, nonetheless; the reasons and reasoning that motivate poet (and poem) are embedded in the world and in the language with which we bring it into view. The resulting praxis is addressed to phenomenological and epistemological concerns.

But it is also a denotatively social and therefore political practice. Poetry comes to know that things are. But this is not knowledge in the strictest sense; it is, rather, acknowledgment—and that constitutes a sort of unknowing. To know *that* things are is not to know *what* they are, and to know *that* without *what* is to know otherness (i.e., the unknown and perhaps unknowable). Poetry undertakes acknowledgment as a preservation of otherness—a notion that can be offered in a political, as well as an epistemological, context.

This acknowledging is a process, not a definitive act; it is an inquiry, a thinking on. And it is a process in and of language, whose most complex, swift, and subtle forms are to be found in poetry—which is to say in poetic language (whether it occurs in passages of verse or prose). The language of poetry is a language of inquiry, not the language of a genre. It is that language in which a writer (or a reader) both perceives and is conscious of the perception. Poetry, therefore, takes as its premise that language is a medium for experiencing experience.

Poetic language is also a language of improvisation and intention. The intention provides the field for inquiry and improvisation is the means of inquiring. Or, to phrase it another way, the act of writing is a process of improvisation within a framework (form) of intention.

In the course of the experiencing of experience, poetic language puts into play the widest possible array of logics, and especially it takes advantage of the numerous logics operative in language, some of which take shape as grammar, some as sonic chains, some as metaphors, metonyms, ironies, etc. There are also logics of irrationality, impossibility, and a logic of infinite speed. All of these logics make connections, forge linkages. That, indeed, is the function of logics; they motivate the moves from one place to another. But the emphasis in poetry is on the moving rather than on the places—poetry follows pathways of thinking and it is that that creates patterns of coherence. It is at points of linkage—in contexts of encounter, at what André Breton called *points sublimes*—that one discovers the reality of *being in time*, of *taking one's chance*, of *becoming another*, all with the implicit understanding that *this is happening*. These notions are central even in the earliest of the essays collected here, though they are most explicit in the later ones.

The essays are presented chronologically. The first, "A Thought Is the Bride of What Thinking," was written in the spring of 1976, and the last, "Happily," was finished on February 1, 1999. For the most part, they have undergone only superficial revision, but each essay is preceded by a headnote describing something of the occasion in and for which it was written. Where I felt it necessary, I have attempted in the headnotes to "update" my thinking on certain topics. I chose to do this updating in headnotes rather than in revisions to the essays because the notion of "changing one's mind" is extremely important in aesthetics as in ethics. The phrase "there are no opposites" appears more than once in the poetry I have written; its companion phrase says "there are no end to contradictions." The headnotes, then, in addition to contextualizing the essays, are meant to assert their hermeneutic character and preserve the spirit of provisionality in which they were first written. That, too, is the spirit in which they are now offered.

The last essays in the book explicitly seek to place poetry in the most complex of experiential situations, that of being "in context." Like George Oppen, I am aware that poets work in the context of "being numerous." These essays were prompted by invitations and called into existence by occasions, but their true context is a community—literary and pedagogical—in which challenges and encouragement, provocations and excitement, contention and insights have been generated over the years in a mode which I would define as friendship of the most supreme kind. The spaces in which meaning occurs are social spaces, ones in which human practice as well as artistic practice is at stake.

These essays, then, are rooted in conversations with and writings by a number of friends, mostly poets and particularly those either closely or loosely associated with Language writing. For almost thirty years now, I have depended on the friendship and on the challenges they have offered. They have provided a context for my work; they have given it meaning and made the undertaking of it meaningful, at least to me. My gratitude for this is enormous.

At an immediate and practical level, this book is indebted to several people.

Hank Lazer was the first to suggest that I consider publishing a collection of essays. Michael Davidson and Charles Bernstein encouraged me to take the suggestion seriously, and it was Charles who first put me in touch with Linda Norton, my editor at the University of California Press. Linda has provided unswerving support to the project and to me as I undertook it, through friendship and, more important, through her understanding of the book itself, in whole and in its diverse parts.

At several points which I perceived as moments of crisis, I have received much-needed technical assistance from Anthony Miller and from Travis Ortiz, and I thank them most sincerely for their generosity and patience.

There are two other persons to whom I owe particular thanks and to whom I feel a magnitude of gratitude that is probably impossible to convey.

Lytle Shaw responded to my initial doubts about the sense and value of these essays (and hence about the worth of putting this book together) by offering not just adamant arguments in favor of the project but also prolonged and meticulous conversations about them. He has read through the contents of this book at every stage of its development, and his lengthy and inspiring commentary and criticism have provided the excitement as well as the ideas and information that made revisions and additions to the manuscript possible. If my arguments still aren't perfect and if my understanding remains incomplete, it is certainly not his fault.

Over the years, the person in conversation with whom I have most passionately tested thoughts and modes of thinking has been Barrett Watten. Without his example and guidance, I would be a far weaker and worse thinker than I am.

And above all, always, I thank Larry Ochs. He inhabits my continuous context and makes it a happy one.

Note

1. William James, *Essays in Radical Empiricism* (Cambridge, Mass.: Harvard University Press, 1976), 42.

A Thought Is the Bride
of What Thinking

Prose is not a genre but a multitude of genres.

Superficially, this says no more than that prose can be (and is) used in the service of one or another of numerous genres (all those, in fact, that are not poetry). But, this being the case, prose, taken in and of itself, may be regarded as the site of numerous simultaneous genres; it is a genre after all, a genre of multitudes.

In 1975, when I wrote the three short works that came to comprise "A Thought Is the Bride of What Thinking," it was in prose and in multitudes—in plethora, surfeit, plenitude, superabundance—that I was interested. One could interpret my interest in the latter as a product of youthful optimism, an affirmation of life in a physically and emotionally lively phase of it, but multitudinousness, as it exists both within and around anything, has been a sustained fascination, and not an untroubled one. Consciousness of the multitudinousness does not necessarily or exclusively warrant optimism.

Intrinsic to the existence of boundless multitudes is the impossibility of comprehensiveness and therefore of comprehension. Living in their midst, one has to acknowledge the impossibility of knowledge and do so in the context of perpetual change and inevitable mortality—of oneself as of everything. It is for this reason that these three prose pieces revolve around questions of order and disorder, capacities and incapacities, and this is why a degree of tension—of exuberant uneasiness—is evident, as the writing addresses, both explicitly and tonally, the conflict between confidence (competence, power) and doubt.

Consciousness of life has a tenacious and ambivalent relationship to it. Consciousness will not let go of life, and it is simultaneously and equally capable of inhibiting it and of enhancing it. Language has a similarly tenacious and ambivalent relation to thinking. (I would be more precise and say "to thinking about reality," but in my opinion there is nothing else to think about. The term "reality" embraces everything; reality is all there is.)

The torque that these relations exert on language is evident in these works.[1] Though I would have phrased it imprecisely at the time, I was in search of a mode of writing that could be multiply referential, densely contextual, with a capacity to be periodically surprised by its own inherent logics, and in the process of constantly either describing or suggesting possible narratives (histories). I also wanted a mode that was maximally enjambed, because I felt things to be under the pressure of abutment, contingency, and contiguity and hence constantly susceptible to change. One had to think quickly if one were to catch the ideas—the relationships—between things, and prose generally has greater velocity than poetry.

And so I found myself writing prose, in what seems in retrospect to be a markedly aphoristic mode—a mode of complete but heterogeneous thoughts. Various statements may seem succinct. Perhaps they are the result of compression, as if all the parts of a syllogism were condensed into a single excessive logical moment, but one with explosive properties. The language is also elliptical, inhabiting gaps but exhibiting gaps within itself also.

An interest in discovering and perhaps creating relationships between things is, in essence, a narrative interest. The anecdotal innuendoes, particularly in "The Virtues of the Dead, or, The Return," can be attributed to this. But they are also a result of the social conditions in which this work was written. From 1972 to 1977, I was living in a radically rural setting, without electricity and at a considerable distance from the nearest town, though not without a few neighbors. Even minor events tended to become subjects of anecdotes, and anecdotes tended to develop into full-blown stories through which things (and ourselves) could become connected to the events. In essence, language was being used to negotiate the boundaries between public and private and to join them.

A Thought Is the Bride of What Thinking was published by my own Tuumba Press (Willits, California, 1976) as the first volume in the Tuumba chapbook series. The works were originally part of a much longer (book-length) man-uscript entitled *The Inclusions,* but, though some of the poetry sections and a few other prose sections from that manuscript did appear in magazines, I eventually decided not to publish the book.

Variations: A Return of Words

Think again . . . the twin . . . its order inscribed.

Thought, or, advances. I have, for the aureate making of things, a further care.

Lucidities, or, lines. The starry angular varieties of recurrent word and changed idea in constellation gather. On the nectarine and on the clarinet distinction casts a light, the two in turn. One has only to look at the one to think to see the other.

Diversions, or, the guitar. It is in rereading one's notebooks, es-pecially the old ones, that one discovers the repetition of certain concerns, the recurrence of certain issues, certain chronic themes that are one's own. You ask that whatever comes out of the books on the shelf be new, but that is impossible. Certain themes are incurable.

(Repeatedly I come upon the ahistorical thought, particularly as it characterizes an idea of private life—an individual's thinking, or wishing to think, of him- or herself not only as unique but as uniquely experiencing. This pertains to thinking as well as to identity: one wants not just oneself but also one's response to life to be unprecedented. What one feels, what one experiences, then, would have more density and weight of life, more vivid clarity, than what others feel or experience. *My* love, *my* suffering, *my* insight, etc., would become incontrovertible—the ultimate assertion.

But it could insist only on the present. To be unprecedented is to take a particular relation to the past—the relationship of no relationship at all. This constitutes a romance, and, periodically, in pursuit of it artists have courted the special status of madness.

But the notion that insanity gives proof of the intensity of one's experience may be a misunderstanding of the case. It is just as likely that insanity represents the divorce of its victims from the actual, producing a state in which a private reality replaces the common one.)

The noble, or, the fierce. If a thing seems real, even if only for a short time, then is it real? Reality is both temporal and temporary; it must have a past tense. A cultural reality may make a change, and even, when what was thought to be characteristic turns out to have been merely apparent, come undone.

But a fantasy is a real thing. And contemporaneity is one form of fantasy, a form fantasy takes in writing. Coherence is not the difficulty.

Combination, or, the metaphor. Someone refers to "the courage of her convictions." The difficulty lies not so much in adhering to one's beliefs as in determining their object—what it is one is having beliefs about. This is particularly problematic in a world that is both overexposed and, at the same time, through the invasive sentimentalization of the private realm, concealed behind the titillating surfaces of public display.

Surrealism, or, the hooves of clattering trolleys. The figure of action is in motion, yet the movement is not what is seen. I hear the war. Is it a depiction of a confusion, or is it a spectacle?

On television the surreal is to be seen in nonrevolutionary form. I am thinking, for example, of the old show in which the hero's mother has returned from the dead in the form of a talking car.

(As I originally imagined this piece, it was to be a series of vignettes depicting varieties of nonsense, but instead of exhibiting pleasure, the result produced a cynicism, a sarcasm, that I didn't really feel. Certain forms of nonsense, apparently, constitute a limitation of pleasure. Poetry shouldn't succumb to piety, even with regard to illogicality and nonsense.)

Style, or, ink. One does throw up these shadows and distortions, casting minute gestures. People say, "Nothing's irrevocable," more to subdue their anxiety than to express a philosophy, as if the roundness of the world guaranteed a return, as if the possibility of a return guaranteed a second chance, and as if that justified a relaxation of intention. Or as if there were something to be read into the moment at which both a yellow warbler and the shadow of a cloud pass over a field—something which, in rendering the convergence of warbler and cloud exemplary, would see them as indifferent in themselves.

Devastation, or, the wreck. One can't write the words "war," "atrocity," "horror," etc., and by using them as names communicate the effect of what's named. This is because of the relation of language (and, in particular, naming) to measurement. The problem (if it is one) is with measurement—with incommensurability and with scale. Either there is one continual horror or there are different, discrete horrors each of which is constituted by one or many horrible occurrences within it. In neither case can a horror be taken as representative—as a horror which has absorbed all others. Horror, war, and atrocity have to be kept in mind as wrecks. And the brutality they produce can only elicit an emotional response, not a written one.

Further thought, or, further advances. This, or this again, in different terms, may serve to add either complication or clarification. In either case, thinking does in some cases contract but in most cases expand one's consciousness (one's consciousness of something but also of thinking). By contracting thought, I mean the painful and narrow circling that taunts the mind. Yet even here, further thought (and not necessarily of a different kind) can serve finally to propel one out of the morbid circle.

(Often what is critical when an idea is first related, is not to know the thought alone but to know who is thinking it, who is "in on" the idea, who is involved in it. This can indicate what's at stake—what's of interest and also (since having an idea does not preclude generosity) what's of disinterest. Take the idea that poetry is an art of linkages. It's an anecdotalist with a photo album who says so. He begins a story illustrated with a color photograph involving a woman in New Jersey and a cheetah, the woman and the cheetah in the photograph posing on the steps of a conventional ranch style home between matching junipers. The door to the house is open behind them. The animal is undeniably a cheetah. Listening to the story, I exercise my will to believe. This is not a matter of gullibility, and it is not merely a willing suspension of disbelief—it is an active, palpable, and I might even say decisive act of volition, and what's at stake is pleasure; it pleases me to believe in the woman in New Jersey and the cheetah. To do so is an act of irreverence, since I use the capacity for belief without rules and "without," as Paul Valéry puts it, "caring too much for the unequal weight of reality in the successive objects of [my] thoughts.")

As chance must lead you first one way and then another, and as comedy does not always sustain laughter but may provoke tears, so here what is reflected is not always what is visible, and art is seen not to be a mirror.

And here are some other representations which perhaps you would want to see with their misshapen letters and numerals, superior, polite, and strange.

If to think is to dance, it is to fall while dancing, as well; it is to dance among geese and elephants. Also, of course, it is to dance among albatrosses.

(The winds are so strong and constant in the Southern latitudes where the albatross is at home that the bird can rest in flight. Beneath it are the constantly rising waters and the battered triangles of their troughs.)

And the curving roofs of old houses in scattered villages.

There is an artistic approach which depends on what could be called a technique of first gestures. One makes a form, sketches it out, looks to see it, and pursues the suggestions it has made. The initial step is a gesture—or the result of a gesture. In writing, one writes out a first word or phrase (less often, a sentence or paragraph); in music, a first sound or texture of sound. These initial objects of one's alertnesses serve as the points of departure for a foray into the world and back again.

My earliest memory (though not necessarily my first) is of a yellow—I've always thought it to have been a single brilliantly yellow flower, a buttercup. From the earliest period of my life, the period before language, come other purely visual memories. I remember, for example, particular wallpapers—the small pink roses on the yellowing paper in my grandmother's room, the dark green unpatterned paper of the long living room, and the pink paper in my room, newly hung, which I tore off the wall in long strips one warm afternoon as I lay bored in my crib through an interminable "nap time." My father was home; it was summer and he was on the porch with his easel, painting.

Probably feelings can be communicated solely because they are much the same for everyone—banalities, in short. This is not to say that they are invalid, or stupid, or even absurd (though like anything else, they may be). Feelings are common to us all, never new, stunning only to the person feeling one or another of them at the time. Thoughts, however, can be effective whether or not one holds them in common with others.

Devastation, or, the wreck again. There have been heavy frosts this spring, and the blossoms on the fruit trees have been blackened. The blossoms are black as saints. The ants writhe in the sugar box.

Distortion, or, error. To err is to wander, probably in an unanticipated direction, inadvertently. The mistake is not necessarily without advantage, though it may be irrevocable.

Ink, or, the guitar. Returning from the middle distances, to the same points, repeatedly, from whatever direction, one homes, like a nomad or migrant. Perhaps that is a function of thought, nomadic homing—undertaken (consciously or not) in defiance of all narratives of progress.

Explanation, or, explication. In one's journal, one need only write a few words and they can serve as emblems for a full thought. But, nonetheless, it is there, in one's journal, that one tends to be most verbose. For oneself, one can write, say, Boot, or Inclusion, and summon the cogent images and their array of meanings. For others, however, explanations are due—and in the journal, they are forthcoming. The journal is not, then, a private document; it is sentimental and public.

(Nonsense [the comedic element that interrupts logic] depends on this, that the existence of a double [everything of which one can be conscious has a double] will always instigate a paradox— a contradictory return. It is comedy that's at stake in any argument. Not harmony but the simultaneity of conditions before and after something appears.)

Now, here is the sun at noon. It tilts even at the moment of telling of it. The vision climbs, the response is in retreat. The circle grows careless. The air quivers with the qua! qua! of fleeing geese, while the thought of their formation in flight lingers.

A Thought Is the Bride of What Thinking

Bravery is what they boast of.

The writer works from the inside out, but never gets out, partially because she can't and partially because, in any case, she doesn't want to.

It is only the mind, with its heart, that recognizes immaterial things; the senses are incapable of doing so.

The very long anecdote is to tell you that no one has been here for awhile.

Of course she made up every story she told, and you still believed them. Her geese kept rolling in the dust like dogs, or they rested like empty bottles.

She had been out in the dark, she said. Walking. There was this fat man staying with her, and he had taken his asthma medicine and they had lain talking in bed for a while. He'd been "visiting" a long time, and she guessed she cared for him, and she was good to his two little children. After a bit he thought to go sit in the garden to get his breath, and there he died. She came back from her walk and there he was in the moonlight among the little lettuces.

With the help of a neighbor she got him into his car and she drove him to the nearest hospital. She was arrested there for transporting a dead body. The children were taken away and put in "foster care."

Hawk this: the kitchen, the gas station, the shoes and socks, the toothpaste, the wooden chair, the box of noodles, the catsup and coffee, the aspirin, the water, the newspaper, the pencil, the coughing.

Every number is a nightfall. Think of tranquillity, feel tranquil— two different things. Of which are we keeping track? And if one came up with a different number, what would it mean, some rationalization of time? of experience? What's our position? the peacetime admiral bellows from his desk. The building hasn't moved in months. This morning the latitudinal and longitudinal figures are what they were yesterday. The admiral has pretended that the pavement is water since the war (which war?) began.

Poetry plays with order, makes order of disorder, and disorder of order. It is unwilling to distinguish reality from veracity, and veracity from tale, and sees what each word thinks to see.

It takes a positive though a pessimistic view of life. Much is amusing as much is disgusting, but there is no question of being afraid.

The Virtues of the Dead, or, The Return

Though the obscurity remains, the leaving off is inevitable. Someone else must rage and sorrow, hovering or thrown over the mortal smoke and wood, the mortal tongues, the mortal swinging and dark green, bricked in with activity. Now she's the patient mother, or the mother of patience itself, though perhaps she wondered what she'd been waiting for, during that last long episode of history.

Often during the last fifteen years of her life, she talked about her death. She told the family that she wanted to be buried in a bronze coffin. When she did die, finally, the request was honored, though no one in the family approved. Their disapproval, in fact, was the main topic of conversation throughout the period before the funeral and afterwards. It was the focus for all their subsequent reminiscences about her.

To what degree can one govern one's personality? or even control the outward signs of one's personality? If one admires quiet people but is naturally garrulous, can one change one's habits and do so permanently? And isn't there something dishonest in artifice at this level?

I am not afraid to curse you.

I am not afraid of anger.

I divide you with my anger; may you fall apart.

May you be separated from what you love, what you love and what you hate.

May your tongue fall out and may all that you had said be forgotten.

May your fingers be frozen and your home lost, but most of all, your tongue and your right eye.

May you be divided in that way.

The pathway to the heart, he said, and a dignified death. Time has a switch on us. You shrink as you stand, of course; but who's to know? Out beyond the stars the hours grow, unhampered by the dirt clods. Here lies a kid only a day old. Beside him, his grandfather, eighty-nine. The life simply went out of him. And here is he whose father and children outlived him, in the dimensions of their present lives.

What was a passion, what now a pencil. What was a sunset going down. What in winter was (an) abandoned (wasps' nest) now writhes. What I wrote was engraved in the typewriter. What was a letter has been sent.

Writing—out of place and as if off the top of one's head—seems much easier with a typewriter than with a pen. The mind remains free of its own particular terms (the terms proper to it) by being distanced, visually and tactilely, from the paper. And the privacy of the thought is shielded by the clatter, just as background music provides a wall of sound which obliterates the presence of everyone, including oneself.

This anonymous privacy renders the moral qualities of the artist irrelevant; she may be a liar and a cheat, a murderer, a sneak and a thief, or indeed a generous and saintly person.

It is important, however, to think about everything—or, at least, anything—but not in such a way that one loses all pleasure.

I believe in the . . . of the cold dark room, pinecone, piano. One responds—it's the responsibility makes me—say, the real is as real does.

Certainty is given to the simple-minded. To know what one thinks under all circumstances, to have definite and final opinions, is a matter of doubt to the ethical intellect. It is matter for doubt. (This doesn't deprive one of the capacity for making decisions, which come in the thick of things, though maybe arbitrarily.)

The room is dark in its four corners. Something drapes the walls.

One wishes for an inclusive art: of what occurs, the corollaries, and to what occurs, the tangents.

On Wednesday afternoon, a friend said, "You can't say anything unless you can say everything; that's not what Hegel said but it's what he meant to say." You can say everything but always only potentially.

To say everything, or to attempt to do so, could be taken as an act of integrity, insofar as integrity may be defined as "the condition of having no part or element taken away or wanting; undivided or unbroken state; material wholeness, completeness, entirety." This shouldn't drive one to "a full confession." Nor to the dangerous purism of a conventional dictionary definition of the ethical ("the condition of not being marred or violated; unimpaired or uncorrupted condition; original perfect state; soundness").

The artistic act has integrity to the extent that it is a generally inclusive reckoning, an outlook, taking anything into account, the diverse and the disparate. The artist, thereby, displays a vast tolerance and an infinite capacity for questioning, and her work exerts the moral force of combination. It constitutes a relation.

She must be both responsive and responsible, since her work will reflect an intensity of response, reciprocal with the world.

In Athens there is a memorial on which is this inscription:

> The People of the Oropians
> to Timarchos, Son of Theodosos
> on Account of His Virtue

George Seferis, in his journal, responded: "I do not know this Timarchos, nor his virtue. Never mind, they felt the need to mention it."[2]

Notes

1. One of the finest discussions of this "torque" occurs in Ron Silliman's essay "The New Sentence," in *The New Sentence* (New York: Roof Books, 1987).

2. George Seferis, *A Poet's Journal*, tr. Athan Anagnostopoulos (Cambridge, Mass.: Harvard University Press, Belknap Press, 1974), 198.

Preface to *Writing Is an Aid to Memory*

In the fall of 1977, not long after my family and I had moved back to Berkeley from Mendocino County (and into a neighborhood very near where I had lived as a child), Geoff Young, the editor of The Figures, invited me to write a manuscript for his press. The result was *Writing Is an Aid to Memory*.[1] In that work, I attempted to explore some epistemological relationships that hold time to language and language to time. This is an area that continued to fascinate me, and I took up the problem again when writing *My Life* (the book that followed *Writing Is an Aid to Memory*), but while in *My Life* I was interested in posing sentences and blocks of sentences (paragraphs) as units of time, in *Writing Is an Aid to Memory* I was working in a mode that was more elemental, more obviously (and more radically) materialist, and my interest was in building time. I wanted to release the flow of accumulated time in syntax and thereby to make time happen. Obversely, I wanted to release the flow of accumulated syntax in time and thereby make sentences (and their concomitant thoughts) happen. In both cases, I felt that formations of knowledge could be made perceptible—offering a picture of knowledge underway.

Language gives structure to awareness. And in doing so it blurs, and perhaps even effaces, the distinction between subject and object, since language is neither, being intermediate between the two.

The Preface was written after the poem, and in substance it can perhaps best be said to consist of traces of it.

I am always conscious of the disquieting runs of life slipping by, that the message remains undelivered, opposed to me. Memory cannot, though the future return and proffer raw confusions. Knowledge is part of the whole, as hope is, from which love seeks to contrast knowledge with separation, and certainty with the temporal. Abridgment is foolish, like a lopping off among miracles; yet times are not enough. Necessity is the limit with forgetfulness, but it remains undefined. Memory is the girth. Mute and blind at its disposal, each can express, say, moral attitudes but does not have the power to say different things at one time with or without different parts or view—a merchant, inventor, politician, and mechanics. Or a body of elements, ideas, such as anything slender with certainty requires—without repetition of bulk, melancholy, or distance. And flesh else like one in clothing and colors to become versatile, sinews and bones in great versatility. One calls from experience origin and ends in a manual activity, seems vain activity, and terminates another at the middle known to one as doubt. Certainty senses which essence is reopened about cessation and open tongues: -vities, -vatives, known and do but the proper commentary. The distant person carries science and lying. Argument demonstrates that truth cannot end. Continuous quantities, like continuous qualities, are endless like the truth, for it is impossible to carry them. It is impossible to carry light and darkness, proximity, chance, movement, restlessness, and thought. From all of these, something spills. The greatest gifts are returned by influences, and sometimes beauty turns my attention by endeavor, where action is beyond praise and courage so increased beyond the true—as if the true were an arithmetic or fame and could increase.

I would add greatly to the beauty by those feeling conversant; but where to put it? With its indispensable side out, where nothing is greater, the laws of shadowy detail, to the smallest detail, even of the corpses of criminals held long in prison, as inhuman medicine, sketching the action from the insides of the bones and exploring what has been a mind, unknown. I am pressed with questions as if posed and feverish with a peculiar greed. Incessant knowledge and the natural sciences of difficulty, brilliance, complexity, and generosity, to please an entire face, where sorrow by the fact is not of true greatness. Work is retarded by such desire, which is anticipation of its certainty, and hence a desire impossible of satisfaction, in the future despite the grand decision to pull it present. It is that interest as lapse of time, that wanting to put too much in, is forgetting, or the forgotten calling attention. The whole has been given away and looking out is a forgetting sent without to end all the commoner.

The trees of street are laid down. A bedroom is cut where I went. Where I mean to will have to come to me. Though we keep company with cats and dogs, all thoughtful people are impatient, with a restlessness made inevitable by language.

Note

1. Lyn Hejinian, *Writing Is an Aid to Memory* (Berkeley: The Figures, 1978; reprinted Los Angeles: Sun & Moon Press, 1996).

If Written Is Writing

"If Written Is Writing" was written in 1978, specifically for one of the first issues of Bruce Andrews and Charles Bernstein's journal L=A=N=G=U=A=G=E, the advent of which seemed to invite (and even demand) response. Like most of the other poets with whom I was in constant conversation during this time, I felt under increasing pressure to write essays—or, rather, to write thinking: to propose, and especially to involve, poetry with politics and metaphysics. Such a project was very much at odds with commonly held notions of poetry as an unworldly enterprise. The sense of being at odds—the frustration of being misunderstood—contributed to the pressure to write theory. But it was the need to discover relations between writing and the world and to relate those discoveries to others that gave the deeper sense of urgency to the task of writing thinking or theory. What was at stake was the definition of poetry, and that mattered a great deal, but also at stake were the ways we could negotiate reality.

The editors of L=A=N=G=U=A=G=E proposed that the theory need not be extrinsic to the poetry. They did not require a normalized, expository style.[1] In "If Written Is Writing" I undertook an integrated style; it is not inappropriate that it has an underlying anti-idealist theme. The argument would go something like this: reality exists; it is independent of what we think though it is the only thing we can think; we are a part of reality but at the same time consciousness of this fact makes us separate from it; we have a point of reentry (a "centrique happinesse"), which is language, but our reentry is hesitant, provisional, and awkward. It is also a never-ending entry, a process which I may have been equating with life, though if so I did not make that equation explicit; the equation of the process of perpetual re-entry with writing, however, is explicit.

Though the hesitant, inefficient, and phrase-based style of the work may mimic speech, it is impossible to construe this piece as spoken; it is obviously writing. The writtenness of it was important, since I wanted to propose writing as a material manifestation, an embodiment, of desire for reality.

This desire drives us backward into the past as well as forward; that is, the reality we desire precedes us, we remember it. That is what the title "If Written Is Writing" attempts to indicate.

I think of you, in English, so frequent, and deserved, and thereby desired, their common practice and continually think of it, who, since the Elizabethans, save Sterne and Joyce, have so trothed language to the imagination, and Melville, of whose *Mardi* the critics wrote, in 1849, "a tedious, floundering work of uncertain meaning or no meaning at all. A hodgepodge. . . . A story without movement, or proportions, or end . . . or point! An undigested mass of rambling metaphysics."[2]

No-one is less negligent than you, to render the difficulties less whether well-protected, in grammar, in which it has been customary to distinguish *syntax* from *accidence*, the latter tending to the inflections of words—inflections, or toward itself, a bending in. The choices have always been fashioned and executed from within. Knowing is right and knowing is wrong. Nodding is, or could be, to you.

In such are we obsessed with our own lives, which lives being now language, the emphasis has moved. The emphasis is persistently centric, so that where once one sought a vocabulary for ideas, now one seeks ideas for vocabularies. Many are extant. Composition is by. The technique is very cut and the form is very close. Such is surprising even now, if overdue. Now so many years ago Donne wrote, "Some that have deeper digg'd loves Myne than I, / Say, where his centrique happinesse doth lie. . . ."[3]

The text is anterior to the composition, though the composition be interior to the text. Such candor is occasionally flirtatious, as candor is nearly always so. When it is trustworthy, love accompanies the lover, and the centric writers reveal their loyalty, a bodily loyalty. Quite partial is necessity, of any text. Marvelous are the dimensions and therefore marveling is understandable—and often understanding. Much else isn't, but comes, from the definite to an indefinite, having devised excuses for meeting, though we have not yet found it recognized, through a selection, or choice. The original scale determines the scope, the mood, the feel, the tone, the margin, the degree, the mathematics, the size, the sign, the system, the pursuit, the position, the mark.

Of centricities, an interior view, there are two sources, perhaps three. One locates in the interior texture of such language as is of the person composing from it, personal and inclusive but not necessarily self-revelatory—in fact, now, seldom so; through improvisatory techniques building on the suggestions made by language itself—on patterns of language which are ideas and corresponding behavior or relevant quirks. This becomes an addictive motion—but not incorrect, despite such distortion, concentration, condensation, deconstruction, and digressions that association by, for example, pun and etymology provide; an allusive psycho-linguism. In the second it is the bibliography that is the text. The writing emerges from within a pre-existent text of one's own devising or another's. The process is composition rather than writing.

There are characteristic, contracting rhythms. The long line, with ramifying clauses, an introductory condition, and other cumulative devices have been fragmented, the rhythm accentuated. You can read. You can write. An unstable condition is given pause. The Elizabethans were given to a long system and we to purchase for pause, though not stop.

A possible third centricity, the perhaps, emerges from the imperatives and prerogatives of grammar. Such might be a work of, say, conjunctions, in which, for example, John Lloyd Stephens writes, "There is no immediate connection between taking Daguerreotype portraits and the practice of surgery, but circumstances bring close together things entirely dissimilar in themselves, and we went from one to the other."[4] And in a guide to French grammar I read, "Linking is rare between a plural noun and a verb or between a plural adjective and a verb except in poetry."

All theory is most inventive when ascribed in retrospect. On the line is an occasion to step off the line. The critic is a good or bad player. The cat gets the chair and you get the edge.

Conclusion:

By usual standing under half.

Notes

1. As a result, of course, they risked inviting a kind of belletrism into existence. And though the risk was well worth taking, since many pieces of enormous power were published in the journal, it was to avoid the superficialities of belletrism that Barrett Watten and I, in editing *Poetics Journal,* encouraged relatively long essays with room for a full development of ideas.

2. Elizabeth S. Foster, Historical Note in Herman Melville, *Mardi* (Evanston and Chicago: Northwestern University Press and The Newberry Library, 1970), 668.

3. John Donne, "Loves Alchymie," in *The Complete Poetry of John Donne,* ed. John T. Shawcross (Garden City, N.Y.: Anchor Books/ Doubleday & Company, 1967), 126.

4. John Lloyd Stephens, *Incidents of Travel in the Yucatan* (Norman: University of Oklahoma Press, 1962), 1:69–70.

Who Is Speaking?

The question "Who is speaking?" is uttered from within the social relationship that binds together the problematics of power and ethicality. As the question was first posed in the early 1980s as a topic for discussion by a group of Bay Area women poets and intellectuals, it constituted a challenge to certain styles of discourse, lest they begin to circumscribe possibilities in the public life of the poetry community. Erudite, authoritative, contentious—that was one of the public voices of poetry. To contribute to its formation, one had to be able to produce commentary with enormous rapidity. One had to know a lot and to know that one did so. One had to feel oneself to be on firm ground, ready to deliver and parry challenges. That this generally came more easily to men than to women was not unpredictable, though not all of the women in the scene felt ungrounded and not all the men in the scene were speaking. The men and women who weren't speaking did not feel powerless, however. To invent other public formations —even to enact an ungrounding—seemed desirable, even necessary, and it certainly seemed possible.

The question "Who is speaking?" was intended as a challenge to a perceived style of asserting power and to the structures of power that were being created by it. It was directed not at any specific group of persons but at the problem of power itself, and—contrary, perhaps, to more typical feminist challenges to power structures of the period—the discussion did not constitute a rejection of power. Instead, it revolved around questions of grounds and goals, of dialogue and efficacy, and to some extent it aspired to an increased impersonal freedom for everyone. We were espousing an admittedly utopian enterprise—one that was attached to a virtually explicit agenda underlying every poetry discussion at the time; it was intrinsic to our poetics, and its clear aim was to improve the world.

The grandiosity of that ambition may at first glance seem laughable. But it is only so if one assumes that "to improve the world" requires that one improve it forever. That ambition is indeed laughable—or it would be if it weren't horrifyingly dangerous and if the history of the twentieth century didn't include so many examples of atrocity perpetrated in the name of improving the world forever. Such an aspiration underlies all totalitarianism and all bigotry. It is inherently transcendental, since a world "improved forever" would be an unworldly world, and its poetry would be a transcendental enterprise.

But the fact of the matter is that the world requires improving (reimproving) every day. Just as one can't prepare an all-purpose meal and dine once and then be done with the preparation and consumption of food forever, so one cannot come to the end of the fight for social justice and ecological safety, for example, forever. Victories are particular, local, and almost always temporary. To improve the world, one must be situated in it, attentive and active; one must be worldly. Indeed, worldliness is an essential feature of ethics. And, since the term poetics names not just a theory of techniques but also attentiveness to the political and ethical dimensions of language, worldliness is essential to a poetics.

Poetics entails involvement in public life. And that involvement, in turn, demands a negotiation with, and a willingness to take on, power.

In this context, the question "Who is speaking?" prompts a second question, one that is addressed to oneself as the speaker of the first: "Am I speaking?"

From this, numerous questions follow: If not, why not? Isn't it incumbent on me to break through others' noise and my own silence so as to speak? If so, how so? Having broken through into speech, what should I say and what should it sound like when I'm saying it? Is it important to speak? Is it necessary to do so? Can one be a participant without speaking? Should silence be construed as protest? As complicity? Who or what is the authority that "permits" one to speak, and on what grounds is that authority established and/or asserted? What authority do I gain by speaking, first, in any particular act (moment) of doing so and second, as one who is often one of the speakers? What is the relationship between private creativity and participation in public discourse? Is a public context a necessary component of private work? What is the relationship of public speech to published writing —are these similar public positions? Is writing formed in a social context, as part of a dialogue, or is writing formed prior to the dialogue, then becoming part of it? Who or what determines (and what are the criteria for determining) that what has been said was "good"? What does it mean when one feels one "doesn't have anything to say"? What is the nature of a community of discourse? Is there a style of discourse that is effective and valuable without being oppressive? Many such questions were formulated in private conversation before asking the original question, "Who Is Speaking?" in public.

If, as many of us have claimed, the practice of poetry, in being a study of language, involves alertness to and critique of its misuse, and if its misuse in the form of public hypocrisy is one of the outstanding problems of our time, then it was incumbent on us to develop modes of invention which were not hypocritical. This should not be interpreted as a demand for the invention of honesty. The notion of honesty tends to be equated with truthtelling, and we felt a genuine distaste for both inherited and discovered notions of Truth. But it did, over time, develop into a demand for honesty of invention. The question "Who is speaking?" asked who was inventing and what was being invented.

A panel discussion on the question took place in San Francisco at Intersection for the Arts on March 26, 1983. The panelists were Gloria Frym, Robert Glück, Johanna Drucker, and myself.[1] This event was the culmination in public of private conversations, but in many ways I see it now as an initial, rather than as a final, step.

It was an early intervention into the process of inventing.

What follows is a slightly revised version of my contribution to that panel. In my manuscript copy of it, it begins with an epigraph in the form of a quotation, unattributed but probably from a news article: "75% of all Americans interviewed prefer death to public speaking."

Invention is central to the private as to the public life of a writer, but it is of the latter that I want to speak on this occasion. At stake in the public life of a writer are the invention of a writing community; the invention of the writer (as writer and as person) in that community; and the invention of the meanings and meaningfulness of his or her writing.

Almost every writer is faced with the relentless necessity of inventing him- or herself anew as a writer every day, and the task of considering the terms in which this can be accomplished is an ongoing one.

But the invention of oneself as a writer in a community is only part of a larger question; it should be accompanied by the necessity for inventing that community, and thereby participating in the making of the terms that, in turn, themselves play a crucial role in making invention possible (or, in bad scenarios, impossible). One must think about the invention of the community in and as consideration of the politics, ethics, and psychology of speaking in it. And one must do all this even while addressing the question of how the community and one's way of being in it influences one's writing.

The question of community and creativity is not one issue but a whole complex of interrelated public and private issues, and as one brings the pressure of one's attention to bear on one of them, another of them rises up, requiring that one adjust one's emphasis. But this adjusting of emphasis is essential to keeping the relationship between oneself and the community viable and productive.

Doing so is not easy. There is an inevitable conflict between community and creativity, and writers very often feel torn between the possibilities of solitude and the requirements of the social. Caught in such conflicts, one might ask why one would want to invent a community in the first place. Do we need community? Do we want one?

One quick way to answer this is to say that, want it or not, we have it. And this is the case not just because the world is with us. To the extent that humans know about humans, community occurs. A community consists of any or all of those persons who have the capacity to acknowledge what others among them are doing. In this sense, even solo sailors and hermits living in total isolation in desert or mountain caves belong to communities—communities, in the broadest sense, consisting of the persons for whom solo sailing or hermitism is meaningful.

These communities do not, as such, preexist the solo sailing or the hermit's retreat. In a profound sense, the person setting forth alone to sail or entering his or her hermit's cave, in doing so summons into existence the community in which to do so makes sense—even if, as will sometimes be the case, it is not a present but a past (though not, strictly speaking, preexisting) or future community, consisting of those whose past or future capacity to understand, that is being invoked.

Any characteristic act—whether it is a sailor's sailing or a hermit's withdrawal or a writer's writing—is an act of reciprocal invocation. It activates a world in which the act makes sense. It invents.

Invention, in the literary as in many other contexts, is a term nuanced toward reciprocity—between the creative imagination and utility, between originality and the world. As an act brings a community into being, the community must be there to provide advocacy (or publication, in the broad as well as literal or literary sense—bringing the act into a public space), social and professional support, intellectual challenge, aesthetic stimulus, etc. The community creates the context in which the work's happening happens. It does so by generating ideas and work that might not have come into being otherwise, and, in the best sense, by challenging everyone involved. In this last respect, a community presents a more difficult milieu than that of the support group. To be simultaneously permissive and rigorous is the challenging task that a highly functional community must attempt. A community that can manage it will be an improvement to the world that is always with us.

A community of discourse develops and is maintained through speaking—by which I mean articulate participation of various kinds. In the course of this constitutive speaking, terms come into use that define the community to a certain extent and, more importantly, charge it. These may be literal terms—key words or phrases that designate particular or general ideas of mutual concern and around which there is some shared excitement (though not necessarily always agreement): *ostranenie, parataxis,* and *the new sentence* are possible examples. Or, in a community of writers, the terms might include the titles of literary works or names of publishers or publications or even literary events—particulars that have extension, structural or thematic; particulars in and from which things are happening.

There is, of course, the danger that such terms can become tyrannical—that they will circumscribe the community or that the power embedded in them is of the kind that some persons can wield over others. Also, and perhaps to some extent this is unavoidable, the terms may appear to be, and so become, exclusionary—marking the difference between the inside and the outside of the community and effectively discouraging participation. Or the terms may serve to edit the speaking of the community rather than encourage it, with the result that speech turns into dialect and the terms become a form of closure, the means to a community's self-destruction.

Silencing in a community, of course, does not always come from the community's terms. Silencings occur that are manifestations of a drama whose history is longer than that of any community. One participates in it fearfully, hesitating or even failing to speak lest doing so will reveal one's presence, or the presence of one's ideas, to a predator or enemy, one who may figuratively if not literally gobble one up. One may refrain from speaking because one is afraid of being wrong, or irrelevant, or intrusive (an idle chatterbox), or inarticulate and intellectually clumsy, or ignorant. One may remain silent, in other words, because one is afraid of being exposed (stripped bare by the bachelors). One may sit in silence feeling intimidated, or confused; one may be bored but ashamed to be bored.

Or one may sit in silence feeling self-righteous. There is a curious virtuousness ascribed to silence. We see it inscribed in such aphorisms as "Silence is golden," "Still waters run deep," or "The wise man speaks little and listens well." Behind such prescriptive dicta are a disdain for explanation and a privileging of action. They can serve as injunctions, and their effect, if not necessarily their intention, is to encourage one to keep one's opinions inviolate and apolitical. Silence in this context renders one apolitical precisely because it removes one from the public sphere— the sphere in which ideas are aired and experiences (stories) exchanged.

But a distinction must be made; the silences that occur in a community are not necessarily silencings. Silence is inherent to speech itself—for speech to be meaningful, there must be not only the speaking of the speaker but the silence of the listener.

Can we call this a communicative silence? a communicating one?

Certainly it can be. Borrowing a phrase from Heidegger's "Logos" essay, one might say that such a silence "gathers everything present into presence, and lets it present itself."

Heidegger, however, was talking not about silence but about *logos*, and, since *logos* is usually translated as word, or speech, or reason, *logos* would seem to be the opposite of silence.

But this need not be the case. *Logos* is the opposite of *silencing*. The *logos* of the listener exists in and as his or her readiness and availability, his or her willingness and capacity to be the one who waits to tell, the one who will make an experience of what the speaker says; it can be a ready silence, a contextualization.

The alternative, the refusal of listening resulting in the experience of not-being-listened-to, is a problem which has always vexed women and other "others." Our speech is regarded as trivial, second-class, since it is held to originate not in the public world (of free men) but in the private and domestic sphere (maintained by women and servants). Because of this, it is also regarded as disgusting, since the domestic sphere is the realm of the body—the *domus* being where the body is kept fed, clothed, and clean, where it procreates, defecates, and regularly retreats into the world of greatest privacy and secrecy, the world of sleep and dreams. And finally, because women have knowledge of things of this sphere, our speech is regarded as frightening.

The question "Who is speaking?" implies, then, yet another question: "Who is listening?" Consideration of how speaking is being heard and what is being heard in and of it involves another address to power. Listening accords power to speech. It grants it its logic by discovering logic in it. In listening as in speaking, both meaningfulness and meaning are at stake. To trace the lines of reciprocity through which they are established is to map a social space, a community.

But this metaphor should be used with caution. A community is not a geography, not a fixed and stable terrain, and any map of it is temporary. Communities are mobile and mutable, and they are not always easily habitable. A demanding community can be exhausting, to speakers and listeners alike, and its participants must be allowed private experiences as well as public ones. If, as a member of a community, one is flourishing, one may not be inclined to ask questions of it. But if one is not, it is crucial to do so, in order to discover and accomplish what is to be done.

Note

1. Robert Glück's panel paper, "Who Speaks for Us: Being an Expert," appears in *Writing/Talks*, ed. Bob Perelman (Carbondale: Southern Illinois University Press, 1985).

The Rejection of Closure

"The Rejection of Closure" was originally written as a talk and given at 544 Natoma Street, San Francisco, on April 17, 1983.[1] The "Who Is Speaking?" panel discussion had taken place several weeks earlier, and with the "Poetry & Philosophy" issue of *Poetics Journal* (volume 3) about to come out, Barrett Watten and I had just decided to devote *Poetics Journal* 4 to the theme of "Women & Language."[2] Within the writing community, discussions of gender were frequent, and they were addressed both to perceptible practical problems (instances of injustice) immediately affecting people's work and lives and to longer-term questions of power and, in particular, the ethics of meaning.

Carla Harryman's signal work, *The Middle,* was published this same year. Originally given as a talk, it is an organizationally radiant critique (one might even say trashing) of conventional (patriarchal) power structures.[3] In *The Middle,* the power of authority gives way to the power of invention, with its plenitudes of focus, and to the power of performance. The subject position is in the middle—an uncontainable presence making meaning.

In "The Rejection of Closure," I give no examples of a "closed" text, but

I can offer several. The coercive, epiphanic mode in some contemporary lyric poetry can serve as a negative model, with its smug pretension to universality and its tendency to cast the poet as guardian to Truth. And detective fiction can serve as a positive model, presenting an ultimately stable, calm and calming (and fundamentally unepiphanic) vision of the world. In either case, however pleasurable its effects, closure is a fiction, one of the amenities that falsehood and fantasy provide.

But if we have positive as well as negative models for closure, why reject it? Is there something about the world that demands openness? Is there something in language that compels and implements the rejection of closure?

I can only begin a posteriori, by perceiving the world as vast and overwhelming; each moment stands under an enormous vertical and horizontal pressure of information, potent with ambiguity, meaning-full, unfixed, and certainly incomplete. What saves this from becoming a vast undifferentiated mass of data and situation is one's ability to make distinctions. The open text is one which both acknowledges the vastness of the world and is formally differentiating. It is form that provides an opening.

Two dangers never cease threatening
the world: order and disorder.
 Paul Valéry, *Analects*

Writing's initial situation, its point of origin, is often characterized and always complicated by opposing impulses in the writer and by a seeming dilemma that language creates and then cannot resolve. The writer experiences a conflict between a desire to satisfy a demand for boundedness, for containment and coherence, and a simultaneous desire for free, unhampered access to the world prompting a correspondingly open response to it. Curiously, the term *inclusivity* is applicable to both, though the con-

notative emphasis is different for each. The impulse to bounded-
ness demands circumscription and that in turn requires that a dis-
tinction be made between inside and outside, between the rele-
vant and the (for the particular writing at hand) confusing and
irrelevant—the meaningless. The desire for unhampered access
and response to the world (an encyclopedic impulse), on the other
hand, hates to leave anything out. The essential question here
concerns the writer's subject position.

The impasse, meanwhile, that is both language's creative con-
dition and its problem can be described as the disjuncture be-
tween words and meaning, but at a particularly material level,
one at which the writer is faced with the necessity of making for-
mal decisions—devising an appropriate structure for the work,
anticipating the constraints it will put into play, etc.—in the con-
text of the ever-regenerating plenitude of language's resources,
in their infinite combinations. Writing's forms are not merely
shapes but forces; formal questions are about dynamics—they ask
how, where, and why the writing moves, what are the types, di-
rections, number, and velocities of a work's motion. The mate-
rial aporia objectifies the poem in the context of ideas and of lan-
guage itself.

These areas of conflict are not neatly parallel. Form does
not necessarily achieve closure, nor does raw materiality provide
openness. Indeed, the conjunction of *form* with radical *openness*
may be what can offer a version of the "paradise" for which writ-
ing often yearns—a flowering focus on a distinct infinity.

For the sake of clarity, I will offer a tentative characterization
of the terms *open* and *closed*. We can say that a "closed text" is one
in which all the elements of the work are directed toward a single
reading of it. Each element confirms that reading and delivers

the text from any lurking ambiguity. In the "open text," meanwhile, all the elements of the work are maximally excited; here it is because ideas and things exceed (without deserting) argument that they have taken into the dimension of the work.

Though they may be different in different texts, depending on other elements in the work and by all means on the intention of the writer, it is not hard to discover devices—structural devices—that may serve to "open" a poetic text. One set of such devices has to do with arrangement and, particularly, with re-arrangement within a work. The "open text," by definition, is open to the world and particularly to the reader. It invites participation, rejects the authority of the writer over the reader and thus, by analogy, the authority implicit in other (social, economic, cultural) hierarchies. It speaks for writing that is generative rather than directive. The writer relinquishes total control and challenges authority as a principle and control as a motive. The "open text" often emphasizes or foregrounds process, either the process of the original composition or of subsequent compositions by readers, and thus resists the cultural tendencies that seek to identify and fix material and turn it into a product; that is, it resists reduction and commodification. As Luce Irigaray says, positing this tendency within a feminine sphere of discourse, "It is really a question of another economy which diverts the linearity of a project, undermines the target-object of a desire, explodes the polarization of desire on only one pleasure, and disconcerts fidelity to only one discourse." [4]

"Field work," where words and lines are distributed irregularly on the page, such as Robert Grenier's poster/map entitled *Cambridge M'ass* and Bruce Andrews's "Love Song 41" (also originally published as a poster), are obvious examples of works in which the order of the reading is not imposed in advance.[5] Any reading of these works is an improvisation; one moves through the work not in straight lines but in curves, swirls, and across intersections, to words that catch the eye or attract attention repeatedly.

Repetition, conventionally used to unify a text or harmonize its parts, as if returning melody to the tonic, instead, in these works, and somewhat differently in a work like my *My Life*, challenges our inclination to isolate, identify, and limit the burden of meaning given to an event (the sentence or line). Here, where certain phrases recur in the work, recontextualized and with new emphasis, repetition disrupts the initial apparent meaning scheme. The initial reading is adjusted; meaning is set in motion, emended and extended, and the rewriting that repetition becomes postpones completion of the thought indefinitely.

But there are more complex forms of juxtaposition. My intention (I don't mean to suggest that I succeeded) in a subsequent work, "Resistance," was to write a lyric poem in a long form—that is, to achieve maximum vertical intensity (the single moment into which the idea rushes) and maximum horizontal extensivity (ideas cross the landscape and become the horizon and weather).[6] To myself I proposed the paragraph as a unit representing a single moment of time, a single moment in the mind, its content all the thoughts, thought particles, impressions, impulses—all the diverse, particular, and contradictory elements—that are included in an active and emotional mind at any given instant. For the moment, for the writer, the poem *is* a mind.

To prevent the work from disintegrating into its separate parts —scattering sentence-rubble haphazardly on the waste heap— I used various syntactic devices to foreground or create the conjunction between ideas. Statements become interconnected by being grammatically congruent; unlike things, made alike grammatically, become meaningful in common and jointly. "Resistance" began:

> Patience is laid out on my papers. Its visuals are gainful and equably square. Two dozen jets take off into the night. Outdoors a car goes uphill in a genial low gear. The flow of thoughts—impossible! These are the defamiliarization techniques with which we are so familiar.

There are six sentences here, three of which, beginning with the first, are constructed similarly: subject—verb—prepositional phrase. The three prepositions are *on*, *into*, and *in*, which in isolation seem similar but used here have very different meanings. *On* is locational: "on my papers." *Into* is metaphorical and atmospheric: "into the night." *In* is atmospheric and qualitative: "in a genial low gear." There are a pair of inversions in effect here: the unlike are made similar (syntactically) and the like are sundered (semantically). Patience, which might be a quality of a virtuous character attendant to work ("it is laid out on my papers"), might also be solitaire, a card game played by an idler who is avoiding attention to work. Two dozen jets can only take off together in formation; they are "laid out" on the night sky. A car goes uphill; its movement upward parallels that of the jets, but whereas their formation is martial, the single car is somewhat domestic, genial and innocuous. The image in the first pair of sentences is horizontal. The upward movement of the next two sentences describes a vertical plane, upended on or intersecting the horizontal one. The "flow of thoughts" runs down the vertical and comes to rest—"impossible!"

The work shifts between horizontal and vertical landscapes, and the corresponding sentences—the details of each composed on its particular plane—form distinct semantic fields. (In fact, I would like each individual sentence to be as nearly a complete poem as possible.)

One of the results of this compositional technique, building a work out of discrete fields, is the creation of sizable gaps between the units. To negotiate this disrupted terrain, the reader (and I can say also the writer) must overleap the end stop, the period, and cover the distance to the next sentence. Meanwhile, what stays in the gaps remains crucial and informative. Part of the reading occurs as the recovery of that information (looking behind) and the discovery of newly structured ideas (stepping forward).

In both *My Life* and "Resistance," the structural unit (grossly, the paragraph) was meant to be mimetic of both a space and a time of thinking. In a somewhat different respect, time predetermines the form of Bernadette Mayer's *Midwinter Day*. The work begins when the clock is set running (at dawn on December 22, 1978) and ends when the time allotted to the work runs out (late night of the same day). "It's true," Mayer has said: "I have always loved projects of all sorts, including say sorting leaves or whatever projects turn out to be, and in poetry I most especially love having time be the structure which always seems to me to save structure or form from itself because then nothing really has to begin or end."[7]

Whether the form is dictated by temporal constraints or by other exoskeletal formal elements—by a prior decision, for example, that the work will contain, say, x number of sentences, paragraphs, stanzas, stresses, or lines, etc.—the work gives the impression that it begins and ends arbitrarily and not because there is a necessary point of origin or terminus, a first or last moment. The implication (correct) is that the words and the ideas (thoughts, perceptions, etc.—the materials) continue beyond the work. One has simply stopped because one has run out of units or minutes, and not because a conclusion has been reached nor "everything" said.

The relationship of form, or the "constructive principle," to the materials of the work (to its themes, the conceptual mass, but also to the words themselves) is the initial problem for the "open text," one that faces each writing anew. Can form make the primary chaos (the raw material, the unorganized impulse and information, the uncertainty, incompleteness, vastness) articulate without depriving it of its capacious vitality, its generative power? Can form go even further than that and actually generate that potency, opening uncertainty to curiosity, incompleteness to speculation, and turning vastness into plenitude? In my opinion, the answer is yes; that is, in fact, the function of form in art. Form is not a fixture but an activity.

In an essay titled "Rhythm as the Constructive Factor of Verse," the Russian Formalist writer Yurii Tynianov writes:

> We have only recently outgrown the well-known analogy: form is to content as a glass is to wine. . . . I would venture to say that in nine out of ten instances the word "composition" covertly implies a treatment of form as a static item. The concept of "poetic line" or "stanza" is imperceptibly removed from the dynamic category. Repetition ceases to be considered as a fact of varying strength in various situations of frequency and quantity. The dangerous concept of the

"symmetry of compositional facts" arises, dangerous because we cannot speak of symmetry where we find intensification.[8]

One is reminded of Gertrude Stein's comparable comments in "Portraits and Repetitions": "A thing that seems to be exactly the same thing may seem to be a repetition but is it." "Is there repetition or is there insistence. I am inclined to believe there is no such thing as repetition. And really how can there be." "Expressing any thing there can be no repetition because the essence of that expression is insistence, and if you insist you must each time use emphasis and if you use emphasis it is not possible while anybody is alive that they should use exactly the same emphasis."[9]

Tynianov continues:

The unity of a work is not a closed symmetrical whole, but an unfolding dynamic integrity. . . . The sensation of form in such a situation is always the sensation of flow (and therefore of change). . . . Art exists by means of this interaction or struggle.[10]

Language discovers what one might know, which in turn is always less than what language might say. We encounter some limitations of this relationship early, as children. Anything with limits can be imagined (correctly or incorrectly) as an object, by analogy with other objects—balls and rivers. Children objectify language when they render it their plaything, in jokes, puns, and riddles, or in glossolaliac chants and rhymes. They discover that words are not equal to the world, that a blur of displacement, a type of parallax, exists in the relation between things (events, ideas, objects) and the words for them—a displacement producing a gap.

Among the most prevalent and persistent categories of jokes is that which identifies and makes use of the fallacious comparison of words to world and delights in the ambiguity resulting from the discrepancy:

—Why did the moron eat hay?
—To feed his hoarse voice.

—How do you get down from an elephant?
—You don't, you get down from a goose.

—Did you wake up grumpy this morning?
—No, I let him sleep.

Because we have language we find ourselves in a special and peculiar relationship to the objects, events, and situations which constitute what we imagine of the world. Language generates its own characteristics in the human psychological and spiritual conditions. Indeed, it nearly *is* our psychological condition.

This psychology is generated by the struggle between language and that which it claims to depict or express, by our overwhelming experience of the vastness and uncertainty of the world, and by what often seems to be the inadequacy of the imagination that longs to know it—and, furthermore, for the poet, the even greater inadequacy of the language that appears to describe, discuss, or disclose it. This psychology situates desire in the poem itself, or, more specifically, in poetic language, to which then we may attribute the motive for the poem.

Language is one of the principal forms our curiosity takes. It makes us restless. As Francis Ponge puts it, "Man is a curious body whose center of gravity is not in himself."[11] Instead that center of gravity seems to be located in language, by virtue of which we negotiate our mentalities and the world; off-balance, heavy at the mouth, we are pulled forward.

> I am urged out rummaging into the sunshine, and the depths increase of blue above. A paper hat on a cone of water. . . . But, already, words. . . . She is lying on her stomach with one eye closed, driving a toy truck along the road she has cleared with her fingers.[12]

Language itself is never in a state of rest. Its syntax can be as complex as thought. And the experience of using it, which includes the experience of understanding it, either as speech or as writing, is inevitably active—both intellectually and emotionally. The progress of a line or sentence, or a series of lines or sentences, has spatial properties as well as temporal properties. The meaning of a word in its place derives both from the word's lateral reach, its contacts with its neighbors in a statement, and from its reach through and out of the text into the outer world, the matrix of its contemporary and historical reference. The very idea of reference is spatial: over here is word, over there is thing, at which the word is shooting amiable love-arrows. Getting from the beginning to the end of a statement is simple movement; following the connotative byways (on what Umberto Eco calls "inferential walks") is complex or compound movement.

> To identify these frames the reader has to "walk," so to speak, outside the text, in order to gather intertextual support (a quest for analogous "topoi," themes or motives). I call these interpretative moves inferential walks: they are not mere whimsical initiatives on the part of the reader, but are elicited by discursive structures and foreseen by the

whole textual strategy as indispensable components of the construction.[13]

Language is productive of activity in another sense, with which anyone is familiar who experiences words as attractive, magnetic to meaning. This is one of the first things one notices, for example, in works constructed from arbitrary vocabularies generated by random or chance operations (e.g., some works by Jackson Mac Low) or from a vocabulary limited according to some other criteria unrelated to meaning (for example, Alan Davies's *a an av es*, a long poem excluding any words containing letters with ascenders or descenders, what the French call "the prisoner's convention," either because the bars are removed or because it saves paper). It is impossible to discover any string or bundle of words that is entirely free of possible narrative or psychological content. Moreover, though the "story" and "tone" of such works may be interpreted differently by different readers, nonetheless the readings differ within definite limits. While word strings are permissive, they do not license a free-for-all.

Writing develops subjects that mean the words we have for them.

Even words in storage, in the dictionary, seem frenetic with activity, as each individual entry attracts to itself other words as definition, example, and amplification. Thus, to open the dictionary at random, *mastoid* attracts *nipplelike, temporal, bone, ear,* and *behind.* Turning to *temporal* we find that the definition includes *time, space, life, world, transitory,* and *near the temples,* but, significantly, not *mastoid.* There is no entry for *nipplelike,* but the definition for *nipple* brings over *protuberance, breast, udder, the female, milk, discharge, mouthpiece,* and *nursing bottle,* but again not *mastoid,* nor *temporal,* nor *time, bone, ear, space,* or *word.* It is relevant that the exchanges are incompletely reciprocal.

> and how did this happen like an excerpt
>   beginning in a square white boat abob on a gray sea . . .
>   tootling of another message by the
>   hacking lark . . .
> as a child
>
>   to the rescue and its spring . . .
>   in a great lock of letters
>   like knock look . . .
>   worked by utter joy way
>   think through with that in minutes
>   already
>
>   slippage thinks random patterns
>   through
>   wishes
>   I intend greed as I intend pride
>   patterns of roll extend over the wish [14]

The "rage to know" is one expression of the restlessness engendered by language. "As long as man keeps hearing words / He's sure that there's a meaning somewhere," as Mephistopheles points out in Goethe's *Faust.* [15]

It's in the nature of language to encourage and, in part, to justify such Faustian longings. [16] The notion that language is the means and medium for attaining knowledge and, concomitantly, power is, of course, old. The knowledge toward which we seem to be driven by language, or which language seems to promise, is inherently sacred as well as secular, redemptive as well as satisfying. The *nomina sint numina* position (that there is an essential identity between name and thing, that the real nature of a thing is immanent and present in its name, that nouns are numinous) suggests that it is possible to find a language which will meet its object with perfect identity. If this were the case, we could, in speaking or in writing, achieve the "at oneness" with the universe, at least in its particulars, that is the condition of complete and perfect knowing.

But if in the Edenic scenario we acquired knowledge of the animals by naming them, it was not by virtue of any numinous immanence in the name but because Adam was a taxonomist. He distinguished the individual animals, discovered the concept of categories, and then organized the various species according to their different functions and relationships in the system. What the "naming" provides is structure, not individual words.

As Benjamin Lee Whorf has pointed out, "Every language is a vast pattern-system, different from others, in which are culturally ordained the forms and categories by which the personality not only communicates, but also analyses nature, notices or neglects types of relationship and phenomena, channels his reasoning, and builds the house of his consciousness." In this same essay, apparently his last (written in 1941), titled "Language, Mind, Reality," Whorf goes on to express what seem to be stirrings of a religious motivation: "What I have called patterns are basic in a really cosmic sense." There is a "PREMONITION IN LANGUAGE of the unknown, vaster world." The idea

> is too drastic to be penned up in a catch phrase. I would rather leave it unnamed. It is the view that a noumenal world —a world of hyperspace, of higher dimensions—awaits discovery by all the sciences [linguistics being one of them] which it will unite and unify, awaits discovery under its first aspect of a realm of PATTERNED RELATIONS, inconceivably

manifold and yet bearing a recognizable affinity to the rich and systematic organization of LANGUAGE.[17]

It is as if what I've been calling, from Faust, the "rage to know," which is in some respects a libidinous drive, seeks also a redemptive value from language. Both are appropriate to the Faustian legend.

Coming in part out of Freudian psychoanalytic theory, especially in France, is a body of feminist thought that is even more explicit in its identification of language with power and knowledge—a power and knowledge that is political, psychological, and aesthetic—and that is a site specifically of desire. The project for these French feminist writers has been to direct their attention to "language and the unconscious, not as separate entities, but language as a passageway, and the only one, to the unconscious, to that which has been repressed and which would, if allowed to rise, disrupt the established symbolic order, what Jacques Lacan has dubbed the Law of the Father."[18]

If the established symbolic order is the "Law of the Father," and it is discovered to be not only repressive but false, distorted by the *illogicality* of bias, then the new symbolic order is to be a "woman's language," corresponding to a woman's desire.

Luce Irigaray writes:

But *woman has sex organs just about everywhere*. She experiences pleasure almost everywhere. Even without speaking of the hysterization of her entire body, one can say that the geography of her pleasure is much more diversified, more multiple in its differences, more complex, more subtle, than is imagined.... "She" is indefinitely other in herself. That is undoubtedly the reason she is called temperamental, incomprehensible, perturbed, capricious—not to mention her language in which "she" goes off in all directions.[19]

"A feminine textual body is recognized by the fact that it is always endless, without ending," says Hélène Cixous: "There's no closure, it doesn't stop."[20]

The narrow definition of desire, the identification of desire solely with sexuality, and the literalness of the genital model for a woman's language that some of these writers insist on may be problematic. The desire that is stirred by language is located most interestingly within language itself—as a desire to say, a desire to create the subject by saying, and as a pervasive doubt very like jealousy that springs from the impossibility of satisfying these yearnings. This desire resembles Wordsworth's "underthirst / Of vigor seldom utterly allayed."[21] And it is explicit in Carla Harryman's "Realism":

> When I'm eating this I want food. . . . The I expands. The
> individual is caught in a devouring machine, but she shines
> like the lone star on the horizon when we enter her thoughts,
> when she expounds on the immensity of her condition, the
> subject of the problem which interests nature.[22]

If language induces a yearning for comprehension, for perfect and complete expression, it also guards against it. Thus Faust complains:

> It is written: "In the beginning was the Word!"
> Already I have to stop! Who'll help me on?
> It is impossible to put such trust in the Word![23]

This is a recurrent element in the argument of the lyric: "Alack, what poverty my Muse brings forth . . . "; "Those lines that I before have writ do lie . . . "; "For we / Have eyes to wonder but lack tongues to praise. . . . "[24]

In the gap between what one wants to say (or what one perceives there is to say) and what one can say (what is sayable), words provide for a collaboration and a desertion. We delight in our sensuous involvement with the materials of language, we long to join words to the world—to close the gap between ourselves and things—and we suffer from doubt and anxiety because of our inability to do so.

Yet the incapacity of language to match the world permits us to distinguish our ideas and ourselves from the world and things in it from each other. The undifferentiated is one mass, the differentiated is multiple. The (unimaginable) complete text, the text that contains everything, would in fact be a closed text. It would be insufferable.

A central activity of poetic language is formal. In being formal, in making form distinct, it opens—makes variousness and multiplicity and possibility articulate and clear. While failing in the attempt to match the world, we discover structure, distinction, the integrity and separateness of things. As Bob Perelman writes:

> At the sound of my voice
> I spoke and, egged on
> By the discrepancy, wrote
> The rest out as poetry.[25]

Notes

1. "The Rejection of Closure" was included in *Writing/Talks*, ed. Bob Perelman (Carbondale: Southern Illinois University Press, 1985),

and, following suggestions from Barrett Watten, in revised form in *Poetics Journal* 4: "Women & Language" (May 1984). More recently, it was anthologized in *Onward: Contemporary Poetry & Poetics*, ed. Peter Baker (New York: Peter Lang, 1996), and extracts appear in *Postmodern American Poetry: A Norton Anthology*, ed. Paul Hoover (New York: W. W. Norton and Co., 1994). The essay has been translated into Serbian by Dubravka Djuric, and that version appeared in *Gradina* 2–3 (1991; Niš, Yugoslavia).

2. *Poetics Journal* 4: "Women & Language" (May 1984).

3. Carla Harryman, *The Middle* (San Francisco: Gaz, 1983), 4. *The Middle* was republished in *Writing/Talks*, ed. Perelman.

4. Luce Irigaray, "This sex which is not one," tr. Claudia Reeder, in *New French Feminisms*, ed. Elaine Marks and Isabelle de Courtivron (Amherst: University of Massachusetts Press, 1980), 104.

5. Robert Grenier, *Cambridge M'ass* (Berkeley: Tuumba Press, 1979); Bruce Andrews, *Love Songs* (Baltimore: Pod Books, 1982)

6. At the time this essay was written, "Resistance" existed only in manuscript form. A large portion of it was eventually incorporated into "The Green" and published in *The Cold of Poetry* (Los Angeles: Sun & Moon Press, 1994)

7. Bernadette Mayer to Lyn Hejinian, letter (1981?).

8. Yurii Tynianov, "Rhythm as the Constructive Factor of Verse," in *Readings in Russian Poetics*, ed. Ladislav Matejka and Krystyna Pomorska (Ann Arbor: Michigan Slavic Contributions, 1978), 127–28.

9. Gertrude Stein, "Portraits and Repetitions," in *Gertrude Stein: Writings 1932–1946*, ed. Catharine R. Stimpson and Harriet Chessman (New York: Library of America, 1998), 292, 288.

10. Tynianov, "Rhythm as the Constructive Factor," 128.

11. Francis Ponge, "The Object Is Poetics," in *The Power of Language*, tr. Serge Gavronsky (Berkeley: University of California Press, 1979), 47.

12. Lyn Hejinian, *My Life* (Los Angeles: Sun & Moon Press, 1987), 14–15.

13. Umberto Eco, Introduction to *The Role of the Reader* (Bloomington: Indiana University Press, 1979), 32. This book was of great help to me as I was considering the ideas expressed in this essay; I was especially interested in Eco's emphasis on generation (creativity on the part of both writer and reader) and the polygendered impulses active in it.

14. Lyn Hejinian, *Writing Is an Aid to Memory* (Los Angeles: Sun & Moon Press, 1996), parts 2 and 12.

15. Johann Wolfgang von Goethe, *Goethe's Faust, Part One*, tr. Randall Jarrell (New York: Farrar, Straus & Giroux, 1976), 137.

16. This idea is reiterated in *My Life*, one of the several forms of repetition in that work. (See *My Life*, 46).

17. Benjamin Lee Whorf, *Language, Thought, and Reality* (Cambridge, Mass.: MIT Press, 1956), 252, 248, 247–48.

18. Elaine Marks, in *Signs* 3, no. 4 (Summer 1978), 835.

19. Luce Irigaray, "This sex which is not one," 103.

20. Hélène Cixous, "Castration or Decapitation?" in *Signs* 7, no. 1 (Autumn 1981), 53.

21. William Wordsworth, "The Prelude" (1850 version), Book VI, lines 558–59, in *William Wordsworth: The Prelude 1799, 1805, 1850*, ed. Jonathan Wordsworth, M. H. Abrams, and Stephen Gill (New York: W. W. Norton & Company, 1979), 215.

22. Carla Harryman, "Realism," in *Animal Instincts* (Berkeley: This Press, 1989), 106.

23. Goethe, *Goethe's Faust, Part One*, 61.

24. Lines excised from Shakespeare's Sonnets, nos. 102, 115, and 106.

25. Bob Perelman, "My One Voice," in *Primer* (Berkeley: This Press, 1981), 11.

Language and "Paradise"

The Guard, the last publication in the Tuumba chapbook series, appeared in September 1984, a year after my first visit to the Soviet Union and my first meeting with the poet Arkadii Dragomoshchenko (to whom *The Guard* is dedicated).[1] "Language and 'Paradise,'" a purported exegesis of portions of that work, was written a year later, after a second, much longer visit to the USSR. There is, then, a Russian context for these two related works—a context which is more fully developed, of course, in my "short Russian novel" *Oxota*. And the figure of the guard(ian) has an identity in this context as well as in the one I explain in the essay. (The figure, both as border guard and as interloper, reappears to play a complex role in *A Border Comedy* and makes an appearance also in *Sight*.).[2]

The Russian context was not only experiential. My involvement with Russian Formalist theory is clear from the references in the essay to writings by Osip Brik and by Yurii Tynianov (I had read Tynianov's *The Problem of Verse Language* while stranded in the Intourist waiting room at Moscow's Sheremetova Airport for 26 hours). Perhaps it is also evident in some of the strategies I use—the delaying of coherence, for example, which results from the paratactic and "plotless" structure of the essay. The notion of delayed coherence was inspired in large part by the essay by Viktor Shklovsky that Barrett Watten and I published in the first issue of *Poetics Journal*,[3] though the term is my own.

"Language and 'Paradise'" was originally written for presentation at the New Poetics Colloquium organized by the Kootenay School of Writing (Vancouver, British Columbia), in June 1985. It was subsequently published in *Line: A Journal of Contemporary Writing and its Modernist Sources*, no. 6 (Fall 1985).

My writings have almost never taken form as single, independent entities. When I finished *The Guard*, I began a notebook project intended to produce or invent an exegesis, amplification, and adjustment to the poem—an extension of its trajectory. The notebook is labeled "Language and 'Paradise,'" which are the last two words of the poem. In this notebook, I've been writing a commentary on the poem, addressing it sentence by sentence.

The decision to examine the poem at the level of the sentence rather than the line was not arbitrary. It is primarily at the level of the sentence, in the moves from one to the next, that the themes of the poem develop; it is at the level of the sentences that one can follow the prevailing current. But this isn't to dismiss the effect of the line (and the line break) on these sentences (and occasionally in the notebook I have focused my attention on those portions of sentences which make a line). The dynamic of the line is different from that of the sentence, and the interplay between the two produces countercurrents, eddies, backwaters, and swirls. The sentence and the line have different ways of bringing meaning into view.

The situation of *The Guard* is a phenomenological one, an unstable situation involving perceiver, perception (or perceiving), perceived, and the various meanings of their interrelationships, which are not at all mild. By "the perceived," I mean not only objects, but also events, emotions, ideas, and the various interconnections that bind them within the world. I assume the reality of everything. Thus, if I can say that the poem includes the *perceived*, it may include sentences, for example, about desire, various domestic and professional events, political opinion, and the fear of death, as well as a good deal of description. In *perception*, since I am thinking about a poem, I locate (just as I in fact experience) the site of the perceiving in language itself. It is here that the interplay between line and sentence is the most important. As I see it, and this is partially in retrospect (which I mention because I want to make it clear that I learned most of these things by writing the poem, not in preparation for it, and that this perceiving from within the writing is a central element of my practical as well as my theoretical poetics; it provides me with the necessity for writing), if the sentence represents the entirety of a perception, a complete thought, then the line might be taken to represent the shape or scale or measure of our consciousness of it. A perception might come at one in segments, and the line represents such a segment, a unit of consciousness. Thus each line is an aspect of an idea, observation, or feeling. When one sentence ends and another begins on a single line, then the connection between the two is part of the plane of consciousness. This may sound slightly abstract, but it is actually a very simple way to read lines. For example, the third line of *The Guard* consists of one complete sentence, plus a single word of the next sentence: "The full moon falls on the first. I" (11). The connection between "first" and "I" is obvious (although it should also be noted that the allusion to the "first person," solipsistic or grammatical, is somewhat ironic). When the poem begins with the question, "Can one take captives by writing," the "one" (first) is "I."[4]

The rhythmic element in a poem is something I am often thinking about when I write, and not solely as an aesthetic quality—as part of the poem's grace or beauty, say, in one place, or its clumsiness or irritability in another. When I am writing, to the extent that the activity is equivalent to thinking, I am doing so with a certain rhythm of attention. And there is another area which perhaps only rhythm can consider, and that is the conflict between time and space which is thematically central to *The Guard*.

Some of my thoughts about semantic rhythms and polyrhythms in poetry—the rhythms of the sentences and the counterrhythms of the lines—derive in part from ideas expressed by Osip Brik in his "Contributions to the Study of Verse Language":

> Verse is not regulated simply by the laws of syntax, but by the laws of rhythmic syntax, that is, a syntax in which the usual syntactic laws are complicated by rhythmic requirements.
>
> The primary word combination in poetry is the line. The words in a line have been combined according to a definite rhythmic law and, simultaneously, according to the laws of prose syntax. The very fact that a certain number of words coexist with the two sets of laws constitutes the peculiarity of poetry. In the line, we have the results of a rhythmico-syntactic word combination.[5]

The counterpoint between line and sentence establishes two series of durations, and in doing so it brings temporality into spaces. And, although it would be inaccurate simply to equate lineation with space and sentences with time, still it seemed to me that in *The Guard*, where the writing includes an aesthetic (and therefore psychological) encounter between lines and sentences as between times and spaces, it was desirable to use a form that reflected the resulting rhythmic complications. I wanted to set the work in motion against itself, so to speak, to establish the inward concentricity, the pressure, the implosive momentum that stands for the struggle that is enacted in the poem.

As for the position of the perceiver in the phenomenological situation—or in the poem, a poem—it is not a self, neutral and stable, but a contextualized and contextualizing subject, a person, and, although the emphasis in *The Guard* is on the middle term, perceiving, the complex condition of the person had to be represented in the poem. To do this, even minimally, the poem had to give indication of such dynamic elements as individual psychology, personal history, the influence of class background and an individual's attempt to challenge it, the times and places in which the person lives, and so forth. Especially, it had to present the language in which such social matter is situated. The following passage from the fourth part of the poem offers perhaps the most overt attempt at this:

> I and my musician friend very love the jazz
> music and very many study if listen your saxophone
> quartet playing, therefore request
> your if no expensive so if would such
> dear send me some jazz records. (23)

This is an unaltered extract from a letter to my husband, who is himself a musician, from a correspondent in Czechoslovakia who signs his letters sometimes "Fan Boy" and sometimes "Jazz Boy." I liked the passage because of its mimetic as well as comedic potential. Jazz/Fan Boy's sense of English syntax seems to be derived from his assimilation of rhythms in the music he likes; the result is a truly jazzy letter. Of course, as an analysis of the perceiver, it is very primitive, since it is merely quoting. A similarly functioning quotation appears in the second part of the poem, in which I embedded a small extract from a column in the *San Francisco Chronicle* called "The Question Man." This particular day's question was, "What is the dirtiest room in your house?"

> The kitchen: everyone eats
> in different cycles—yeah
> the dishes are all over the counter . . .
> yeah, food's left out, things are on the stove
> yeah, the floor's filthy—that's amazing!
> have you been here before? (15)

I'm going to present various passages from the notebook to *The Guard*, but not in sequence. I am not taking the sentences in the order in which they appear in the poem. In some instances the notebook attempts an exegesis of a given sentence; in others, a sentence serves simply as an instigation to only obliquely related thoughts. I selected these particular pages from the notebook and arranged them so that they might suggest several possible constellations of concern, in the work and after it.

This notebook, I should add, became the site not only of a retrospective reading of *The Guard* but a medium for writing into what became my next project, the series of poems called "The Person."[6] There are a number of lines in "The Person" that derive from my comments about *The Guard*, and thus, to that extent, material for the one project was generated by the previous one. *The Guard*, in terms of "The Person," remained (or became) unfinished. Indeed, I don't like to regard any of my work as finished. I don't want to resist "the book," but it is an extremely problematic entity if and as it implies a finished work.

I begin in the middle—of my own writing and of the larger project which writing represents. It is only after the beginning and before the end that things and thinking about them can begin anew.

In citing this extensive, productive "middle," I must acknowledge Carla Harryman's important work of that title.[7] But I also would point to a line from the first canto of Dante's *Divine Comedy*, the canto which was the source of the original impulse for *The Guard*. I began writing the poem propelled by the charged aporia that is fundamental to the lyric, and in which Dante finds himself: "Midway this way of life we're bound upon, / I woke to find myself in a dark wood."[8] The poet sees a path and follows it through the dark wood until he comes to a portal, one whose threshold he must cross if he is to begin his journey through Hell and Purgatory and make his way to Paradise. There at the portal Dante meets the poet Virgil, a figure both guide and guard, who will serve as his companion, accompanying him not only through the portal into the landscape of the afterlife but also, and perhaps more significantly, through the portal into the poem itself. *The Divine Comedy* is, after all, a poem, though through it the poet seeks to go beyond the poem, to cross the very limit of language, and thus reach an unmediated, beatific experience of Paradise— one which, however, were it indeed to be such an unmediated experience, would be unspeakable; Paradise can only be experienced in silence. Dante, in other words, must cross the poem and then exit it at the very point where it *is* "Paradise," since the poem, as such, even as it admits the poet into vivid realms of experience, will always also be rendering that experience approximate and bordered by the very language in which it exists. The figure of Virgil, whom Dante calls "my author" and who personifies poetry, can take Dante (and Dante's poem) as far as "paradise" but on reaching it he will have to turn back—if only to return and try again.

> If the world is round & the gates are gone. . . .
> The landscape is a moment of time
> that has gotten in position. (11)

This "midway" topos is a condition of consciousness; the middle serves as both context and content to consciousness.

. . .

> *The tree*
> *stands up aching in the sun.* (12)

This and the several following lines of the poem attempt to cast time into visual and hence spatial imagery. The idea was to point out vertical and horizontal traces of time's passage or of events which could only occur over time. Recognizing the occurring inherent to things—recognizing that they could only exist after "taking some time"—produced an increasingly dense accrual of moving images, until "The sky was packed // which by appearing endless seems inevitable" (13).

What I was after was not "eternity" but an impression of temporal heterogeneity, not timelessness but a strange simultaneity, a current array of disparately time-bound things. "Here" and "there," "then" and "now," "this" and "that," are registered differently in each of them, but all of these are contextualizing terms, and it is by virtue of this that one can speak of simultaneity and temporal heterogeneity in the same passage.

Despite an analytic or investigatory impulse underlying my writing generally, I am keenly aware of the nonisolability of objects and events in the world, our experience of them, and our experience of that experience. I assume that there is reality in the world and in this poem I have focused on perception and on the language that serves as its site—or, more specifically, on the poem as the site of the consciousness of perception.

At points where temporality is dominant in a work, it exerts a particular pressure (hence, here, the tree's "aching in the sun"), and one's response is likely to include restlessness and sometimes anxiety. Time challenges the span of the self, and for that reason a sense of temporal pressure in or on a work can serve as an incitement to activity. In contrast, where the spatial dominates the work, the experience of the work may include a sense of tranquillity. Landscape is reassuring, "Like the wind that by its bulk inspires confidence" (15). The pressure of time and the consolation of space can both produce desirable aesthetic effects, but they are very different. At the end of *The Guard*, I suggest that that may be the difference between language and "paradise."

. . .

Paradise encouraged cuppings. (32)

Meanwhile, in the seventh part of the poem, I was becoming increasingly aware that, wherever there is a fragility of sequence, the particular character of diverse individual things becomes prominent; their heterogeneity increases the palpability of things.

This palpability has both metaphysical and aesthetic force, which is to say that these particulars are not isolated, but to understand their relations under conditions in which sequential logic is in disarray, one must examine other connections. The most basic and most resilient is that of the simple conjunction, *and.* It is fundamental to all paratactic presentations, it is the signal component of collage, and it is the first instrument through which children begin to offer accounts of the world. All relations begin with *and.*

And yet it would be a mistake to consider *and* a "primitive" conjunction. In this section of *The Guard*, however, it is the primary one, even though its presence is more often implicit than explicit. And its function here, I hoped, was to take on something more complex than a listing of coexistents. I wanted to resist the synthesizing tendency of the syllogism and the aphorism; I wanted to subvert the power of "therefore" and, wherever one of a series of terms (sentences) might threaten to subsume others (the sort of sacrifice that the dialectical tends to make in its quest for categorical clarity), to deny it the capacity to do so.

■ ■ ■

The tongue
becomes observant and the tongue gets tough
inevitably, like a fruitskin. (28)

Physiology must take into account the things that persons perceive. The body itself is historical. It gives an account of experience.

The mouth, certainly, bears the history of the languages it speaks—its acquired habits of movement circumscribe the sounds it can make, whether mimetic (clickings, shushings, poppings, tootings, etc.) or descriptive (of the click and thump of horses crossing a bridge, water gushing from a pipe, fish snapping as it fries, a steam train in a park).

But are mimesis and description necessarily opposed? Don't they both, albeit in different ways, not only perform perception but, in doing so, also experience that perception in and as perceiving itself? In the sixth chapter of *The Phenomenology of Perception*, a chapter addressed to "The Body as Expression, and Speech," Merleau-Ponty speaks of the "intentionality and sense-giving powers" of the body, granting it "a unity distinct from that of the scientific object." And, he goes on, "In trying to describe the phenomenon of speech and the specific act of meaning, we shall have the opportunity to leave behind us, once and for all, the traditional subject-object dichotomy."[9]

Such a statement would seem to refute the notion that language is always and inevitably mediate. It serves as a guide to phenomena, certainly, bringing us face to face with them, but it stands as a guard against our being "ultimately at one" with them, since language is the principal medium through which we objectify things and our experience of them. But is this latter necessarily the case? is it even an accurate characterization of the circumstance of description? It's through language, after all, that we discover our nonautonomous being. The very fluidity of meaning that we note in the relation of words to things, signifier to signified, makes fluid what might otherwise become rigid.

. . .

Loosely a bullfrog exits a pond. (28)

This line is descriptive, but elements in the sentence are burdened with the choices made in its composition. "Loosely" for example is emphatic because it comes first. And there's a gap, a momentary delay, between it and the verb it governs; through that gap the grammatical subject makes its appearance, a bullfrog.

Or is it only "loosely" a bullfrog—is it merely something like a bullfrog?

And why apply the adverbs "only" and "merely" to the ambiguous identity of the figure?

But I *was* thinking of a bullfrog. The figure is there for its rotundity and folds, and for the sake of the play of the conceptually complex folds against the "exits," the round vowels and rolling l's against the bright vowels and sibilant *x* and *ts*. "Exits," the verb, is in the simple present tense but denotes an unspecified time—present, yes, but when? Its "now" is the time of the utterance; the bullfrog exits in the temporal context of saying so, and, as far as we can determine, only in that context. No other is indicated.

The gap between loosely and exits, then, is a gap that the word "exits" names. The bullfrog appears in its exit, the time of the sentence and of the poem.

. . .

> *We take up*
> *an unconventional position between two posts*
> *(whenever I hear "opposition" I vomit).* (29)

Somewhere within the disputed territory of reference that separates "word" from "thing" stands that peculiar being, the grammatical first person(s).

The parenthetical plural is always part of her condition. And her subject-object, I-we, public-private status becomes ever more pronounced in the "unconventional position" which constitutes the writing posture. This comes about in part because of increased self-awareness, distance, the onset of a stage that comes *after* a first, as it were unmediated, encounter, a stage which culminates as "I" isolates something and, as if to figure it out, becomes objective, which is to say in polar opposition to it, isolating herself in the process. But such extreme, polarizing (and sickening) objectification is off at some far edge of the poem, if it is in it at all. Rather, with its many positions, the poem (and not only this one) exists between poles ("posts") within the period of surprise at the actual existence of something coming into view when its moment, so to speak, has arrived.

This sentence has its source in a letter to me from the Russian poet Arkadii Dragomoshchenko, to whom *The Guard* is dedicated. Writing from what was then Leningrad, he said:

> But about this subject, the hatred and love (I vomit when I come across the word "opposition") of the things and names given to the poet to comprehend—he destroys the connection . . . , he struggles in his creation of appropriate places for everything and everybody. . . . But the language of meanings (definitions)—in spite of numerous formulas—becomes something Roman, moving toward myth, crossing borders but not finding its destiny. . . . I foresee going ahead of language into the high world where vision, hearing, memory, the body are not the first, the second, nor third element, no longer need time nor space, nor God, because they are not within *this* framework, within *this* condition. There is "the sadness of language."

. . .

Hunger and thirst very different and different
yet again from their ineluctable peppiness
the twitching of number
in what would have been vacancy. (22)

Time is the violent element that can make spatial configurations appear irrational. It severs, disjoins, postpones, even as it enumerates, even as it makes things count. Time sets the conditions for the surge of desire—whether erotic or epistemological—that is a central theme of the poem and that repeatedly casts the things of which it speaks (including desire itself) forward, into a distance in which they appear "different" and then again "different." Each thing, in its vivacity, its living condition, is itself and itself again. This is the secret of its identity over time—it is the same thing the second time as it was the first.

Numbers, though they function grammatically as adjectives or pronouns, have a strong prepositional inflection, since in themselves they express relational concepts: *with, after, beside, beyond, inside, including, among, before, by means of, together with, after, excluding*, and so on as well as prepositionlike adjective-conjunction constructions such as *more than* and *less than*.

Like the preposition, number refers to its frame of reference at the same time that it is specific within the frame, the name of the whole as well as the part.

Number, itself semantically inflected, is one of the few grammatical categories that contributes inflection (usually by adding an *s*) to other words in English.

. . .

Can people take captives by writing (11)

This is the opening line of *The Guard.* Here at the outset, to quote Dante, "I turn the face of my words towards the poem itself, and address it" (a comment from which I quote directly in the fourth section of the poem: "The windows resort / to equivalence as spring to cruelty / with evenly-hovering attention, and turn / the face of its words to me / just as water melts in the fire" [22]).

Windows, with their transparent/reflective surfaces, can seem to imitate the revealing/concealing character of words, and, within their frames, they can seem to imitate pictures. The windows turn my attention's words back to face "me"; this is a self-reflexive moment, forecast by the question which begins the poem. In this sense, as in certain others, "I" am the captive of the poem.

But "I" am not its sole captive. Nor am I necessarily held against my will or without avenues of escape. Indeed, "I" may be a captor, too, and certainly, even as I'm framed, I am a constructor of frames. "It's / as if I were seeing myself / propped on my hand with . . . " (27).

The aspiration to "capture the world in words" is frequently implicit in writing, and, despite the ugly exercise of power the metaphor implies, the impulse is usually directed more toward some form of historiography than toward oppression. One longs to diminish the inevitable loss of oneself and one's experience that time and mortality bring about.

Humans repeat themselves not only in the sense that history

is said to do so, and not simply because they are given to habit, but because, in telling of things, they tell of themselves. "In fact," as Paul Valéry notes, "there is no theory that is not a fragment, carefully prepared, of some autobiography."[10]

. . .

We will never know a true confession. (15)

Stirred by language, explanatory and encyclopedic in character, the confession reflects something of a Faustian obsession with knowledge. But a confession, or at least an unforced confession, is motivated by a yearning to be understood, in all senses of the term—a desire to know but also a desire to make known—and, beyond that, in the release of knowledge, in total context, to be known. The confession gives an account of how one was in the world; it tells of one's worldliness and reveals one's temporality.

Here there is more to the confession than a mere demand for the witnessing of a self-exposure. The act is of more interest and exhibits greater ambition than its abject psychological component or potential for manipulativeness would suggest. The confession reaches through and beyond its obvious quest for forgiveness or absolution. It is directed toward another kind of psychological gain. It seeks ultimately to overcome time.

To "tell all" does more than disclose facts and reveal "the truth" of events; in this sense, it is not objective. It reaches across events to another person and attempts to introduce a witness, someone who is omniscient. This witness will become a first and original as well as complete knower of the narrative, apprehending it all at once, all as one.

A confession begins as a particular kind of narrative; it recounts a sequence of events with consequences. It is a narrative that is under the pressure of time, and in it, the narrator's relationship to time is fraught with anxiety—a sense of guilt, perhaps, or remorse, fear, or a sense of loss. The aim of the confession, then, is to relieve the related narrative of consequentiality and hence of meaning. The confession is a strange form of aestheticization.

▪ ▪ ▪

My heart did suck . . . to fidget, soothed
. . . by seawater, restless . . . against
the unplugged phone. (28)

Visible throughout this sixth part of the poem are numerous traces of the erotic—sex, hunger, restless intellectual and emotional urges, aesthetic passions, etc., when they are felt in the body, when they seem to be lodged in the heart or stomach or liver, producing effects which range from ecstasy to irritability. This is not, of course, the first evidence of the erotic condition in the poem. It appears in the opening section, where even the weather and the very air itself are drawn to us viscerally through "the open mouths of people" which "are yellow & red" (11), gaping and inflamed with appetite or speech, disclosing the colors of fires in industrial furnaces or of a ripe peach. "Such air / always flies to the heart and liver, faces nature / with its changing pan, floating boats on the bay / far from authority, sent truly / speaking in little weights" (13–14).

Because it follows the sentence (discussed above) "Loosely a bullfrog exits a pond," a reader is inclined to attempt to make the phrase "My heart did suck" develop logically from it. And if there is a controlling logic here, one which can overleap the disjuncture, it is associative. The bullfrog (its rhythmic two-phase beat not unlike that of a heart) exits the pond, and the heart (a pumping muscle not unfroglike in its form and motion) empties it.

But neither association nor resemblance induces one thing to flow seamlessly into another. The heart is still bound in its membrane, and the bullfrog still lives in its skin.

It is true that earlier in the poem I have said, "The skin contains endlessness" (18), but this is not to suggest that an entity has escaped from or is anywhere but within its skin, nor that it is amorphous, eternal, or even infinite. The condition of being bound or bordered is what allows for distinction and difference, and therefore for encounter and experience: "The skin containing character" (14). Seams apparent, this is the form of an entity's "endlessness."

Though the passage under discussion articulates semantic thought (thought rendered logical through its inhering to language), and though links in the chain of association may be discovered (or invented), this passage does not represent a "stream of thought." There is semantic rhythm, incremental movement, cognitive pulse, but there are real gaps and discontinuities here as well as stillnesses and lulls. An unpsychologized unconscious is incorporated into the poem's phrasing, an unconscious which is not unthinking and not unexperienced. The ellipsis marks represent this contradiction. They are not the opposite of language, they are not arrayed against it, but they depict the contrariness within it.

This passage is not the first in which ellipses occur in the poem. Indeed, the first line of the poem ends with one, and as the poem proceeds, it accumulates these nonterminal, interstitial dots. From between them the poem seems to stagger, impeded by temporal and cognitive discontinuities as well as by recurrences, going forward through its own intrinsic postponements and deferrals.

The desire to tell within the conditions of a discontinuous consciousness seems to constitute the original situation of the poem. The discontinuity of consciousness is interwoven through the continuity of reality—a reality whose independence of our experience and descriptions must be recognized. In response, the poetic impulse, attempting (never successfully) to achieve the condition that the phrase "language and 'paradise'" names, seeks to extend the scope and temporal continuity of consciousness.

■ ■ ■

They too live half in a shoe. (17)

This is an anxious moment in the poem. The work encounters an impasse.

There is more to the sentence, but this is its opening clause. It is not an opening *line*, however, since the clause forms the last line of a stanza. Between the semantics of the clause (both with respect to sense and to syntax) and the structure of the stanza, contrary impulses are in play, setting up resistance within the poem.

It is not until two stanzas later that something like a resolution occurs: "And the other half in a shoe too," (18) (and this line occurs likewise at the end of a stanza and serves as the opening into a longer sentence).

Poetry frequently makes a trope of resistance. At the most basic level, resistance serves as a figure for a central concern that poetry addresses to itself, "the problem with language" (our sense of its notorious inadequacy, its ambiguities, and the perpetual crisis of meaning inherent to it). As resistance makes itself felt, it awakens intelligence and demands what Dante termed "novelty of the meaning"[11] and the acts of inquiry that go with it, even where this produces further resistance. Resistance forces shifts and displacements, and it is in the context of resistance that poetry's fascination with metamorphoses can be best understood— as the refiguring of the world, as a mode of figuring it out.

. . .

You match your chair. (11)

Within "the problem with language" lurks a comedic element. It is unpredictable but involves prediction—anticipation and expectation at the linguistic as well as the experiential level, a foretelling whose fulfillment produces not only resolution but also pleasure, the eruption of something uncontrolled.

It was Bob Perelman who turned to me and said, "You match your chair." We were in a classroom at San Francisco State University waiting for a poetry reading by Carla Harryman and Alan Davies to begin. The chairs in the room were upholstered in purple, and, prompted by Bob's comment, I noticed that many of us in the room were wearing similar shades of purple. We all matched our chairs.

But of course not perfectly. Obviously, we and our chairs did not merge into that continuum which constitutes true identity.

In a match, a contestation is taking place, one between the several matching elements and another between those and the expectations their observer feels regarding them. And it is "feeling" that occurs here, not analysis and not synthesis but a quick emotional apperception of what is relevant. To match is to take two predictably related elements and make them unpredictably relevant. Matching in this way generates what the Russian formalist writer, Yurii Tynianov, calls oscillating signs, a type of which is the pun.

It is in the lengthy second chapter of *The Problem of Verse Language* that Tynianov discusses this linguistic element and its function in poetry. He identifies within the usage of words three fundamental signs of meaning. What he calls "the principal sign" is a word's primary meaning, the "lexical unity" which allows a word to be used in diverse instances and still hold steadily to a sensibly single referent (e.g., the word *land* in the phrases "he reigned on land and sea," "your cattle are on my land," "this is my native land," "this is bad land for growing carrots," etc.). The secondary sign provides the word's connotative nuances and "semantic overtones," those elements which make the four instances of the word *land* differ. And the oscillating sign is one in which two principal signs jostle for primacy, as in the pun.[12]

Generally speaking, the comic employs oscillating signs. We laugh because they fit.

．　．　．

It takes a very normal person to create
a new picture. (20)

This person revels in its education, because education is full of details. In the general excitement, everything is repeatedly new, if not in itself, then in its relation to composition—to concentricities of composition. Its nonisolability restores and guarantees its newness. And it insures its relevance.

This is what I had in mind in the second part of the poem, also, when I wrote, "So sociable the influence of Vuillard" (I was thinking of the richly detailed and patterned prominent backgrounds in his paintings), "so undying in disorder is order" (14). After writing this, I had a dream in which the poem was subjected to analysis, not as a linguistic or literary object but as if it were a mind. In the dream, the poem was undergoing "psychoanalysis." The procedures, however, seemed closer to mathematical problem solving, or to a parody of them, since the activity was comical and pointedly ironic. All that had been written was now separated into *logical units* (that's what they were called in the dream)—words, phrases, occasionally entire sentences—and each was to be divided by *N*, a *unit of normalcy*. This "composes" a fraction, and the fraction (logic divided by normalcy) "gives us" (so it was said in the dream) *imagination*.

The attempt to divide things up with the systematic rigor of mathematics in order to bring the imaginary into view is quixotic, to say the least. And to a large extent, "the guard" of the poem's title, who serves both as the guard of and the guide through the poem (a role accorded to Virgil in Dante's *Divine Comedy*), is indeed a quixotic presence—enthused over details, impressionable, capricious, optimistic, impractical, idealistic. Unable to see the forest for the trees, it sets its own terms, it identifies itself as the norm for normalcy. And as such, it is always in the middle of things. Since the concept of a norm presupposes the existence of a standard on whose basis the norm is determined, and since it presupposes an already existing reality to which it might apply, it cannot have the first word. And since the determination that something matches the norm or that the norm has been properly applied has to come from something apart from the norm and after its application, it can never have the last word.

Notes

1. Lyn Hejinian, *The Guard* (Berkeley: Tuumba Press, 1984); reprinted in Lyn Hejinian, *The Cold of Poetry* (Los Angeles: Sun & Moon Press, 1994). Numbers following the quoted lines refer to page numbers in *The Cold of Poetry*.

2. Lyn Hejinian, *A Border Comedy* (forthcoming); Lyn Hejinian and Leslie Scalapino, *Sight* (Washington, D.C.: Edge Books, 1999).

3. See Viktor Shklovsky, "Plotless Prose: Vasily Rozanov," tr. Richard Sheldon, in *Poetics Journal* 1 (January 1982).

4. For a parallel, see Lyn Hejinian, *My Life* (Los Angeles: Sun & Moon Press, 1987), 81: "In the sentence, 'One turns onto 261 from 101 and follows it to the 5 point 73 mile marker, where a steep dirt road goes off to the right, up which one climbs for two miles, until one reaches a crest which is not the highest point on the ridge but from which there is for the first time a long view to both east and west, where one leaves the car and follows a path past two big oaks up a small hill for a quarter mile to the cabin,' I am the one."

5. Osip Brik, "Contributions to the Study of Verse Language," in *Readings in Russian Poetics*, ed. Ladislav Matejka and Krystyna Pomorska (Ann Arbor: Michigan Slavic Contributions, 1978), 122.

6. Included in Lyn Hejinian, *The Cold of Poetry*.

7. Carla Harryman, *The Middle* (San Francisco: Gaz, 1983).

8. Dante Alighieri, *The Divine Comedy: 1 Hell*, tr. Dorothy Sayers (New York: Penguin Books, 1984).

9. Maurice Merleau-Ponty, *The Phenomenology of Perception*, tr. Colin Smith (London: Routledge & Kegan Paul, 1962), 174.

10. Paul Valéry, *The Art of Poetry*, tr. Denise Folliot (New York: Bollingen Foundation and Pantheon Books, 1958), 58.

11. "It is a practice of an orator in certain situations to address someone indirectly, directing his words not at the person for whom they are intended, but rather towards another. And this method is what is really used here, because the words are directed at the *canzone*, but the meaning to men. I say, then, 'I believe, *canzone*, that they will be rare,' that is, few in number, those who will understand you clearly. And I give the cause, which is twofold. First, because the discourse is 'fatiguing' . . . ; second, because the discourse is hard—I say 'hard' referring to the novelty of the meaning." Dante Alighieri, *Literary Criticism of Dante Alighieri*, tr. and ed. Robert S. Haller (Lincoln: University of Nebraska Press, 1977), 71.

12. Yurii Tynianov, *The Problem of Verse Language*, tr. and ed. Michael Sosa and Brent Harvey (Ann Arbor: Ardis, 1981), 64ff.

Two Stein Talks

In 1933 my father, Chaffee Earl Hall Jr., an aspiring writer (he became an academic administrator and a notable painter), wrote to Gertrude Stein. He was a college student, attending the University of California in Berkeley, to which he commuted from his parents' Oakland house. Like Stein, he too had grown up in Oakland, or more precisely in an enclave within Oakland known as Piedmont, in what was to him a terrifically stifling middle-class milieu. He was most certainly a misfit there, with a personality and interests that were largely incomprehensible to his parents and peers, and with dreams of getting out of there (which he did). Presumably, he was seeking out some sort of fellow feeling in writing to Stein; I don't have a copy of his letter, although I do have the short letter that Alice B. Toklas wrote him on behalf of Stein and sent from 27 rue de Fleurus along with a copy of "her" *Autobiography,* inscribed to him by Stein. The letter is dated "15th January 1934." "My dear Mr. Hall, Miss Gertrude Stein desires me to thank you very warmly for your letter of the fourth of December in which you write of your appreciation of her work and its influence upon you and upon your writing. She send [*sic*] you every good wish for the success of the book you are now working upon and for your future work. Miss Stein sends you her greetings and to Piedmont too. I am very sincerely yours, A. B. Toklas, Secty."

Gertrude Stein was a canonical figure in the culture of my father. And, in a profound sense, I credit him not only with the origin of my own interest in Gertrude Stein, but also with a sense of my own artistic possibilities. Thanks to my father's crediting Gertrude Stein, a woman, with genius, I took it that gender would not be a bar to my own attempts to be a writer.

In the culture of the 1950s in which I was growing up, gender did seem to preclude my becoming a scientist, which was a possibility I also considered, and it wasn't until later, I think, that I was able to discern the scientific tendencies within Stein's work. Those I discovered—or at least was able to articulate—in an altogether different context, when in 1981 I undertook a three-night residency at 80 Langton Street, an artistic space in San Francisco, and devoted it to "American Literary Realism." It was in researching the topic that I came upon the conjunction of scientific notions with artistic ones, and the modeling of artistic methods on those of science. This is particularly clear in Emile Zola's appropriation of ideas from the physiologist Claude Bernard's *Introduction à l'étude de la médecine expérimentale* (Introduction to the Scientific Study of Medicine). Bernard's goal was to change medicine from an intuitive art to a scientific discipline based exclusively on observation and deduction, and Zola, in *Le Roman expérimental* (The Experimental Novel) expressed a similar agenda: "An experiment is basically only a provoked observation," Zola says. "I have then reached this point: the experimental novel is a result of the scientific evolution of the age; it continues and completes physiology, which itself leans on physics and chemistry; for the study of the abstract, the metaphysical man, it substitutes study of the natural man subject to physio-chemical laws and determined by the influences of environment; in a word it is the literature of our scientific age."[1]

To use science as a model for artistic researches into reality remained at the heart of the various "realisms" that emerged from the mid–nineteenth century on, culminating, perhaps, in Gertrude Stein's work. Positivist assumptions and a promise of progress (toward more and better knowledge resulting in a more ample and better world) are inherent in the scientific model, and the tendency was initially optimistic. The enterprise was taken to be collective rather than individualist, and it allowed for a paradoxically amoral ethics, one which in Theodore Dreiser's work, for example, develops into remarkably generous sympathies made intelligent rather than patronizing or pitying by his own embittered sense of irony. In the works of the American realists, especially, where the word "force" replaces "causality" as a key term, observation and experience tended to undermine optimism and to deny the existence of progress, testifying instead (in the novels of Frank Norris, for example) to a mechanistic determinism which overpowers purpose and worth.

Much of the material that I presented at the 80 Langton Street talks was incorporated into the talks on Gertrude Stein during a residency at New College of California during the spring semester of 1985 and which were in turn the basis for the "Two Stein Talks" that follow.

The "Two Stein Talks," in only slightly different form (and under the title of "Two Talks on Gertrude Stein") appeared in *Temblor 3* (Spring 1986). The essay was reprinted in *Revista Canaria de Estudos Ingleses* 18 (ed. Manuel Brito), and Janet Rodney produced the essay in a magnificent limited edition at her Weaselsleeves Press in 1995. I would like to take this opportunity to thank the editors of these publications, and also to acknowledge my gratitude to Craig Dworkin, who was enormously generous in helping me track down quotations from Stein's work that I had neglected to footnote when, in first composing these as talks, I had thought their presentation would be limited to an oral one.

Language and Realism

Well, I read 30 or 40 pages, and said,
"this is a fine new kind of realism—
Gertrude Stein is great!"
William James to Gertrude Stein,
May 25, 1910

The fact (if it is one) that we live in a real world has been of vary-
ing importance at different periods to culture and its art forms.
At times the question of "reality" and of the relation of art to it
has taken on considerable urgency, and since the Industrial Revo-
lution this, in turn, has taken on political and even economic res-
onances as well as epistemological ones. Theorizing and produc-
ing work in the name of various "realisms"—durational realism,
dynamic realism, external realism, formal realism, magical real-
ism, national realism, objective realism, plastic realism, poetic
realism, socialist realism, visionary realism, to name a few—or
under the guise of naturalism (stark realism), a number of writers
have attempted to make art simultaneously an analytic tool and a
source of perception and to make the real—usually construed as
the ordinary—world its focus.[2]

In recent years I have argued for a rethinking of realism in
terms of contemporary writing practice, both with respect to its
methods and its intentions. But in order to understand what such
a rethinking of it might yield, it is necessary briefly to account for
what has been meant by realism, in literary and art critical history.

The various "realisms" seem generally *not* to have taken on the
question of what constitutes the realness of reality—what gives
things realness. That problem seems to have been reserved for
philosophy (with significant contributions from political and eco-

nomic theory). The Industrial Revolution, along with the science that preceded it, had the effect of objectifying reality. Or perhaps it was the other way around; perhaps in the wake of industrialization and the technologies that made it possible, culture has increasingly assigned to the category of "reality" all (but only) those things which could be objectified. In any case, historically artistic realisms have assumed the existence of reality and posited it as the condition—circumstantial and particular—of lived life.

The term as applied to painting and to writing came into use in the middle of the nineteenth century, more or less simultaneously in Russia and in France and doubtless elsewhere as well. In Russia it seems to have been used first to talk about literary issues, and in France it was first applied to painting. Both Turgenev and Flaubert were credited with the paternity, but it was Emile Zola and his followers who made the term and its array of concepts current.

Given that I intend to relate this term to Gertrude Stein's writing and to her thinking about writing, it is interesting to note that Zola was a close social and intellectual companion of Cézanne, whom in turn Stein so admired. Cézanne and Zola were schoolboys together and comrades later as artists. They believed, at least for a very long time, that they were seeking solutions to the same, or very similar, artistic questions—though Cézanne's, it seems to me, was the far more complete solution.

In *The Experimental Novel* (1880) Zola identified the task of the writer with that of the scientist, taking a position that explicitly rejects the methods and subject matter of the romanticism which had been the dominant literature of the time: "No more lyricism, no more big empty words, but facts, documents," he wrote.[3] "Today we are rotten with lyricism, we wrongly believe that a great style is made of a sublime disorder, always ready to tumble over into madness; a great style is made of logic and clarity."[4]

Or, as Martin Eden, the eponymous hero of Jack London's realist novel, puts it, "The science professors should live. They're really great. But it would be a good deed to break the heads of nine-tenths of the English professors—little microscopic-minded parrots!"[5]

The basic concerns of the realist writers in the nineteenth century were methodological. Paul Alexis, who, along with others of Zola's group including Guy de Maupassant, was an exponent of Zola's ideas, wrote: "Realism is not a 'rhetoric,' as is generally believed, but something of greater seriousness, a 'method.' A method of thinking, seeing, reflecting, studying, experimenting, a need to analyze in order to know, but not a special way of writing."[6]

The frame of reference was philosophical. The intention was to treat the real rather than the ideal, the everyday rather than the unusual, the common rather than the exceptional. Realism rejected the loftiness and exoticism characteristic of romanticism and turned to ordinary life for subject matter. The technique was to be based on models from science. "The chain of reasoning will be very simple," said Zola; "if the experimental method has been capable of extension from chemistry and physics to physiology and medicine, then it can be carried from physiology to the naturalist novel."[7]

Realist literature attempted to confront two essential and quite separate issues. One was metaphysical; that is, the writer questioned the nature of the real, the relationship of the real to appearances, the distinction between the simulacrum and the original, the accuracy of perception, the problem of perception's susceptibility to illusion, and, finally, the capacity and sufficiency of art to translate, transfer, or become itself real. The other issue was ethical; that is, the writer questioned the relationship of art to truth, the relevance of sincerity and/or simulacra, and posited some practical value for the work, suggesting that literature can and should be useful. Realism, in this case, may be regarded as an attempt to get at both verisimilitude and veracity. "The extent of all realism is the realm of the author's pen, and a true picture of life, honestly and reverentially set down, is both moral and artistic whether it offends the conventions or not," wrote Theodore Dreiser. "Truth is what is; and the seeing of what is, the realization of truth."[8]

It is in Paul Alexis's statement that we see the limitations of the project already defined: "a need to analyze in order to know, but not a special way of writing." In fact, it is precisely a special way of writing that realism requires.

"Gertrude Stein, in her work," wrote Gertrude Stein in *The Autobiography of Alice B. Toklas*, "has always been possessed by the intellectual passion for exactitude in the description of inner and outer reality. She has produced a simplification by this concentration, and as a result the destruction of associational emotion in poetry and prose. She knows that beauty, music, decoration, the result of emotion should never be the cause, even events should not be the cause of emotion nor should they be the material of poetry and prose. Nor should emotion itself be the cause of poetry and prose. They should consist of an exact reproduction of either an outer or an inner reality."[9]

Stein's personal history was peculiarly directed toward the study of reality and of our perceptions of reality, which may or may not differ from or alter reality itself (to determine whether it did so and how formed part of her studies), as well as toward the study of the language which, on the one hand, apparently mediates between us and reality and, on the other hand, is for most of us the constant, ready, everyday, and natural medium for discovering, defining, and asserting reality—making use of it, expressing it, and, perhaps, creating it.

Indeed, perhaps it was the discovery that language is an order of reality itself and not a mere mediating medium—that it is possible and even likely that one can have a confrontation with a phrase that is as significant as a confrontation with a tree, chair, cone, dog, bishop, piano, vineyard, door, or penny—that replaced her commitment to a medical career with a commitment to a literary career. If so, she would have similarly realized that her writing was potentially as social and as useful as doctoring might be.

> That is a speech. Anybody will listen. What is romantic. I was astonished to learn that she was led by her head and her head was not with her head her head was leading when her heart stood still. She was certain to be left away with them.
> . . .
> Speeches are an answer. . . .
> The scene opens and they have a valley before them.[10]

The spirit of artistic commitment to the world, and the designation of that as realism, had in the nineteenth century followed on a rejection of religious (transcendent, inspirational) and secular (escapist) fantasies as the principal function of writing. But it was a response also to the emerging significance of science and its values—research, experimentation, persistence even to the point of drudgery, and belief in the passionate force of discipline.

Stein's later interest in detective fiction is something of an intellectual pun on this. It is useful to consider, because detective fiction parallels when it doesn't parody the essentially bourgeois values implicit in nineteenth-century realism and coincident with radical political and social values also present there.

Detective fiction asserts social optimism, a triumph over grim context. Detective stories are not about guilt and innocence, that is, not about morality; they are about details. The clue is a detail that solves a specific crime when appropriately observed by a detecting person. The purpose and function of these as of all the other details are to bury the specific crimes and crime in general—criminality.

The point of detection is to uncover the incontrovertible relationship between logic and justice. In the course of being detected, things—that is, objects, events, and ideas—that seem arbitrary and indiscriminate are rendered logical and relevant.

The nature of detail, the foregrounding of certain details and their transformation into clues, forces the trivial to become moral, even humanitarian. The specialness of the detective lies in his or her ability to combat the inexact and muddy, since it is they that cause or conceal the crime. The detective turns a detail into a clue by heightening the particular; he or she replaces false or insufficient with true or adequate detail. As Stein put it in "Subject-Cases":

> Parlors and parlors and for their parlors and in the parlors
> and to the parlor, to the parlor into the parlor for the parlor
> and in fact for it and in fact more than a fact. A fact is a fact.

It is a fact, and facing and replacing, in replacing, to replace, to replace here and there, and so much. In so much and so quoted and as quoted and so forth and for the most of it, for almost all of it and so and in that way not investigated. As to investigating reasonably preparing, preparing to do so. Do so and do so and to do so and as it were to be as if it were to have contributed and further more not more than as to stating. To state. Behind them to state, behind them and not to wait, behind them and more frequently and as it was very frequently they were merely as to have it attributed. Attributed to all of it and so satisfactorily as stated.[11]

Thus the detective buries the crime under the inexorable logic of infinite unlimited unquenchable details. "So indeed and so indeed a parlor settles that."[12] (The resemblance between the English *parlor* and the French *parler*, to speak, sets up a pertinent pun.)

At Radcliffe College, or what was then called Harvard Annex, Gertrude Stein studied with William James, who was not yet the philosopher William James but still a psychologist.

For James, psychology meant the study of consciousness—the contents and forms of consciousness. His methods were experimental, involving laboratory work and hence using laboratory methods. His principal work was the study of perception, our consciousness of perception, and the consciousness of the consciousness of perception—a trajectory from which one can hear the rumble of an approaching philosophy of language. James thoroughly understood, and Stein animated in practice, the vital, even vivacious, relationship of language forms and structures to perception and consciousness. James's psychology assumed people's natural inclination to seek truth, however multiple and variable it might turn out to be. (Obviously a truth based on and derived from perception will be as multiple and variable as the things perceived and persons perceiving.) But for Stein, it was not truth but understanding that was of value—a shift of emphasis, from perceived to perceiving, and thus to writing, in which acts of observation, as complex perception, take place. James's emphasis on the importance of (primarily perceptual) experience and its relationship to the structures and development of meaning had already extended to a study of language as a function of experience. Stein took the concept further. Language, as she thought and felt it, does far more than simply offer names for our experiences; indeed, a dependency on names (nouns) tends to obscure experience, by replacing what we experience with a pre-established concept, a "simulacrum," of it. It was on this discovery that Stein based her radical challenge to the primacy and centrality of the noun. States of consciousness exist as full sentences; the topography of consciousness consists of a rich verbal landscape. In imagining it, we have to bear in mind its porosity and observe the range of activity on its surface. We must acknowledge our sensation of *of*, *if*, *the*, and *some* as well as *tree*, *smoke*, *shed*, and *road*.

Tender Buttons was written between 1912 and 1913, after Gertrude Stein and Alice B. Toklas made their first trip to Spain, where, as Stein herself has said, Spanish light and Spanish ways of arranging things, the light flat but the compositions round, had a profound effect on her perception of things—their composition and the syntax of seeing them. *Tender Buttons* is in three sections, titled "Objects," "Food," and "Rooms." There are fifty-eight objects, or object poems; the table of contents of "Food" lists thirty-nine titles but there are fifty-one "poems" in the section; and "Rooms" is a continuous piece in paragraphs. The relative weights of the three sections are about equal, and the things portrayed are ordinary—ordinary objects, mostly domestic; ordinary food, plain and wholesome, not haute cuisine; domestic rooms, averagely adorned.

In a pair of articles that were first published in the *New York Review of Books* in 1982,[13] Charles Rosen and Henri Zerner, reviewing an exhibition and catalogue focusing on realism and the realist tradition, point out that subject matter taken from the ordinary world retains its integrity and ordinariness and even banality in conjunction with a highly visible artistic means. The realism of the means—the materiality and palpability of the poetic language, for example—is a precise manifestation of the artist's attention to the particularity of the subject matter.

It is in this respect that the pronouncement from Zola's circle, namely that realism doesn't involve a "special way of writing," becomes inadequate and mistaken. Somewhat paradoxically perhaps, it is the autonomy of the writing—the high visibility of its devices and even its intrusive strangeness—that authenticates the accuracy of its portrayals and gives the work itself its authority. "It is the guarantee of the truth of what is being represented."[14]

To some extent, then, a writer's candor with regard to his or her own means can be taken as the representation of a general truthfulness with regard to objects. Rosen and Zerner make a further point with regard to mundane subject matter whose aesthetic value is of no significance: "If contemporary life was to be represented with all its banality, ugliness, and mediocrity undistorted, unromanticized, then the aesthetic interest had to be shifted from the objects represented to the means of representation."[15]

In this, the opposite of realism is not imagination (which exists within style) but idealism (which is imposed on subject matter).

> Flaubert's prose, distinguished and beautiful in itself, does not disturb the banality of the contemporary life he represented. . . . [Art] can lay a double claim, first to absolute truth undistracted by aesthetic preconceptions, and then to abstract beauty, uninfluenced by the world that is represented. Art for art's sake and Realism are not polar opposites . . . but two sides of the same coin. It was the avant-garde that succeeded in uniting them. . . . In avant-garde Realism there is an extreme insistence on the means of representation; the rhythm of the prose or the patterns of the brush strokes are always obtrusively in evidence. A work of avant-garde Realism proclaims itself first as a solid, material art object, and only then allows us access to the contemporary world it portrays. In avant-garde Realism, consequently, the beauty of the book or the picture always appears to be irrelevant to what is being represented. Stylistic forms that idealize had to be avoided at all cost.[16]

"Art ought," wrote Flaubert, "to rise above personal feelings and nervous susceptibilities! It is time to give it the precision of the physical sciences, by means of a pitiless method."[17] Similar ideas occur repeatedly in twentieth-century avant-garde theory. So Viktor Shklovsky wrote: "Thus in order to restore to us the perception of life, to make a stone stony, there exists that which we call art."[18] And Francis Ponge: "In order for a text to expect in any way to render an account of reality of the concrete world (or the spiritual one) it must first attain reality in its own world, the textual one."[19]

"What seems beautiful to me"—this is Flaubert again, in one of his famous and remarkable letters to Louise Colet—"what I should like to write, is a book about nothing, a book dependent on nothing external, which would be held together by the internal strength of its style . . . a book which would have practically no subject, or at least one in which the subject would be almost invisible, if that is possible."[20] It might almost have been in response to this that Gertrude Stein wrote of *Tender Buttons:* "Now that was a thing that I too felt in me the need of making it be a thing that could be named without using its name. After all one had known its name anything's name for so long, and so the name was not new but the thing being alive was always new."[21] And, she added, several pages further, "I had to feel anything and everything that for me was existing so intensely that I could put it down in writing as a thing in itself without at all necessarily using its name. The name of a thing might be something in itself if it could come to be real enough but just as a name it was not enough something."[22] It is thus that she arrived at *Tender Buttons*, a poem, or group of poems, in which the liveliness of anything recurs artistically within the scope of a radical force of attention.

This ambitious, exquisite work raises a number of issues—current issues, relevant to contemporary writing. There are three areas from which one can triangulate a reading of the work. The first is linguistic: the work questions the nature of language as the basis for knowing anything and explores the effect of technical aspects of language (parts of speech, sentence structure, grammar, and the size and shape of the writing) and poetic devices (images, patterns, paradoxes, etc.). The second is psychological, by which I mean, in Jamesian terms, it investigates the character of consciousness and, in particular, of a consciousness that is based on perception and elaborated by the perceiver through encounters with the world. And the third is philosophical, best seen in terms of phenomenology, insofar as it addresses and tests empirically available material—things that can be viewed "objectively," which is to say viewed as objects but also viewed in the process of coming into objecthood.

"What is the difference between a thing seen and what do you mean," as Stein posed the issue.[23] "Now what is the difference between a sentence and I mean."[24] In *Tender Buttons* Stein attempted to discover uses of language which could serve as a locus of meaning and even of primary being; to do so she had to disassemble conventional structures through which language, in mediating between us (thought) and the world (things), becomes instead a barrier, blocking meaning, limiting knowledge, excluding experience.

If one accepts Merleau-Ponty's definition of phenomenology, *Tender Buttons* might be read as a phenomenological masterpiece, a work that guarantees writing a role in the exploration of "realness." In the preface to *Phenomenology of Perception*, Merleau-Ponty says:

> Phenomenology is the study of essences; and according to it, all problems amount to finding definitions of essences: the essence of perception, or the essence of consciousness, for example. But phenomenology is also a philosophy which puts essences back into existence, and does not expect to arrive at an understanding of man and the world from any starting point other than that of their "facticity." . . . It is also a philosophy for which the world is always "already there" before

reflection begins—as an inalienable presence; and all its efforts are concentrated upon re-achieving a direct and primitive contact with the world. . . . It is the search for a philosophy which shall be a "rigorous science," but it also offers an account of space, time, and the world as we "live" them. It tries to give a direct description of our experience as it is.[25]

Putting "essences back into existence" was the practical work that Stein undertook in *Tender Buttons* and the portraits of that same prewar period. She described her intentions in her lecture "Portraits and Repetition":

> I began to wonder at at about this time just what one saw when one looked at anything really looked at anything. Did one see sound, and what was the relationship between color and sound, did it make itself by description by a word that meant it or did it make itself by a word in itself. All this time I was of course not interested in emotion or that anything happened. . . . I lived my life with emotion and with things happening but I was creating in my writing by simply looking. . . . I became more and more excited about how words which were the words that made whatever I looked at look like itself were not the words that had in them any quality of description. . . . And the thing that excited me so very much at that time and still does is that the word or words that make what I looked at be itself were always words that to me very exactly related themselves to that thing the thing at which I was looking, but as often as not had as I say nothing whatever to do with what my words would do that described that thing.[26]

The first poem in *Tender Buttons* is titled "A Carafe, That Is a Blind Glass."

A kind of glass and a cousin, a spectacle and nothing strange
a single hurt color and an arrangement in a system to point-
ing. All this and not ordinary, not unordered in not resem-
bling. The difference is spreading.[27]

A carafe is a container, a glass one, which, if filled with a thick
liquid, that is a colored one, might be, so to speak, blind, opaque.
A blind glass might also be a blank mirror, or a draped window—
a window with the blinds drawn. A glass might be a magnifying
glass, or some other eyeglass—a spectacle—though it's unusual
to use it in the singular (as it is to speak of a scissor or a trouser).
The meaning (or meanings) of the title depends on whether the
phrase after the comma is an appositive or whether the comma is
like the copula "and" in the sentences of the poem that follows.
In the former case, one thing is seen in two aspects; in the latter,
two things are joined in a pair. The pattern of unfolding laid
against infolding, or of doubles set in dualities, continues in the
poem until the last sentence, which might be read as a statement
or commentary on the rest.

"A kind in glass and a cousin": a kind binds carafe and blind
phonically. The two words in the two halves of the title are con-
densed into one, while the simple phrase, a kind of glass, under-
goes a bit of distortion, becoming a kind *in* glass. A kind of glass,
or some kind of glass thing, which is a carafe, has something *in*
it—the way ideas fill words.

A cousin is a relationship—a familiar one, "nothing strange."

A spectacle has a double meaning, in that it is both that
through which one sees, "glass," and also what one sees through
them: "What a spectacle!" and "Don't make a spectacle of your-
self." Seeing through, seeing with, seeing at, seeing in, and see-

ing beside—a fully prepositional situation. As William James re-marks in *Principles of Psychology:*

> There is not a conjunction or a preposition, and hardly an adverbial phrase, syntactic form, or inflection of voice, in human speech, that does not express some shading or other of relation which we at some moment actually feel to exist between the larger objects of our thought. If we speak objectively, it is the real relations that appear revealed; if we speak subjectively, it is the stream of consciousness that matches each of them by an inward coloring of its own. . . . We ought to say a feeling of *and*, a feeling of *if*, a feeling of *but*, and a feeling of *by*, quite as readily as we say a feeling of *blue* or a feeling of *cold*.[28]

This raises one sense in which one might interpret Stein's "an arrangement in a system to pointing"; a "system to pointing" might mean descriptive language (though significantly "not or-dinary" language, bearing in mind the distinction between ordi-nary and poetic languages)—descriptive not with recourse to naming but relationally. Pointing itself, the gesture, is relational, in that it locates a thing relative to the position of the pointing person and implies the presence of contiguous or neighboring things beside which or among which the thing-pointed-to sits, and among which it might be "lost" if it weren't pointed out. Af-ter all, if it sat alone the pointing would be redundant—an empty gesture.

The first sentence of the poem is a trio of twos, in which *a cousin*, *nothing strange*, and *an arrangement* (the second terms of each pair) are aligned and face *a kind in glass*, *a spectacle*, and *a single hurt color*. A single hurt color might be interpreted as an imperfect perception—imperfect in being single—thus in need of the first term of the next sentence: "All this."

"I tried to include color and movement,"[29] Stein said, meaning that she wanted generally to understand the qualities of things, in themselves (their color) and also as they color our feelings and thoughts, as they qualify them, "in the stream of consciousness," as James puts it, "that matches each of them by an inward coloring of its own." Or as Stein says, "Beside beside is colored like a word beside why there they went."[30]

As for movement, Stein wanted to understand things not in isolated rigidity, which falsified and monumentalized conditions which were fluid, but as present participants in ongoing living—outpouring, fountainous living. How does a carafe move? In an arrangement. By being larger than a cup and smaller than a pitcher; by containing less liquid than before; by reflecting light (and thereby color); by being or containing the same color as a piece of paper; by having a vase with flowers not of that color set to the left of it from here but to the right of it from there, and so forth.

Stein's analysis, in this sense, is lateral; she does not trace things back to their origins, her investigation is not etymological. That would reduce things to nouns, and Stein's concern was to get away from the stasis (and the phallocentric monumentality) of the name. She saw things in a present continuity, a present relativity, across the porous planes of the writing. "Not ordinary." And "not unordered in not resembling." Not chaotic, despite the rapidly multiplying abundance of singularities, by virtue of the differences. Differences keep things separate and distinct.

As Donald Sutherland put it: "The great welter of what seem to be particularities and trivialities in *Tender Buttons* comes from a 'religious' attitude toward everything as simple existence." Stein has perceived that the experience of "simple existence" comes about through "the change . . . from feeling that everything was simply alike to feeling that everything was simply different."[31] Differences, as Stein has discovered, are at the heart of discernment. As she says in "Composition as Explanation," "It was all so nearly alike it must be different and it is different, it is natural that if everything is used and there is a continuous present and a beginning again and again if it is all so alike it must be simply different and everything simply different was the natural way of creating it then."[32]

It is precisely differences that are the foundation and the point of devices such as rhyming, punning, pairing, parallelisms, and running strings of changes within either vowel or consonant frames. It is the difference between rod and red and rid that makes them mean. Wordplay, in this sense, foregrounds the relationship between words. "A sentence means that it looks different to them. Considerably. A sentence means that it is as different as it looks."[33]

The carafe in *Tender Buttons'* first poem is only the first of a number of various things that can be thought of as containers or enclosures. With regard to language (signification, sense), the concept of containment is one that opens questions regarding words' and sentences' ability to "hold" meaning. Stein is probing the fraught relationship between the semantics of perception and the syntax of the language in which it is expressed and described—or in which, perhaps, it actually takes place.

Across the motif of containment, there is a series of words relative to destruction, or, at the least, change—process, alteration, and natural transformations, as well as cracks, holes, punctures, piercing, gaps, and breakage, as well as the possible spill with which the first poem ends. Variations on the motif recur, and they refer in part to Stein's concerns about the means and adequacy of writing—of capturing things in words. As she put it a in "Americans," a work of the same period, "A gap what is a gap when there is not any meaning in a slice with a hole in it. What is the exchange between the whole and no more witnesses."[34]

The contrast between the containment motif and the motif of water and fluidity is obvious. The flow of water is rather like the abstract nature of color. It can take place in or on a thing but it is always as a part of a larger, more abstract entity that it has its character. Blue, or the sea. "Why is there a single piece of any color," Stein asks in "Rooms."[35] Perhaps the allusions to water are simultaneously allusions to consciousness, that consciousness which, said William James, "does not appear to itself chopped up in bits . . . it is nothing jointed; it flows. . . . It is [the] free water of consciousness. . . . Every definite image in the mind is steeped and dyed in the free water that flows round it. With it goes the sense of its relations, near and remote."[36] The term "stream of consciousness" recurs over and over in James's writings on psychology.

I myself don't always experience consciousness as a "stream." Instead it often does appear broken up, discontinuous—sometimes radically, abruptly, and disconcertingly so. It would seem that Stein wondered about this:

Will she be kneeling beside the water where the water is flowing and will she be losing it and will she furnish a house as well and will she see some one as she is advancing and will she be a christian and will she furnish a house as well. Will she be kneeling beside the water. Will she advance and will she furnish the house as well. Will she be kneeling there where the water is flowing. She attached to it this, she attaches to it.[37]

Box, bottle, carafe, cup, shoe, tumbler, book. Containers and their covers—concealment—colors, and dust, dirt, darkness, polish, shine. "A shine is that which when covered changes permission. An enclosure blends with the same that is to say there is blending. A blend is that which holds no mice and this is not because of a floor it is because of nothing, it is not in a vision."[38]

Does a thing contain itself? Does it contain its own reality? Do we perceive a thing as it is in itself? Do the words in which we speak of a thing capture our perception, our thought of it? Containers and enclosures question the integrity both of things and of our claims to convey a sense of them at many levels. Speaking of the objects in *Tender Buttons*, Stein said:

> Instead of giving what I was realizing at any and every moment of them and of me until I was empty of them I made them contained within the thing I wrote that was them. The thing in itself folding itself up inside itself like you might fold a thing up to be another thing which is that thing. . . . If you think how you fold things or make a boat or anything else out of paper or getting anything to be inside anything, the hole in the doughnut or the apple in the dumpling perhaps you will see what I mean.[39]

For Stein, the container was from the start an interesting problem. To regard description—or the page of writing—as a container was to betray the nature of the thing described, the flow of its existence, and the flow of the consciousness perceiving it. "An eyeglass, what is an eyeglass, it is water."[40]

To resolve this, she conceived of her work not as a medium for emptying herself of ideas nor as a formalized language holding the contents of the objects which emptied themselves into it, but of the writing as "the thing that was them"—which means that things take place inside the writing, are perceived there, not else-where, outside it. It is the nature of meaning to be intrinsic, in other words, as the meaning of any person is, of me, *is* me, the person. That is how the poem means. Concentric circles draw more and more in as they radiate out; more and more lake is con-tained by the stone.

Tender Buttons can be read as a hard-edged, rigorous, analyti-cal, merciless, impassioned realism which

1. is patient and thorough in regarding things in the world;
2. sounds the psychological density of language;
3. keeps its techniques bristling with perceptibility;
4. is motivated by the cathexis of language itself in relation to knowledge;
5. is successful in achieving the inability to finish what it says.

Grammar and Landscape

1

Landscape, in and of itself, is a model of longevity. It has the virtue of never being complete, and so of seeming permanent—eternal. As a form, therefore, it is solemn and vacant, because nothing can match it. No condition, or set or array of conditions, achieves a finalized form of landscape—which makes landscape an exemplary case, a spread of examples. As the biologist D'Arcy Thompson says in his classic *On Growth and Form* (1917), "Some lofty concepts, like space and number, involve truths remote from the category of causation; and here we must be content, as Aristotle says, if the mere facts be known. But natural history deals with ephemeral and accidental, not eternal nor universal things; their causes and effects thrust themselves on our curiosity, and become the ultimate relations to which our contemplation extends."[41]

For Gertrude Stein, landscape was an empty form, or rather a form free of prediction, a vibrational field of reversible effects. The exactitude—the "realism" that she claimed for her analyses (as nameless naming) of single objects in *Tender Buttons*—could be repeated over and over if she could get not only the object but its position and the condition of its being in position. And this could be multiplied; there could be many objects and then therefore many relationships, simultaneously—coincidents, which are the most reversible of relationships.

To "Act so that there is no use in a center"[42] proposes landscape with its perspective spread over a largish surface, located on innumerable nonisolating focal points. In terms of writing, this meant, for Stein, that the vanishing point might be on every word.

Stein, in her *Lectures in America*, and especially in the one called "Plays," tracks the development of her understanding of landscape in terms of plays—at first in the theater, and in terms of temporal rather than spatial problems, but more and more as writing rather than theater, and in response to local landscapes— in Spain both on the trip that influenced *Tender Buttons* and on subsequent visits, and then in the French countryside: "and there I lived in a landscape that made itself its own landscape," she says,[43] as if identifying as a natural condition, or a condition in nature, that which was the made condition of her own descriptive writing in *Tender Buttons*: "I made them" (that is, the objects as descriptions in the poems of *Tender Buttons*) "contained within the thing I wrote that was them. The thing in itself folded up inside itself like you might fold a thing up to be another thing which is that thing inside it that thing . . . ," as she said.[44] The landscape "that made itself its own landscape" was bright and substantive, heavy, burdened, under the tension of its own sufficient and complicated activity, its habitual readiness, a form of charged waiting, a perpetual attendance; this is very much the way a child feels its life, and the way saints, as Stein saw them, feel theirs. One thinks of the opening of *Four Saints in Three Acts*, a play which for Stein was primarily and pointedly a landscape:

> Two saints prepare for saints it two saints prepare for saints
> in prepare for saints.
>
> A narrative of prepare for saints in narrative prepare for
> saints.
>
> Remain to narrate to prepare two saints for saints.[45]

But if one is to consider the landscape as a form of charged, redolent waiting, one can't help but think too of Flaubert, and his recurrent oblique or lateral stylistic influence on Stein.

> Full and flushed, the moon came up over the skyline behind
> the meadow, climbed rapidly between the branches of the
> poplars, which covered it here and there like a torn black
> curtain, rose dazzling white in the clear sky, and then, sail-
> ing more slowly, cast down upon the river a great splash
> of light that broke into a million stars, a silver sheen that
> seemed to twist its way to the bottom, like a headless snake
> with luminous scales; or like some monstrous candelabra
> dripping molten diamonds. The soft night was all about
> them. Curtains of shadow hung amid the leaves. Emma, her
> eyes half-closed, breathed in with deep sighs the cool wind

that was blowing. They did not speak, caught as they were in the rush of their reverie. Their early tenderness returned to their hearts, full and silent as the river flowing by, soothing-sweet as the perfume the syringas wafted, casting huger and more melancholy shadows on their memory than those the unmoving willows laid upon the grass. Often some night-animal, hedgehog or weasel, would scuffle through the undergrowth as it started after its quarry; now and again a ripe peach could be heard softly dropping from the tree.[46]

2

It is at just that moment that the night is repeated, received repeatedly surrounding the foggy morning, a rainy noon, the hot sun, the clouds in moonlight moving from left to right. That is, despite the forward momentum, the gravitational drag that keeps us characteristically active, despite the inclination to look without specificity of thought or focus into the distance and gaze at the blue-gray diffusion and soothing yellow-gray silhouettes on the horizon that soak up details, one concentrates instead (perhaps, in search of forms) on the foreground branches of a middle-sized tree just within reach to the left. On their underside, the leaves are a dusty gray with a powdery texture, and green and greasy above, bisected by a bulging vein. It takes more breeze to move the tree than to shake the gradual grass that goes down a slope over a mound that begins above the tree in rocks and green and exposed maroon concave faces on the hill. "The rope attached to the mountain is for the benefit of those who roll the rocks down the mountain and the umbrella and the mechanical motion is hers who is breaking the rocks open and she is observing that the grass is growing nearly four times yearly."[47] The young grass grows more broadly than tenderly and is most pervasive in the middle distance, since the dirt in the foreground and the dying yellow and matted gray and brown moldy tangle blot it out over some ants. In the interim: bees, a wire fence, cows, shadows, picnics, and a game, a siren in the distance that reaches us in waves after it sounds. Several seasons, and an entire day move by, and if you now think of language, both loosely and particularly, as radiating structures and as behavior in sentences, the relationship between grammar and landscape, while still vague, may begin to be perceived, at least in the imagination.

To suggest that there is a relationship between grammar and landscape in Stein's work—or to suggest that we can usefully imagine one in order to understand the meaning of a form of poetic language in her writing—is really not an imposition, since landscape and grammar were what Stein herself was simultaneously writing and thinking about (the two for her are almost inseparable) during the twenties and early thirties, the years in which she wrote a number of plays (many of them included in *Operas and Plays*), *Lucy Church Amiably*, and the works collected in *How to Write*. One can read these various works in conjunction, that is as a ground for the examination of temporal and of spatial scales in the world of things and persons and in language, which determines just as much as it reflects our sense of measure and scale. Cows, roses, shadows, exclamations in appreciation, rivers, spouses, poplar trees, fences, conversations, and sentences in description, for example. What occurs as time and what occurs as space, the movement, have grammatical value and can be understood as such at least incompletely—by which I mean that it is likely that the understanding remains unfinished.

3

Stein once said of dances and battles that they construct landscapes, since persons go in and out of them and fill them with movement back and forth. The resulting landscapes constitute plays.

> The landscape has its formation and as after all a play has
> to have formation and be in relation one thing to the other
> thing and as the story is not the thing as any one is always
> telling something then the landscape not moving but being
> always in relation, the trees to the hills the hills to the fields
> the trees to each other any piece of it to any sky and then any
> detail to any other detail, the story is only of importance if
> you like to tell or like to hear a story but the relation is there
> anyway. And of that relation I wanted to make a play and I
> did, a great number of plays.[48]

The first of the plays of this period was "Lend a Hand or Four Religions" (1922). She said of it later, "This play has always interested her immensely, it was the first attempt that later made her *Operas and Plays*, the first conception of landscape as a play."[49]

Although "Lend a Hand or Four Religions" precedes *Four Saints* by several years, it bears a strong relation to it and to *Lucy Church Amiably*. The milieu is bucolic—"natural" but inhabited, or at least attended. The repetitions that occur suffice for action, ordinal numbers provide sequence and thus temporality, and the patterns that develop provide what there is of plot. Seasonal activity, counting and minding, form the meditative motifs which develop into the character traits of the Four Religions.

Four Saints in Three Acts was written in 1927, the same year as *Lucy Church Amiably*. In *Four Saints*, Stein said, "I made the Saints the landscape. All the saints that I made and I made a number of them because after all a great many pieces of things are a landscape all these saints together made my landscape. These attendant saints were the landscape and it the play really is a landscape."[50]

The activity, or characteristic movement (both literal and conceptual—i.e., not perceived but known), that takes place in the plays and the novel is patterned rather than plotted, and the works are not without vista, romance, and even melodrama. What is in place from the outset and continuously occurring are all-over relationships of greater or lesser complexity that include things, persons, and events—lists (one of the plays, in fact, is called "A List"), shifts ("What is the difference between reserve and reverse"),[51] cycles that are both rhythmic and arrhythmic, like acceleration and deceleration in time or crescendo and diminuendo in space, comings and goings, and the dynamics of emotional and motivational relativity.

That the form in which this takes place is called landscape, rather than story, makes it easier to understand how Stein perceived and felt about event, adventure, and meaning—what constituted these for her. Of course, *nonlinear* is a key term here, and it is against this that grammar becomes complicated and interesting.

In the opening paragraphs of the lecture "Plays," Stein herself associates her studies of grammar with her interest in plays as landscape. She repeats a discovery that she had recorded in *How to Write* regarding the emotions in relation to linguistic structures ("paragraphs are emotional and sentences are not")[52] and she goes on to announce her discovery of a disjuncture between the emotional time of the play and the emotional time of the audience watching the play. This causes a troubling "syncopation," as she calls it—an unpleasant and debilitating anxiety. "The thing seen and the emotion did not go together."[53] Perceptual participation is blocked, and the result is devitalization and hence devaluation. For Stein vitality—liveliness—is a supreme good; the first and highest value of anyone (or anything) lies in their "being completely living," and so this problem with the conventional theater is an important one. "I felt that if a play was exactly like a landscape then there would be no difficulty about the emotion of the person looking on at the play being behind or ahead of the play because the landscape does not have to make acquaintance. You may have to make acquaintance with it, but it does not with you, it is there. . . . "[54]

And so Stein arrived at the question, What is a landscape and what relationship does a landscape have with a sentence and a paragraph? Or, What are the qualities that are characteristic of a landscape? And what is it about landscapes that lead Stein, and through her us, to think about grammar? "Grammar is the same as relative."[55] "Grammar in relation to a tree and two horses."[56]

It is customary and to an extent automatic to think of landscape as a space, as a framed spatial configuration enclosing natural phenomena. But to think about time as it takes place in a landscape makes it much easier to understand some of Stein's central concepts and the literary strategies that develop out of them, since so many of them concern temporal structures of perception. "The sense of time is a phenomenon of nature," she said in "Natural Phenomena."

It is what adds complexity to composition. There can be past and present and future which succeed and rejoin, this makes romantic realistic and sentimental and then really the three in one and not romantic and not realistic and not sentimental. The three in one makes a time sense that adds complexity to composition. A composition after all is never complex. The only complexity is the time sense that adds that creates complexity in composition. Let us begin over and over again. Let us begin again and again and again.[57]

It is the convergence of these elements—that is, time and space —with language that provides the excitement of grammar. "It makes me smile to be a grammarian and I am."[58]

4

The characteristics exhibited by space in landscape are easily recognizable. As Donald Sutherland puts it, it is a "composition of motions."[59] Things in space expand or wither, the expanse is more or less framed from any particular point of view in it. Trees bend to the wind; the color of the grasses shifts under shadows; bushes bloom and receive birds; cows, deer, a bicyclist, squirrels, a dog, lizards, etc., pass through. A rock rolls down the slope. Any unit of this space, however large or small, is complete in itself as a landscape. The style of activity anywhere bears a resemblance to the style of activity elsewhere. The space is filled, so to speak, with long-wave and short-wave sympathetic vibrations. "Would it be very certain that rain and its equivalent sun and its equivalent a hill and its equivalent and flowers and their equivalent have been heard and seen and felt and followed and more around and rounder and roundly. Is there also a hesitation in going slower. She said yes."[60]

A self-contained landscape where "what is seen is contained by itself inside it" in direct and precise distances, divisions, and situations is the point here. The "going slower" becomes obsessive. The movement, if one can put it this way, becomes a fixation. The activity that maintains between events is arrested and detail is flattened. It is in this sense that Stein could observe, as she put it in "Plays," "A landscape does not move nothing really moves in a landscape but things are there." It is a matter of simple observation. "Magpies are in a landscape that is they are in the sky of a landscape, they are black and white and they are in the sky of the landscape in Bilignin and in Spain, especially in Avila. When they are in the sky they do something that I have never seen any other bird do they hold themselves up and down and look flat against the sky."[61] In essence the landscape, by virtue of its own laws, is transformed under attention into a tableau, a *tableau vivant*; episodes become qualities. "All that was necessary was that there was something completely contained within itself and being contained within itself was moving, not moving in relation to anything not moving in relation to itself but just moving."[62] It is thus that Stein can envisage battles and charging up or down hills as landscape events—flattened out onto the names of the hills. Events are presences:

1. A stain with a lily.
Second. A girl with a rooster in front of her and a bush of strange flowers at her side and a small tree behind her.
3. A guardian of a museum holding a cane.
4. A woman leaning forward.

5. A woman with a sheep in front of her a small tree behind her.

6. A woman with black hair and two bundles one under each arm.

7. A night watchman of a hotel who does not fail to stand all the time.

8. A very stout girl with a basket and flowers summer flowers and the flowers are in front of a small tree.[63]

5

The way in which Stein depicted landscape is radically different from that of the American nineteenth-century landscape painters, though I think one can trace their influence on the work of other twentieth-century American poets. Either directly or indirectly drawing on the writings of American Renaissance writers (particularly Emerson and Thoreau), the painters of the Hudson River Valley school interpreted landscape as the "book of God," as a wilderness in which Spirit is Immanent, as a solitude (their attitude toward humans is full of conflict), an abode of melancholic euphoria, a retrospection of Eden. Their landscapes are saturated in loss. The burdening of a sense of place with the past (whether its own or some imported past) continued to hold significance for certain later American modernist poets. I am thinking, for example, of the mystique of place in Charles Olson's work, where Gloucester becomes history, with etymology as its paradigm, the noun or name taking on increasing weight, until it becomes a heroic task (the task of the poet) simply to say it. Landscape is not a site of play but of drama.

Stein's sense of landscape seems more painterly than theatrical, but the painters who were influencing her were Braque, Picasso, Matisse, and, above all, Cézanne. Certainly the use of a flat or planar perspective for purposes of intensification comes from Cézanne. His landscapes are presented, so to speak, broadside, and more than one area is present with full force. Similarly, Stein distributes value or meaning across the entirety of any given work; the emphases are panoramic.

In some respects, Stein in the landscape works is discovering for herself the fundamental distinction that the Swiss linguist Ferdinand de Saussure had articulated in his lectures on linguistics.[64] Saussure's distinction pertained to the definition of the terrain we call language and alternative (though not mutually exclusive) approaches to it. Language may be considered diachronically, that is historically, in terms of its etymologies and developing syntactic usages and strategies over time; at the same time, that same language may be regarded synchronously, as a system in use and complete at any given moment. Indeed, the distinction between synchrony and diachrony proves extremely fruitful for regarding almost any kind of system. What we have is two continuums (or continua), one of which, the diachronous, we may think of as vertical, an historical swathe or a current of contiguous time lines trailing behind every object, idea, and event. The second continuum, that of the synchronous present, on a plane extending over the full expanse of the moment, is characterized by an existential density in which present relationships and differentiations, to the extent that we can take them in, are the essential activity. The diachronous is characterized by causality, or one could say narrativity; the attachments of one thing to another are consequential. Whereas the synchronous is characterized by parallelism. One notices analogies and coincidences, resemblances and differences, the simultaneous existence of variations, contradictions, and the apparently random. Stein's landscapes are resolutely synchronous.

Key elements coexist with their alternatives in the work. Nothing is superseded. A phrase or sentence is not obliterated when an altered or even contradictory version of it appears. In this regard, the frequent use of "and" in Stein's work is an important indicator of inclusion, just as the use of the gerundive is an important indicator of the continuation of anything. One must be careful not to read any sequence of sentences as a series of substitutions or cancellations, not even as a "progress" of thought. "A sentence is never displaced."[65] And although any reading, like any writing, has to occur over time, Stein set herself the difficult task of attempting to sustain everything in any of her works as concurrent. The effects she was seeking are landscape effects, producing an experience less mediated than those produced in historical stages.

6

What adds figurative interest to the synchronic-diachronic opposition is that, although the synchronic is obviously a temporal concept, it projects a spatial figure—one could say a landscape— "a moment of time that has gotten in position."[66] The syntax of time is juxtaposed against the syntax of space, rather as the sentence runs across the line in poetry. There are the two sets of conditions governing the composition.

Barrett Watten, in discussing Robert Smithson's sculpture in the title essay of his book *Total Syntax*, says, "*Space* is the exterior syntax; it is physical and cultural, starting from the actual site of the work. *Time* is the interior syntax; it is structural and psychological and begins with the response to the work in language."[67] But in Stein's work—that is, in *Lucy Church Amiably* and in the plays of the same period—*both* space and time are psychological and interior, and both are structural vis-à-vis language, which remains exterior, as the *site*. Time is pressed onto and spread out over the imagined spatial plane, and it is in language that details, and especially temporal details, are specified and, as it were, made physical. Distinctions must occur—activity takes place—across the language plane itself. In terms of spatial syntax, configurations and relationships occur in sets rather than in sequence, so that the perceptual activity, which has taken the form of writing, makes essential comparisons, oppositions, and distinctions. As Saussure put it, "In language there are only differences."[68] Or as Stein said, "Grammar makes it be different."[69]

This occurs at its simplest level with the word itself, and accounts in part for Stein's exploration of the significance of homonyms and rhymes and the effect of changing single vowels or consonants across a set of words. "Natural phenomena are or are not to cease. There is a pleasant difference between a crease cease and increase. There is a pleasant difference between when they had been very fortunate in deciding everything and when they had it little by little all the time."[70] And in "Sentences," "Supposing it is ours a dress address name can be opposed to name and tame."[71]

The change and exchange of names is one of Stein's recurrent devices, and can be read as instrumental in the construction (and questioning of) the relationship of sound to meaning (it is, also, of course, a highly suggestive component in Stein's concepts of identity and entity). "Nobody knows which name is the one they have heard," she comments. "Helen Mary how many how many how many Helen Marys are there to be had as many as every time every every every time time of day. . . . "[72] Beyond the obvious (and important) musicality of such passages, they also contain psychological resonances, particularly with regard to mood. "Simon when and fall Simon Church out loud. Simon Ethel out loud. Simon Edith out loud. Simon William out loud. Simon Elizabeth out loud. Simon Couttall out loud. Simon Charles Simon with it. Simon very well Simon Alice very well I thank you. Simon South who went about and said it is very nicely evident that they exchange wire for west and it is their pleasure. It is the pleasure of the very different difference every afternoon after noon."[73] Like Heidegger, Stein has discovered that every relation with phenomena is colored in mood. But whereas Heidegger, in *Being and Time*, concentrates on the moods of "boredom" and "anxiety," Stein's are more diverse and include pleasure and humor. She is often in mood amused.

Indeed, Gertrude Stein was often a comic writer; funniness has something to do with the vibrational movement that she achieved. On the other hand, she was almost never ironic, perhaps because irony comes from being of two minds, and Stein was, by choice, significantly singleminded. And for the same reason she is seldom metaphorical. In fact, metaphor for Stein is a suspect device, since it is a secondary characteristic of perception, and it is primary perception that Stein sought in her work. Directly in sentences.

7 Seasons

Sentences of which present attention is the sole antecedent; the thought begins here. "A sentence is an imagined frontispiece."[74] Candor without confession, not neutral but frontal. In the thickening of the sentence. "A grammar means positively no prayer for a decline of pressure."[75] Stein's open aphoristic style must come from writing one sentence at a time. As a consequence of its irreducibility, a sentence like "A sentence is not natural" is the kernel of an analysis, but so too is "A sentence is not not natural."[76]

Despite the beauty and even the usefulness of William James's metaphor of consciousness as a stream, and despite the inextricable correspondences between language and thought, to think of grammar as a river is likely to lead to silly consequences. Sentences give our senses form, which is why a river or stream is such an outrageous model for location and stability, even when the landscape is taking its name from the river, as in the Loire Valley, for example.

> A river separates water and so it should.
> A river separates water and so it should.
> A river separates water and so it should.
> A river.
> A river separates water and so it should.[77]

The entrance of the sentence into metaphysics may produce a landscape, but the sentence itself is grammatical. Its words and meaning are engaged as grammar, motivated temporally and spatially. The sentence moves in large or small increments, depending on the specific sentence; conventionally, it advances the story, the argument, the information, or the melody-line. And conventionally it is led by the noun-verb configuration (which can only take place in sentences anyway—that is, words are simply vocabulary until they take place in a sentence; it is the sentence which renders them malleable, making their plasticity operative and relevant).

But in Stein's writing, the word values, which are conventionally hierarchical, are often instead spread out within the sentence. The role of noun and verb gets shifted or bounced back and forth across the sentence, and words trade functions, something which is relatively easy in our scarcely inflected English where words like *paddles value sentences reverse part* and so on may be nouns verbs or in some cases adjectives without any alteration—so the movement is multidimensional, multirelational. "A sentence is an interval in which there is a finally forward and back."[78]

This does approximate consciousness, but its workings are less analogous to a stream or river than to bird flight, to use an alternative metaphor from the "Stream of Thought" chapter in William James's *Principles of Psychology:*

> As we take . . . a general view of the wonderful stream of our consciousness, what strikes us first is [the] different pace of its parts. Like a bird's life, it seems to be made of an alteration of flights and perchings. The rhythm of language expresses this, where every thought is expressed in a sentence, and every sentence closed by a period. The resting-places are usually occupied by sensorial imaginations of some sort, whose peculiarity is that they can be held before the mind for an indefinite time, and contemplated without changing; the places of flight are filled with thoughts of relations, static or dynamic, that for the most part obtain between the matters contemplated in the periods of comparative rest. . . .

The truth is that large tracts of human speech are nothing but *signs of direction* in thought. . . . These bare images of logical movement . . . are psychic transmissions, always on the wing, so to speak, and not to be glimpsed except in flight.[79]

In his combination of metaphors, James presents a view of language that gives it panoramic capacity. He gives a view of a landscape that is a temporal-spatial configuration and describes a language that operates within and across it, a language that is in and of it and that makes it possible for Stein to write "a sentence that comes in the midst not in the midst of other things but in the midst of the same thing."[80]

An example of a polyvalent sentence, one that scans both outward and into the shifting features of its own interior landscape, is the short poem in *Tender Buttons* called "Roast Potatoes."

Roast potatoes for.[81]

The dominant word, when the sentence is first uttered, is *for*, in part because of the word's terminal position and the oddity of a preposition's appearing in that position. And this disequilibrium is simultaneously syntactic and semantic. We give the word prominence as we attempt to compensate for foiled grammatical expectation and to adjust our semantic balance.

In subsequent readings of the poem, the word "roast" goes through various permutations. It may be an adjective, defining potatoes, and if so, in one reading of the sentence, it is a redundant one—namely, if one reads "for" as a pun on the French word *four* (roast potatoes in French are *pommes de terre au four*)—and here the redundancy frames the "potatoes" and performs the function of establishing balance (horizontality) to the sentence.

But rather than an adjective, "roast" may be a noun, in which case one might read the sentence as if it were an entry in an index: Roast, potatoes for (one has to supply a "missing" comma—but one often does so in reading Stein).

Or again one might take "roast" as a verb, perhaps in the imperative. In all of these (and in other possible readings), the noun, "potatoes," remains stable—as real potatoes certainly tend to do—and the poem remains planar and horizontal; it is viewed full face.

In longer sentences, the number of meaning events, and the possible range of combination and recombination, is much greater. "A sentence," says Stein, "is made to be divided into one two three six seven starting with one."[82] "Roast potatoes for" might be a "one." Another "one," certainly, is "Place praise places."[83]

The comment "A sentence is made to be divided into one two three six seven starting with one" has obviously to do with stress and emphasis, and also with a notion of equivalence between possible units—the meaning units, so to speak—that are foregrounded as planes. Stein follows the comment with examples: "A sentence divided in three. He is never to be allowed / to continue to commence / to prepare to wait" (I've inserted slashes to indicate the tripartite phrasing) and "A sentence divided into six. Théy háve púrchased what théy have béen to sée."[84]

Where the reader makes the divisions may be somewhat subjective, dependent on one's particular rhythm of comprehension, how fast one thinks, how large a unit one can hold before having to drop it for the next, and the nature of the background activity in the sentence—its field of reference. In the sentence divided into three, for example, the nearly perfect grammatical balance is poised within a temporal warp. The logic is displaced—that is, it is possible "to continue to prepare" and "to commence to wait" but it is unlikely that one would "continue to commence."

"A sentence is made by coupling meanwhile ride around to be a couple there makes grateful dubeity named atlas coin in a loan." This is the first sentence of "Sentences."[85] Here the phrasing is interlocked, rather than displaced. If one parses the sentence, almost every phrase does multiple duty, holding the sentence together as a complex thought, or web of thoughts, and serving as a so-to-speak hospitable ground for the meanings that adhere to it. There are radical shifts going on in the sentence, such as "the grateful dubeity" that "a couple there makes" and the change in scale from "atlas" to "coin" and from "coin" (some specific one, e.g., a penny) to "coin in a loan" (coinage in general, money)—though here it is also possible that "coin in" is a verb, meaning something like to "cash in" or "convert into money." A couple (lovers?) rides around a rich world in or on a sentence. Such love might be thought of as "grateful dubeity"—headlong tentativeness, grateful in being given the opportunity to doubt.

"We do know a little now what prose is," Stein says in "Poetry and Grammar." "Prose is the balance the emotional balance that makes the reality of paragraphs and the unemotional balance that makes the reality of sentences and having realized completely realized that sentences are not emotional while paragraphs are, prose can be the essential balance that is made inside something that combines the sentence and the paragraph."[86]

As Ron Silliman points out in his essay "The New Sentence," what Stein means here is "that linguistic units integrate only up to the level of the sentence, but higher orders of meaning—such as emotion—integrate at higher levels than the sentence and occur only in the presence of either many sentences or, at least Stein's example suggests this, in the presence of certain complex sentences in which dependent clauses integrate with independent ones."[87] Language generates sentences, which taken as forms of frontal grammar are the verbal planes from which consciousness constructs that of which it is conscious. That is, one realizes consciousness by positioning sentences in the landscape of consciousness.

Sentences are made wonderfully one at a time.[88]

This is a sentence.[89]

A sentence thinks loudly.[90]

A sentence is happily rough enough.[91]

A sentence is primarily fastened yes as a direction, no as a direction.[92]

I return to sentences as to a refreshment.[93]

A sentence says that the end of it is that they send in order to better themselves in order to sentence.[94]

A balance in a sentence makes it state that it is staying there.[95]

The great question is can you think a sentence.[96]

Notes

1. Emile Zola, "The Experimental Novel," in *Documents of Modern Literary Realism*, ed. George J. Becker (Princeton: Princeton University Press, 1967), 165, 176. (Zola's *Le Roman expérimental* is a full-length work, a portion of which appears in *Documents of Modern Literary Realism*.)

2. For excellent short studies of realism, see Damian Grant, *Realism* (London: Methuen & Co., 1970) and Lilian R. Furst and Peter N. Skrine, *Naturalism* (London: Methuen & Co., 1971).

3. Quoted in Grant, *Realism*, 40.

4. Zola, "The Experimental Novel," 192.

5. Jack London, *Martin Eden* (New York: Macmillan, 1978), 186.

6. Paul Alexis, "Naturalism Is Not Dead," in Becker, 408.

7. Zola, "The Experimental Novel," 169.

8. Theodore Dreiser, "True Art Speaks Plainly" (1903), in Becker, *Documents of Modern Literary Realism*, 156 and 155.

9. Gertrude Stein, *The Autobiography of Alice B. Toklas*, in *Gertrude Stein: Writings 1932–1946*, eds. Catharine R. Stimpson and Harriet Chessman (New York: The Library of America, 1998), 865–66.

10. "Saving the Sentence," in *How to Write* (Barton, Vt.: Something Else Press, 1973), 14.

11. "Subject-Cases: The Background of a Detective Story," in *As Fine as Melanctha* (New York: Books for Libraries Press, 1969), 17–18.

12. Ibid., 21–22.

13. Charles Rosen and Henri Zerner, "What Is, and Is Not, Realism?" *New York Review of Books*, February 18, 1982, 21–26, and March 4, 1982, 29–33. Versions of these articles are reprinted in Charles Rosen and Henri Zerner, *Romanticism and Realism: The Mythology of Nineteenth-Century Art* (New York: The Viking Press, 1984).

14. Rosen and Zerner, *New York Review of Books*, February 18, 1982, 26.

15. Ibid., 25.

16. Rosen and Zerner, *New York Review of Books*, March 4, 1982, 29.

17. Gustave Flaubert, letter to Mademoiselle Leroyer de Chantepie, December 12, 1857, quoted in Becker, *Documents of Modern Literary Realism*, 95.

18. Quoted in Viktor Erlich, *Russian Formalism* (The Hague: Mouton Publishers, 1955), 76.

19. Francis Ponge, *Pour un Malherbe*, quoted by Serge Gavronsky in

his Introduction to Francis Ponge, *The Power of Language*, intro. and ed. Serge Gavronsky (Berkeley: University of California Press, 1979), 8.

20. *Letters of Gustave Flaubert 1830–1857*, ed. Francis Steegmuller (Cambridge, Mass.: Harvard University Press, 1980), 154.

21. "Poetry and Grammar," in *Gertrude Stein: Writings 1932–1946*, 330.

22. Ibid., 334.

23. "Hotel François Ier," in *Mrs. Reynolds and Five Earlier Novels* (New York: Books for Libraries, 1969), 302.

24. "Sentences and Paragraphs," in *How to Write*, 31.

25. Maurice Merleau-Ponty, *The Phenomenology of Perception*, tr. Colin Smith (London: Routledge & Kegan Paul, 1962), vii.

26. "Portraits and Repetition," in *Gertrude Stein: Writings 1932–1946*, 303.

27. Gertrude Stein, *Tender Buttons*, in *Gertrude Stein: Writings 1903–1932*, eds. Catharine R. Stimpson and Harriet Chessman (New York: The Library of America, 1998), 313.

28. William James, *The Principles of Psychology* I (Cambridge, Mass.: Harvard University Press, 1981), 238.

29. "Portraits and Repetition," in *Gertrude Stein: Writings 1932–1946*, 302.

30. "Saving the Sentence," in *How to Write*, 13.

31. Donald Sutherland, *Gertrude Stein: A Biography of Her Work* (New Haven: Yale University Press, 1951), 73. Stein's discussion of this appears in "Composition as Explanation," in *Gertrude Stein: Writings 1903–1932*, 520–29.

32. *Gertrude Stein: Writings 1903–1932*, 525.

33. "Sentences," in *How to Write*, 146.

34. "Americans," in *Geography and Plays* (New York: Something Else Press, 1968), 39.

35. *Gertrude Stein: Writings 1903–1932*, 349.

36. William James, *Psychology: Briefer Course* (Cambridge, Mass.: Harvard University Press, 1984), 145, 151.

37. "Lend a Hand, or Four Religions," in *Useful Knowledge* (Barrytown, N.Y.: Station Hill Press, 1988), 173.

38. *Gertrude Stein: Writings 1903–1932*, 346.

39. "Portraits and Repetition," in *Gertrude Stein: Writings 1932–1946*, 308.

40. *Tender Buttons*, in *Gertrude Stein: Writings 1903–1932*, 331–32.

41. D'Arcy Thompson, *On Growth and Form* (Cambridge, England: Cambridge University Press, 1961), 3.

42. *Tender Buttons*, in *Gertrude Stein: Writings 1903–1932*, 344.

43. "Plays," in *Gertrude Stein: Writings 1932–1946*, 262.

44. "Portraits and Repetition," in *Gertrude Stein: Writings 1932–1946*, 308.

45. *Four Saints in Three Acts*, in *Gertrude Stein: Writings 1903–1932*, 608.

46. Gustave Flaubert, *Madame Bovary*, tr. Alan Russell (New York: Penguin Books, 1950), 210.

47. "Lend a Hand, or Four Religions," in *Useful Knowledge*, 185.

48. "Plays," in *Gertrude Stein: Writings 1932–1946*, 264–65.

49. *The Autobiography of Alice B. Toklas*, in *Gertrude Stein: Writings 1903–1932*, 864.

50. "Plays," in *Gertrude Stein: Writings 1932–1946*, 267.

51. "Sentences and Paragraphs," in *How to Write*, 27.

52. "Plays," in *Gertrude Stein: Writings 1932–1946*, 244.

53. Ibid., 245.

54. Ibid., 263.

55. "Arthur a Grammar," in *How to Write*, 49.

56. "A Grammarian," in *How to Write*, 111.

57. "Natural Phenomena," in *Painted Lace* (New York: Books for Libraries, 1969), 221.

58. "A Grammarian," in *How to Write*, 107.

59. Sutherland, *Gertrude Stein: A Biography of Her Work*, 126.

60. "Natural Phenomena," in *Painted Lace*, 174.

61. "Plays," in *Gertrude Stein: Writings 1932–1946*, 267.

62. "Portraits and Repetition," in *Gertrude Stein: Writings 1932–1946*, 310.

63. "A Saint in Seven," in *What Are Masterpieces* (New York: Pitman Publishing Corporation, 1970), 42.

64. Saussure's Course on General Linguistics was held in Geneva between 1907 and 1911, and there is no reason to believe that Stein would have known of his work.

65. "Sentences," in *How to Write*, 143.

66. Lyn Hejinian, "The Guard," in *The Cold of Poetry* (Los Angeles: Sun & Moon Press, 1994), 11.

67. Barrett Watten, *Total Syntax* (Carbondale: Southern Illinois University Press, 1985), 68.

68. Ferdinand de Saussure, *Course in General Linguistics*, ed. Charles Bally and Albert Sechehaye with Albert Reidlinger, tr. Wade Baskin (London: Peter Owen, 1960), 120.

69. "Arthur a Grammar," in *How to Write*, 95.

70. "Natural Phenomena," in *Painted Lace*, 226.

71. "Sentences," in *How to Write*, 115.

72. *Lucy Church Amiably* (Millerton, N.Y.: Something Else Press, 1972), 36, 183.

73. Ibid., 56–57.

74. "Sentences," in *How to Write*, 123.

75. "Arthur a Grammar," in *How to Write*, 40.

76. "More Grammar for a Sentence," in *As Fine as Melanctha* (New York: Books for Libraries Press, 1969), 366, 374.

77. *Lucy Church Amiably*, 94.

78. "Sentences," in *How to Write*, 133.

79. William James, *Principles of Psychology* I, 136, 144.

80. "Sentences and Paragraphs," in *How to Write*, 30.

81. *Tender Buttons*, in *Gertrude Stein: Writings 1903–1932*, 339.

82. "Sentences," in *How to Write*, 125.

83. "Hotel François 1er," in *Mrs. Reynolds*, 301.

84. "Sentences," in *How to Write*, 125.

85. "Sentences," in *How to Write*, 115.

86. "Poetry and Grammar," in *Gertrude Stein: Writings 1932–1946*, 326.

87. Ron Silliman, "The New Sentence," in *The New Sentence* (New York: Roof Books, 1987), 87.

88. "Sentences and Paragraphs," in *How to Write*, 34.

89. *Ibid.*, 31.

90. More Grammar for a Sentence," in *As Fine as Melanctha*, 375.

91. "Sentences," in *How to Write*, 157.

92. Ibid., 164.

93. "Sentences and Paragraphs," in *How to Write*, 26.

94. Ibid., 33.

95. "Sentences," in *How to Write*, 125.

96. "Sentences and Paragraphs," in *How to Write*, 35.

Line

My brief comment on "the line" was written in 1988, prompted by an invitation from Bruce Andrews and Charles Bernstein to contribute to the "L=A=N=G=U=A=G=E Lines" section of a book on *The Line in Postmodern Poetry*.[1] The topic was of interest to me because, after a prolonged period of working with sentences, I was eager suddenly to disrupt their integrity, escape their confines. For me, the "new sentence"[2] had taken on declarative properties so pronounced that they were (as Bob Grenier pointed out one day in conversation) beginning to sound like imperatives; to me they had become claustrophobic, oppressive.

Almost ten years before writing this comment, I had given a talk (now lost) comparing lines of poetry to lines of sight, lines of investigation, horizon lines, cartographer's lines, and to lines of travel—routes, paths, etc. The comparisons were not gratuitous, and my purpose in making them was more than metaphorical. The comparisons and the metaphors they produced ("avenues of thought," etc.) seemed empirically sound; the line in poetry required literal travel of hand, eye, and mind and its relation to purpose could be taken as analogous to that of explorers, mapmakers, surveyors, and wanderers. But in the question and answer period immediately follow-ing the talk, Ron Silliman challenged the metaphorical premises of the talk by suggesting that I had been comparing apples to oranges. In reconsidering the comparisons, however, I thought they were apt, accurate, and logical.[3] In fact, there may be considerable logic in comparing apples to oranges.

How now, in 1999, might one compare lines to sentences? One can see that they have overlapping but not identical semantic ranges, with a sen-tence offering a complete (i.e., "whole") thought while a line need not (and often adamantly does not). And in being complete, a sentence is apt to have more stability than a line (though it is possible to destabilize the sentence from within—as in Bernadette Mayer's *The Desire of Mothers to Please Oth-ers in Letters,* for example, or, I hope, in my own "Happily" at the end of this volume.) Both lines and sentences make a demand for other lines or sen-tences, linkages, but they do so in different ways and according to different syntactic and logical operations. Sentences may incorporate articulation of this kind within themselves, whereas principal articulation occurs between lines rather than inside them. Meanwhile, the conceptual space between sen-tences is greater than that between lines, so that the effort to achieve link-age between sentences may have to be greater.

Because whatever is going to happen with sentences does so inside them, sentences offer possibilities for enormous interior complexity at nu-merous contextual levels. Or they can be opened outward, through the in-tervention of lines.

I turn to the line in order to begin.

I do so at many points within a work. But if the line is a start-ing place of and within the work, it is also its actual achievement —it provides for both the instigation of an idea and its realiza-tion. Of late, this has been especially the case, given my recent uncertainty about the sentence (or at least my own uses of it) except as it is modified by the line (which discontinues the sentence without closing it).

If there is such a thing as a perceptual rhythm (and it seems that there is), the line would be its gauge in my work. The line affixes detail to time, and it is rhythmic at least in that regard.

It is for me the standard (however variable) of meaning in the poem, the primary unit of observation, and the measure of felt thought. The "writing" of the line begins as an act of observation, and it is completed by recognition of the thought that it achieves there. The tension set up by the coexistence of beginning and end at each point excites the dynamics of the work, and this tension is vital to my thinking within it.

Even as an observation, the line is selective and expressive with regard to perception; it is already complex—that is, a number of decisions have been made before there is a line.

A musical analogue to the line might be the thematic phrase, which initiates the piece and serves as the focus of its parts and devices, but in a poetry in which every single line is internally complete and is of equal weight and importance, the situation is considerably more complex. In this imaginary musical composition, the diverse elements of the piece work to elaborate and fulfill its central theme, whereas in the poem all of the poem is about any single line in it, and any line is basic and central.

In positing the line as the basic unit of the work, I realize that I am denying that function to the word (except in one-word lines). In this sense, syntax and movement are more important to me than vocabulary (the historically macho primacy of which I dislike in any case).

A poem based on the line bears in it a high degree of semantic mutability. Lines, which may be rigid or relaxed, increasing or decreasing, long or short, ascending (questioning) or descending (decisive), predisposed (necessary) or evolving (speculative), representative of sequence or of cluster, redistribute meaning continuously within the work.

The integrity of the individual line, and the absorbing discontinuities that often appear between lines—the jumpiness that erupts in various sections of the work (whether the result or the source of disjunctive semantics)—are so accurate to my experience that they seem inevitable. And so, at this point, it seems logical to me to write with them.

Notes

1. Charles Bernstein and Bruce Andrews, eds., "L=A=N=G=U=A=G=E Lines," in *The Line in Postmodern Poetry*, ed. Robert Frank and Henry Sayre (Urbana: University of Illinois Press, 1988).

2. See Ron Silliman, *The New Sentence* (New York: Roof Books, 1987).

3. I seem, at some level, to still be arguing about this with Ron Silliman in formulations like, "Comparing apples to oranges is metonymic" (see "Strangeness") and "It is not surrealism to compare apples to oranges" (see "Barbarism").

Strangeness

The metonymic association that justified (to my mind) a comparison between lines of travel, lines of investigation, and lines of poetry in the early talk (see the previous essay, "Line") did so on empirical grounds. This talk was one of a series curated by Bob Perelman and it was given at the San Francisco Art Institute, probably in 1979. I no longer have a copy of the talk nor of any notes I used in preparing it, but I remember the occasion with particular clarity. I derived the logic motivating the talk very much as I derived that of "Strangeness," out of associations between poetry and "science" which are not themselves scientific. They are, in fact, tropic, and therefore antithetical to strict scientific methodologies. But they are not antithetical to all forms of empiricism and certainly not to the radical empiricism that William James elaborated and for which I have an ineradicable interest.

In "A World of Pure Experience," while applauding "a loosening of old landmarks, a softening of oppositions, a mutual borrowing from one another on the part of systems anciently closed, and an interest in new suggestions," he notes the risk of a resulting vagueness and warns against the metaphysical flimsiness of purely conjunctive relations ("Merely to be 'with' one another in a universe of discourse is the most external relation that terms can have, and seems to involve nothing whatever as to farther consequences").[1] What interests James (as it interests me) are not so much the things, which simple conjunction leaves undisturbed, but the transitions between them and between them and us.

It is in these transitions that the activity of being is exercised—the work of being in the world, perceptible and, in the case of sentient things, perceiving, or, in the case of nonsentient things, susceptible to the influence, the causative capacities, of other things, sentient or not. These interrelated transitions form a system of perceptible effects. For James, these are the materials of cognition and hence of consciousness. "Knowledge of sensible realities thus comes to life inside the tissue of experience. It is made; and made by relations that unroll themselves in time."[2]

The emphasis on the experiencing of transitions is what allows James to call his empiricism "radical." "To be radical, an empiricism must neither admit into its constructions any element that is not directly experienced, nor exclude from them any element that is directly experienced. For such a philosophy, the relations that connect experiences must themselves be experienced relations, and any kind of relation experienced must be accounted as 'real' as anything else in the system."[3]

"Strangeness" addresses "knowledge of sensible realities," and makes its case for the value of that (and for poetry's role in achieving it) via analogy with a certain tradition of scientific work. But, as Barrett Watten has pointed out to me in conversation, one might look in another direction to discover another pertinent methodology. James's seemingly apolitical ("natural") scientific interests, like those of the Enlightenment science which precedes it, bear certain methodological similarities with those of political science in the Marxian tradition, with its concern for "the synchronic system of social relations as a whole."[4] In particular the examination of modes of structural causality and the expressive nature of effects in the work of Louis Althusser is worth looking at in this context.

In the realm of the political as in that of the material world around us, "knowledge of sensible realities" is vital, and if I have argued that poetic language contributes critically to making realities sensible, it must address both the material character of the political and the political character of the material.

And why should it want to heighten the sensibility of realities and add to knowledge of them? The answer might be the same as that which Wittgenstein posited in response to his question, "What is your aim in philosophy?—To shew the fly the way out of the fly-bottle."[5]

"Strangeness" was first presented as a talk sponsored by the Kootenay School of Writing in Vancouver, B.C., in October 1988, and it was published in *Poetics Journal* 8: "Elsewhere" (1989). The essay was translated into Russian by Arkadii Dragomoshchenko and selections appeared in *Stilistika i Poetika* (Moscow State Institute of Foreign Languages, 1989). It was republished in *Artes* 2 (Swedish Academy, 1990), in *Revista Canaria de Estudos Ingleses* 18 (Universidad de la Laguna, Tenerife, 1989), and in *An Anthology of New Poetics,* ed. Christopher Beach (Tuscaloosa: Univ. of Alabama Press, 1998).

I stand in awe of my body, this matter
to which I am bound has become so
strange to me. . . . Talk of mysteries!
Think of our life in nature,—daily to
be shown matter, to come in contact
with it,—rocks, trees, wind on our
cheeks! the *solid* earth! the *actual*
world! the *common sense! Contact! Contact!* Who are we? where are we?

      Henry David Thoreau, "Ktaadn"

July 10, 1988

Because there is a relationship between the mind and the body, there are inevitable experiences of instability and therefore of loss and discontinuity.

Loss of scale accompanied by experiences of precision.

July 11, 1988

Scale and precision do not contribute to a theory of description but rather to a poetics of description, which I'm here deriving from examples of its exercise on two strange terrains, the terrain of dreams and the terrain of what was in the seventeenth and eighteenth centuries *terra incognita*, hence the terrain of exploration.

By description I don't mean after-the-fact realism, with its emphasis on the world described (the objects of description), nor do I want to focus on an organizing subjectivity (that of the perceiver-describer); nor, finally, am I securing the term to a theory of language.

I propose description as a method of invention and of composition. Description, in my sense of the term, is phenomenal rather than epiphenomenal, original, with a marked tendency toward effecting isolation and displacement, that is toward objectifying all that's described and making it strange.

Description should not be confused with definition; it is not definitive but transformative. Description, in the examples here, is a particular and complicated process of thinking, being highly intentional while at the same time, because it is simultaneous with and equivalent to perception, remaining open to the arbitrariness, unpredictability, and inadvertence of what appears. Or one might say that it is at once improvisational and purposive. It is motivated thus by simultaneous but different logics, oscillating inferentially between induction and deduction.

Although my argument will be based on examples of non-literary description—dream reports and explorers' journals—description obviously involves problems of writing. Vocabulary and grammar are themselves an intense examination of the world and of our perceptual relations within the experience of it. One may agree with Ludwig Binswanger's aphoristic comment, "To dream means: I don't know what's happening to me,"[6] but the description of a dream is intended as a means of finding out.

Description then is apprehension.

August 4, 1988

The term *apprehension* is meant to name both a motivating anticipatory anxiety and what *Webster's Dictionary* calls "the act or power of perceiving or comprehending."[7] Apprehension, then, is expectant knowledge.

Both anxiety and a sense of anticipation or expectation excited by particles occur in dreams, or as dreams.

Apart from whatever psychological insights they may offer, descriptions of dreams, or dream reports, are of enormous interest in offering specific writing problems. The very writing down of a dream seems to constitute the act of discovering it (one "remembers" more and more as one writes until one wonders if it's the writing itself that "dreams") but it is also and problematically an act of interpreting it.

The attempt to describe a dream raises a challenge to selection, questioning not only the adequacy or accuracy of what one (or one's memory) has selected but the very act of selecting itself, since peripheral items may turn out to be central after all, and because details may have been lost in the instability of the dream terrain or in one's own forgetfulness. In this case, dreams present reportage problems, not unlike the reportage problems that are an issue in explorers' journals (those of Captain Cook, for example, or those of Lewis and Clark), in the classic literature of exploration (Darwin's *The Voyage of the Beagle* or Henry Walter Bates's *The Naturalist on the River Amazons*, for example) or in the writings of naturalists at home (e.g., William Cobbett's *Rural Rides* or Gilbert White's Selborne journals).[8] There is a disconcerting similarity between records of dreams and records made by the explorers—the same apparent objectivity, the same attempt to be precise and accurate about details and to be equally accurate about every detail (presumably because one doesn't know which details are the important ones, either in Tahiti or in the dream).

The dream description also presents problems of framing. It questions the relationship between subject and object, since the "I" of a dream is often either unassimilated or diversely identifiable, so to speak reversible, wavering between selves called Me and Not-me.

"I," the dreamer, is not of necessity identical to the "I" of waking life. When, for example, I write of a dream, "I am in a locker room in a prison and use a key to unlock handcuffs so that three of us escape," who am "I"? Did it really feel (in the dream) that I was there in the way that it would if I were there?

In dreams, the opposition between objectivity and subjectivity is a false one. In fact, the dream's independence from binarisms like form-content, male-female, now-then, here-there, large-small, social-solitary, etc., is characteristic and makes polarity irrelevant or obsolete. Instead deliberate and complex disintegration, dispersal, and elaboration occur, in some instances with terrifying effect.

> It affected my health. Terror loomed ahead. I would fall again and again into a heavy sleep, which lasted several days at a time, and when I woke up, my sorrowful dreams continued. I was ripe for fatal harvest, and my weakness led me down dangerous roads to the edge of the world, to the Cimerian shore, the haven of whirlwinds and darkness. I had to travel, to dissipate the enchantments that crowded my brain. (Rimbaud)[9]

August 8, 1988

Dream of September 28, 1987: A dress, or a woman wearing blue or black. She is a mannequin or a living woman. The figure is seen full-face or maybe in silhouette. A view then or afterwards of a saddle-stitch stapler and a book nearby.

Dream of January 31, 1987: K has written a novel—it is a large old oak desk, or maybe only the drawers of the desk. The top drawer is out of the desk, I think K is holding it. The bottom drawer is on the floor in front of C. B and C and K and I are discussing the novel. K explains that the first chapter sounds as if it had been written by someone who was "going nuts, which it was." This is a problem—he doesn't want it to sound like that. He is worried, too, that nothing happens in the novel. I say, "Going nuts is something." K and B break the drawer apart. "I could have an auction." says K. "I had to spend the whole first chapter naming things, but the readers could find out what they are when people bid for them."

"Someone might bid for a dog," I say. This is very funny

and everyone laughs. I'm pleased to have made a joke, but actually I'm only repeating what I thought I heard one of them say. It occurs to me that you really need a studio if you are a novelist, since novelists have to build things. All of this dream is occurring in a room, which is maybe a small backstage area. The light is "natural," but dim, more white than yellow—I'm not thinking about it, I don't notice that I notice, but I do notice the dust and some black and white decor, maybe just panels, maybe just white ones and not black ones.

Now we are examining the end of the novel. Another drawer. It is falling apart, too—the back is separating from the drawer, so there are gaps between the sides. I think to myself that it won't hold water. C is talking about the chapter. B is at the back of the desk, hammering a nail into its side.

Dream of November 2, 1986: I am taking part in a project to measure the planetary system. Other people are involved, including a tall thin man and a woman with enormous breasts. In the project to measure the planetary system each participant slips into place between other participants to form a sphere. We are like sections of a citrus fruit. Once in place, hanging upside down, we form a sphere and ride around pressed against each other for twenty-four hours. I am afraid of being smothered by the woman's enormous breasts. We pull out of the sphere and discuss ways to come up with a better design for measuring the planetary system.

Among the things one notices about these dreams, keeping in mind that they are presented here as writing problems rather than psychological events, is that nonetheless persistent figuring occurs in them; the descriptions, like the dreams, proceed by virtue of various calculations and determinations and produce tropes and images. The dream of planetary measuring is exemplary of this, since it is *about* figuring, and about the metamorphic processes that result. What appears to be a search for the right word is more often and more accurately a search for the right object, itself as unstable as a word and located in an unstable terrain. The figuring that occurs in moving through the mobility of the dream, and the literal refiguring of figures in the dream, take place also in the course of writing. In this sense, the process of writing, like the process of dreaming, is a primary thinking process. Thinking explores, rather than records, prior knowledge or an expression of it.

August 9, 1988

It would be inaccurate, inappropriate, and even ludicrous, to characterize the dream as an example of self-expression. I'm not even sure one can regard it precisely as an act of introspection, though it is impossible to think of dreams as myopic in this respect. But if dreams are not introspective, properly speaking, they nonetheless exhibit some of the effects of introspection on our experience of experience—which, at least in my case, often occurs as writing.

My use of the term *introspection*, and my sense of the introspective method and its effect on experience and ultimately their emergence in poetics, are indebted to William James's philosophy of consciousness and thereby of language. But it is Gertrude Stein who extended James's philosophy into literary practice, a practice foregrounding the consciousness and its linguistic character. In essence, Stein proposes the act of writing as the organization and location of consciousness in legible units, and not just of consciousness but of the consciousness of consciousness, the perceiving of perception. As she says in "Poetry and Grammar," "One of the things that is a very interesting thing to know is how you are feeling inside you to the words that are coming out to be outside of you."[10] Coming into consciousness of consciousness or perceiving perception is, for Stein as for James, the proper function of introspection.

The introspective method has certain consequences. James argues that consciousness can best be described as a stream—he speaks at length of the "stream of thought" and the "stream of consciousness"—but introspecting the contents of that stream, and, more precisely, a particular item floating along it, interrupts the streaming, arrests the item, detaches and isolates it.

> Let anyone try to cut a thought across in the middle and get a look at its section, and he will see how difficult the intro-spective observation of the transitive tracts is. . . . As a snow-flake crystal caught in the warm hand is no longer a crystal but a drop, so, instead of catching the feeling of relation moving to its term, we find we have caught some substantive thing, usually the last word we were pronouncing, statically taken, and with its function, tendency, and particular mean-ing in the sentence quite evaporated. The attempt at intro-spective analysis in these cases is in fact like seizing a spin-ning top to catch its motion, or trying to turn up the gas quickly enough to see how the darkness looks.[11]

If one looks at my dream of September 28, 1987, one sees a se-quence of substantives lacking their transitives. And this is true in several senses. There is a kind of oscillation, even reversibility, between the dress and the woman, which seem to be metonyms for each other, existing spatially (which is to say substantively) but atemporally (intransitively). The dress and the woman may stand for each other, but they are not synonymous nor even overlapping. The objectified figure, even if perhaps a live woman, is static, while the dreamer-observer, from whom "I" have been stripped or withdrawn, sees her or it from several vantage points: "full-face or maybe in silhouette." The female figure is then replaced by a stapler and a nearby book.

"I," the dreamer-observer, experience no self-consciousness. I exist as if absorbed into an audience, or as if no one at all. But the female figure is me. I know this because of the familiar blue or black clothes. The saddle-stitch stapler I recognize as the particular heavy antique one that I used in putting together the Tuumba Press books. Now I have loaned it more or less permanently to someone who publishes a magazine. It is emblematic of certain things I've done and know how to do—make books, for example, both by writing them and by printing and publishing them—and of certain attitudes I have regarding literary communities.

The woman appears first in the dream, and the other three things are elements in a description of her. The dress, stapler, and book are three metonymic entries in a description. I recognize these various elements as me; however, they are entirely displaced—we are shifted apart from each other; indeed there are numerous removes, in a complex of dispossession. "To the psychologist," says James,

> the minds he studies are *objects*, in a world of other objects.
> Even when he introspectively analyzes his own mind, and
> tells what he finds there, he talks about it in an objective way.
> He says, for instance, that under certain circumstances the

color gray appears to him green. . . . This implies that he compares two objects, a real color seen under certain conditions, and a mental perception which he believes to represent it, and that he declares the relation between them to be of a certain kind. In making this critical judgment, the psychologist stands as much outside of the perception which he criticizes as he does of the color. Both are his objects.[12]

August 10, 1988

Introspection has writing as its exemplar, as a radical method with disintegrating and dispersive effects.

The dream about measuring the planetary system may be an attempt to counter this, but "we pull out" in the end.

August 12, 1988

The elements in the September dream are atemporal, only spatial, though remarkably without the sense of continuity that is provided by landscape. They are like props, picked up by perception and then put back. They don't do anything, in a temporal sense.

On the other hand, the person, so-called "I," in the dream of planetary measurement is notably caught in a temporal figure, one which occasions a kind of spatial disintegration—first "I" am afraid of being smothered, and then, I ("we") break the figure apart in order to regain some sense of integrity.

The disjuncture or discontinuity between the spatial existence and the temporal existence of a person ruptures the connection between body and the mind—it is a paradigm for all models and experiences of discontinuity, that fountain of postmodernity and anxiety. And it is the noncoherence of dreams, or of the objects in dreams, that is exactly what makes us suspect them of being unreal. It is thus that our dreams pose an epistemological problem to philosophy.

> Objects of sense, even when they occur in dreams, are the most indubitably real objects known to us. What, then, makes us call them unreal in dreams? Merely the unusual nature of their connections with other objects of sense. . . . It is only the failure of our dreams to form a consistent whole, either with each other or with waking life, that makes us condemn them.[13]

This is true only until our examination of the "real" is such that its components too are dispossessed of their obviousness and necessity. They are, at least in my experience, not so much decontextualized as arrested, until the entire universe of context seems to implode into them, abandoning the observer. It is the dreamer, the observer, the writer who is dispossessed. This is equally true when the object of inquiry is the self. As Adorno puts it,

> Absolute subjectivity is also subjectless. The self lives solely through transformation into otherness; as the secure residue of the subject which cuts itself off from everything alien it becomes the blind residue of the world. . . . Pure subjectivity, being of necessity estranged from itself as well and having become a thing, assumes the dimensions of objectivity which expresses itself through its own estrangement. The boundary between what is human and the world of things becomes blurred.[14]

This is one of the principal strategies of poetry, although perhaps "strategies" is not an accurate term in all cases—inquiry to such a degree is sometimes the motivation of poetry and sometimes furthermore the effect that poetry produces.

August 16, 1988

If one posits descriptive language and, in a broader sense, poetic language as a language of inquiry, with analogies to the scientific methods of the explorers, then I anticipate that the principal trope will be the metonym, what Roman Jakobson calls "association by contiguity." The metonym operates within several simultaneous but not necessarily congruent logics, oscillating inferentially between induction and deduction, depending on whether the part represents the whole (reasoning from the particular to the general) or whether the whole is being used to represent the part (reasoning from the general to the particular). Or, again, an object may be replaced by another adjacent one, the cause by the effect or the effect by the cause, spatial relations may replace temporal ones or vice versa, an action may replace the actor or vice versa, and so forth. Metonymy moves attention from thing to thing; its principle is combination rather than selection. Compared to metaphor, which depends on code, metonym preserves context, foregrounds interrelationship. And again in comparison to metaphor, which is based on similarity, and in which meanings are conserved and transferred from one thing to something said to be like it, the metonymic world is unstable. While metonymy maintains the intactness and discreteness of particulars, its paratactic perspective gives it multiple vanishing points. Deduction, induction, extrapolation, and juxtaposition are used to make connections, and "a connection once created becomes an object in its own right." [15] Jakobson quotes Pasternak: "Each detail can be replaced by another. . . . Any one of them, chosen at random, will serve to bear witness to the transposed condition by which the whole of reality has been seized." [16]

August 17, 1988

Metonymic thinking moves more rapidly and less predictably than metaphors permit—but the metonym is not metaphor's opposite. Metonymy moves restlessly, through an associative network, in which associations are compressed rather than elaborated. Metonymy is intervalic, incremental—it exists within a measure. A metonym is a condensation of its context.

But because even the connections between things may become things in themselves, and because any object may be rendered into its separate component parts which then become things in themselves, metonymy, even while it condenses thought processes, may at the same time serve as a generative and even a dispersive force.

August 18, 1988

Comparing apples to oranges is metonymic.

August 19, 1988

With respect to dream descriptions, psychological interpretation focuses primarily on identification and symbolism (metaphor), but a literary interpretation depends on the metonym (displacement and synecdochic condensation).

In my dream of K's novel, the novel is not a metaphor, and neither is the desk. They enter the dream as metonyms. The word *novel* (in the sense of new) means K, whose real-life job includes writing for a company newspaper. Also I know that K has used lines from newspapers in some of the poems he has recently shown me. But novel means me, too. I've tried to make use of lines from newspapers in imitation of K, though I can't seem to get anywhere with it. And then there is the news itself, of course, dismaying in content and raising the question, over and over, of the efficacy (or inefficacy) of poetry in relation to the course of events; to read the news is to be reminded of the seeming imperviousness of the world to such improvements as might be suggested by artistic work and artistic thought.

The dream, then, is about writers and writing. The desk is writing—the place of production is substituted for the thing produced—agency replaces effect. In the dream we are improving the news; it is not irrelevant that several of us are working together to do so.

The phrase "going nuts" is initially metaphorical—the head looks like a nut, or it is hard on the outside and meaty on the inside like a nut, or it hangs on the neck like a nut. But the plural is interesting; when one suffers from insanity one is transformed into a figure with several heads—one develops or suddenly has a fragmentary or multiple sense of self. The dreamed phrase captures, albeit somewhat humorously, my own experience of extended introspecting, undertaken until the self is utterly unfamiliar and threatens to disperse into separate and apparently foreign parts. When I say in the dream that "going nuts is something," I think I mean that introspection is in fact a real activity and a worthwhile one—not a self-indulgence but a committed study. It is not withdrawal but action.

Perhaps the dream arrived at the word "auction" by association with "action," not quite a homonym. K is saying, Auctions are stronger than words. The dog that someone might bid for and the water that won't be held by the drawer actually belong together—the reference is to a group of poems I wrote and abandoned long ago, a sequence called "Water and Dogs," in which I meant to juxtapose quiescence and vivaciousness, the elemental and the quotidian. Nothing seems more timeless than water to me and nothing more daily than dogs. My obvious worry is that the fragility of the poem can't contain information on the scale of water. We are apparently trying to patch it up.

August 21, 1988

The metonym, as I understand it, is a cognitive entity, with immediate ties to the logics of perception. To the extent that it is descriptive, or at the service of description, as is true in my own work, it also has a relationship to empiricism. That is, to the extent that metonymy conserves perception of the world of objects, conserves their quiddity, their particular precisions, it is a "scientific" description.

The science that I have in mind is that which is manifest in the writings of explorers and the natural historians who accompanied them in order to examine and describe what they encountered. Roman Jakobson, engaged in scientific research of his own (in his study of the cognitive uses of metonymy and metaphor based on work with aphasics), remarks, "The primacy of the metaphoric process in the literary schools of Romanticism and Symbolism has been repeatedly acknowledged, but it is still insufficiently realized that it is the predominance of metonymy which underlies and actually predetermines the so-called Realist trend."[17]

August 23, 1988

A conception of the metonym as a cognitive, perceptual, logical unit can be found in the writings on language and knowledge undertaken by Sir Francis Bacon, writings which have had an enormous influence, eventually on literary language but originally on scientific language. The project he called "The Great Instauration," of which only two parts were completed, the *Advancement of Learning* (1605) and the *Novum Organum* (1620), was to be a description of all knowledge, with an elaboration of the methods for obtaining it, in which writing figured prominently and essentially.

> Even after an abundance of material from natural history and experience, as is needed for the work of the understanding or of philosophy, is ready at hand, the understanding is still by no means capable of handling this material offhand and from memory, any more than one should expect to be able to manage and master from memory the computation of an astronomical almanac. Yet up to now thinking has played a greater part than writing in the business of invention, and experience has not yet become literate. But no adequate inquiry can be made without writing, and only when that comes into use and experience learns to read and write can we hope for improvement.[18]

Bacon goes on to speak of the "great number of particulars, an army of them you might say," lying "so scattered and diffuse as to distract and confuse the understanding." These must be presented as "tables of discovery—well organized and, as it were, living" so as to be available as a "subject under inquiry." And then, on the basis of "that experience that I call literate," philosophers (scientists) may invent "another form of induction . . . from that in use hitherto." "It is not feathers we must provide for the human understanding so much as lead and heavy weights, to restrain all leaping and flying."[19]

In essence, Bacon set in motion a reformation of learning, demanding that scientific attitudes be purged of established systems and prior opinions. Instead, the observer should experience direct and sensuous contact with the concrete and material world, in all its diversity and permutations, and unmediated by preconceptions. Bacon and the philosophers of science who followed him were convinced that the components of the natural world are eloquent of their own history. The materials of nature speak.

The concept of nature as a book appears as early as Plotinus, who compares the stars to letters inscribed in the sky, writing as they move. It recurs in literature from the Middle Ages on, and it played a significant role in the literary and philosophical writings of the American transcendentalists. Barbara Maria Stafford, in her compendious study *Voyage into Substance: Art, Science, Nature, and the Illustrated Travel Account, 1760–1840*, quotes the geologist John Whitehurst, who, in his *Original State and Formation of the Earth* (1778), wrote of a particular geological formation that its history "is faithfully recorded in the book of nature, and in language and characters equally intelligible to all nations."[20] The belief in the cosmic scope and universal intelligibility of the language of nature is important.

During the late seventeenth and early eighteenth centuries there was a great deal of speculation about the origin of languages, and diverse projects were undertaken in hopes of discovering a universal language in past or present cultures analogous to that which seemed to occur in nature. Leibniz, while in England in 1673, set out to discover what he called "the real character" (what present day semioticians would call a "sign") "which would be the best instrument of the human mind, and extremely assist both the reason and the memory, and the invention of things."[21] Scientists and philosophers of science of the period were seeking to determine and define the basics of such a language. In many ways this simply continued efforts initiated by Bacon in the *Advancement of Learning* to develop a scientific style capable of examining and encapsulating an analogy between words and things. Interest in a universal language grew out of Bacon's insistence that knowledge should be communicated in what he called "aphorisms," a mode that condenses material and thus bears strong similarities with the inductive method he was proposing as the definitive mode of inquiry. Unfurbished, compact, and vivid, the aphorism was basic, likewise, to the "plain" style that Baconians advocated for delivering information taken directly from particulars.

In their speculation about the origins of language, and under the impact of writings by travelers and explorers in Egypt, some theorists turned their attention to hieroglyphs. In 1741, William Warburton, in the second book of his *Divine Legations of Moses Demonstrated*, argued that hieroglyphs were not secret symbols written by priests but rather public communication of the best kind; based on forms found in nature and intended to convey information directly to the eyes, they are universal, condensed, and efficient. In addition, they are uncluttered by the trappings of allusive, metaphoric or symbolic meanings. Rather, the hieroglyph is a "plain and simple imitation of the figure of the thing intended to be represented, which is directly contrary to the very nature of a symbol, which is the representation of one thing by the Figure of another."[22] It functions, that is, metonymically; it represents as a fragment of concrete nature might.

If the individual hieroglyph presents a single fragment of natural reality, a "paragraph" or collection of them could only be organized paratactically. Parataxis is significant both of the way information is gathered by explorers and the way things seem to accumulate in nature. Composition by juxtaposition presents observed phenomena without merging them, preserving their discrete particularity while attempting also to represent the matrix of their proximities.

August 25, 1988

Bacon's model for the practice and description of the New Science had an enormous effect on a period when the world was opening into a field of inquiry and in which no hierarchy of inquirers had yet been established. Men (although not women) of letters were as "scientific" as anyone else, and they could and did travel to previously unknown regions as reporters of all that they saw. Thus a whole literature of description developed, and with it a theory (or, actually, a multiplicity of theories) of language, some of it the parent of linguistics and some of it the parent of poetics.

About twenty years after the publication of Bacon's *Novum*

Organum, the Royal Society was established in England on Baconian principles, first as a forum for the discussion of new scientific discoveries and later, as the organization grew into a financial institution as well as an intellectual one, as a principal resource for funds for experiments and voyages of discovery and exploration, with the purpose of accumulating large stocks of data.

Bishop Thomas Sprat's *The History of the Royal-Society of London, for the Improving of Natural Knowledge* (1667) was its first history, written to defend the Society from critics who felt that its scientific work was unholy. The volume serves both as a polemic and an anthology of the goals and achievements of the Royal Society's members and protégés.

> They have been . . . most rigorous in putting in execution . . . a constant Resolution, to reject all the amplifications, digressions, and swellings of style: to return back to the primitive purity, and shortness, when men deliver'd so many things, almost in an equal number of words. They have exacted from all their members, a close, naked, natural way of speaking; positive expressions; clear senses; a native easiness: bringing all things as near the Mathematical plainness, as they can: and preferring the language of Artizans, Countrymen, and Merchants, before that, of Wits or Scholars.[23]

Sprat insisted that the incorporation of new scientific data into poetry would make it comprehensible to everyone, since it could thus take advantage of the universal character of scientific language. He attacks the "trick of Metaphors, which impose their deceptive beauty and, in doing so, obscure information and limit learning." Linguistic descriptive tasks, whether intended for representation or evocation, should be identical with scientific observational ones.

According to seventeenth- and eighteenth-century philosophers of science, there is a specifically scientific way of seeing, which looks at, not over, the object of inquiry. Thus prospect, view, scene, and panorama are essentially unscientific—and the extent to which a metaphor is scenic is further ground for disqualifying it from realist description.

Description may narrate nature but it does so principally by exhibiting its particulars. To the extent that metaphors can be said to give things names which properly belong to other things, they were held to be inconsistent with a respect for particularity. Ultimately, conditions are incomprehensible without the use of analytical conceptual structures, but an initial, essential recognition of difference—of strangeness—develops only with attention to single objects, while others are temporarily held in abeyance. The popularity of the explorers' writings was due, at least in part, to the narrative tension that was established between perceptually immediate details (events) and the suspenseful deferral of complete comprehension.

August 28, 1988

Explorers were in many respects required to be literary men. Information about what they saw, and what they knew about natural and new realities as a result of having seen them, could only be transmitted through descriptions and through the drawings and paintings made by the artists who often accompanied them on their voyages. The explorers' methods of discovery involved a nonmetaphoric examination of particulars, and this became a significant aesthetic element in their writings. Explorers and scientists sought to discover the tangibility and singular distinctness of the world's exuberant details and individualities without spiriting them away from each other. One important result was that the particular, under the pressure of persistent and independent seeing, emerged in the "low," antiaesthetic genre of the travel narrative to restore intensities normally associated with "high" genres and the "elevated" emotions provoked by sublime and heroic features in them. A "literature of fact," intended for the instruction of the public, developing in response to the demand for verifiable truth enunciated by philosophers and scientists, revitalized literature just when it seemed to have become trivialized with "too much art and too little matter."

August 30, 1988

When the term *realism* is applied to poetry, it is apt to upset our sense of reality. But it is exactly the strangeness that results from a description of the world given in the terms "there it is," "there it is," "there it is" that restores realness to things in the world and separates things from ideology. That, at least, is what Sir Francis Bacon argued and what the practicing and theorizing empiricists believed, though argument over the adequacy or inadequacy of such a description, and of the knowledge we acquire from such a description, has propelled Western philosophy ever since— through Hume, Kant, Hegel, Russell, Wittgenstein, to the present. The ontological and epistemological problem of our knowledge of experience is, to my mind, inseparable from the problem of description.

An evolving poetics of description is simultaneously and synonymously a poetics of scrutiny. It is description that raises scrutiny to consciousness. And in arguing for this I am proposing a poetry of consciousness, which is by its very nature a medium of strangeness.

Notes

1. William James, *Essays in Radical Empiricism* (Cambridge, Mass.: Harvard University Press, 1976), 21, 23.

2. Ibid., 29.

3. Ibid., 22. The italics are James's.

4. Fredric Jameson, *The Political Unconscious: Narrative as a Socially Symbolic Act* (Ithaca: Cornell University Press, 1981), 36. I am grateful to Barrett Watten for pointing me to this volume and especially to its first chapter.

5. Ludwig Wittgenstein, *Philosophical Investigations*, tr. G. E. M. Anscombe (New York: Macmillan, 1958), 103.

6. Ludwig Binswanger, "Dream and Existence," in *Being-in-the-World: Selected Papers of Ludwig Binswanger*, tr. Jacob Needleman (New York: Harper & Row, 1963), 247.

7. *Webster's Ninth New Collegiate Dictionary*, s.v. "apprehension."

8. See James Cook, *The Journals of Captain James Cook on his voyages of discovery*, ed. J. C. Beaglehole (Cambridge, England: The Hakluyt Society at the Cambridge University Press, 1955–74); Meriwether Lewis and William Clark, *The History of the Lewis and Clark Expedition*, in three volumes, ed. Elliott Coues (New York: Dover Publications, [1979?]); Charles Darwin, *The Voyage of the Beagle*, ed. Leonard Engel (New York: Anchor Books, 1962); Henry Walter Bates, *The Naturalist on the River Amazons* (Berkeley: University of California Press, 1962); William Cobbett, *Rural Rides* (New York: Penguin Books, 1967); Gilbert White, *The Natural History of Selborne* (New York: Penguin Books, 1977).

9. Arthur Rimbaud, "A Season in Hell," in *Arthur Rimbaud: Complete Works*, tr. Paul Schmidt (New York: Harper & Row Publishers, 1976), 208.

10. Gertrude Stein, *Gertrude Stein: Writings 1932–1946*, eds. Catharine R. Stimpson and Harriet Chessman (New York: Library of America, 1998), 313.

11. William James, *The Principles of Psychology*, vol. 1 (Cambridge, Mass.: Harvard University Press, 1981), 236–37.

12. Ibid., 183–84.

13. Bertrand Russell, *Our Knowledge of the External World* (London: Allen & Unwin, 1926), 85, 95.

14. Theodor Adorno, *Prisms* (Cambridge, Mass.: The MIT Press, 1981), 262.

15. Roman Jakobson, *Language in Literature* (Cambridge, Mass.: Harvard University Press, Belknap Press, 1987), 312.

16. Boris Pasternak, quoted in Jakobson, *Language in Literature*, 312.

17. Jakobson, *Language in Literature*, 111.

18. Sir Francis Bacon, *Novum Organum*, tr. and ed. Peter Urbach and John Gibson (Chicago: Open Court, 1994), 109.

19. Ibid., 109–11.

20. Barbara Maria Stafford, *Voyage into Substance: Art, Science, Nature, and the Illustrated Travel Account, 1760–1840* (Cambridge, Mass.: The MIT Press, 1984), 285.

21. Quoted in Stafford, *Voyage into Substance*, 310.

22. Quoted in Stafford, *Voyage into Substance*, 311.

23. Thomas Sprat, *The History of the Royal-Society of London, for the Improving of Natural Knowledge* (London: Royal Society, 1667), 113.

Materials
(for Dubravka Djuric)

On April 2, 1990, the Serbian poet Dubravka Djuric wrote to me from Belgrade with some interview questions for a short essay to accompany her translations into Serbian of sections from *My Life*. The essay, interview, and translations appeared in the journal *Polja* in December 1990.

The questions were fairly basic, as was appropriate for their context, but in looking back over them now, I particularly appreciate Dubravka Djuric's interest in the relationship between social materiality and literary praxis. The point that there is such a relationship (that poetry is a socially material practice), and that I had exploring it in mind, is one of the obvious features of *My Life*, the work with which Djuric was most concerned. But I would argue that the baring (and bearing) of social materiality was fundamental to Language writing generally, though how this was carried out differed very much from text to text.

Poetry's embrace of language is not uncomplicated, of course. On the one hand, writing cannot help but transport into itself at least some of the ideological material that comes with the language in which it occurs; the language has been saturated by ideology, it is not at all an objective ground. On the other hand, Language writing often attempts to block that ideology (by jamming the system or by cutting the flow of communication, for example) or to embarrass it (by subjecting it to disclosure and critique). In other words, literary devices—disjuncture, the use of parallelism rather than sequence, ellipses, the incorporation of brutal discourse into work, code shifting, and indeed all devices that accomplish a semantic shift—were used with political intent, and both social and literary material regimens were brought into confrontation.

The political character is not inherent in the devices but in the intention motivating their use. A central concern of writing that views such devices as socially material is not subjectivity but agency.

DUBRAVKA DJURIC: Could you tell me about your first poems and other writings, about the fields of interest that were initial and important for you in your beginnings?

LYN HEJINIAN: One of the too rarely considered features of what we term *language* is its multiple character, its polymorphism. Language is qualitatively different from other artistic mediums in that it isn't, strictly speaking, one thing, a single type of material. Language consists of a vast array of strategies and situations for discovering and making meaning. It not only exists in multitudes of context, it is multitudes of context.

My first "writings" were made when I was nine or ten years old, and they were unremarkable in themselves. This isn't surprising, since I in fact didn't particularly care what it was I was writing. I never, for example, thought that words could capture the world or capture my experience (although perhaps during my adolescence I thought that writing might be able to apologize for my existence), and I was never engrossed in "looking for the right word" for something. Instead, my earliest inspirations were my father's typewriter and the two stacks of paper, one clean and the other covered with type, on either side of it. My father, during the first decade or so of my life, spent the evenings and weekends writing a series of novels. None of them was ever published. He also worked as a university administrator, first at the University of California and then at Harvard University, and when I was around ten years old he abandoned novel-writing and returned to an earlier interest in painting. I was given his typewriter.

My earliest writings were, strictly speaking, typing. I was happy to type almost anything, and although I wrote some poems and a short picaresque novel in the guise of a diary kept by a ten-year-old boy (it is no doubt significant that I wrote in the unmarked first person, that is, as a boy), the writing activity that I remember most clearly and with the most pleasure was a series of melodramas based on a popular radio show called "Bobby Benson and the B Bar B." I wrote the plays in collaboration with a friend, and if I remember correctly, she made up the stories and I simply typed what she dictated to me.

I've always had difficulty making up plots, perhaps because I have difficulty imagining people's motivations. It was the material world of writing that first attracted me to it. Because it was material, it was sensual, and despite being material, it was also unpredictable. The urge to write was sparked sometimes by the mere physical activity of writing and sometimes by individual words, but in either case, the urge preceded knowing what I could or wanted to write about. The typewriter and the dictionary together offered me the promise of projects and discovery.

I don't know when it was that I first encountered poetry, but I do know that T. S. Eliot was an early discovery. Thirteen lines from *Four Quartets* were included in an anthology my parents had given me for my fourteenth birthday. It was called *Imagination's Other Place: Poems of Science and Mathematics* and the passage from *Four Quartets* began:

> We shall not cease from exploration
> And the end of all our exploring
> Will be to arrive where we started
> And know the place for the first time.[1]

What I now recognize as fairly orthodox religiosity, at the time I thought was a study of time and knowledge. Time in its ceaselessness and the eternal changes, displacements, substitutions that it brings about, made everything unknowable (and even, perhaps, meaningless), but the resulting aporia didn't seem the least discouraging. On the contrary, the inevitability of uncertainty seemed to open up the possibility of infinite varieties of meaningfulness. I was discovering a peculiar relationship between sense and not-yet-sense in Eliot, a metaphysics that couldn't be detached from language.

Meanwhile, my parents were guiding me to read other poets; Robert Browning, Stephen Vincent Benet, Robert Frost, and Langston Hughes were favorites. My father admired Gertrude Stein enormously (he had grown up as she had in Oakland, California), and my mother loved Coleridge (she had me read "The Rime of the Ancient Mariner" aloud to her over the course of several summer afternoons when I was 9 or 10). I was unacquainted with European poetry, and I hadn't yet made a distinction between English and American poetry, considering it all "ours." I was profoundly impressed by Chaucer.

DD: Please describe the stages of your writing procedure. You have said that the writing process is "composition rather than writing"—could you explain this statement?

LH: The writing process is probably not very cogently divisible into stages. Progress occurs, but not always and strictly in stages. But perhaps I could identify three distinct elements of the process: the scrutinizing attention that both searches and hovers; the strategic force that language itself is; and the conscious writing of the poem and what results, unforeseeable but fully intended. These elements are often present simultaneously and they always overlap, so to use the word "stages" would be misleading; they don't constitute a developmental sequence. And even to name different elements risks obscuring the reality, which is that writing is really an indivisible process. One wants to ask how one gets going, how one keeps going, and how one knows what is going on. One wants to ask where the ideas are and how one sets the whole order of ideas in motion. And underlying these essentially practical, technical aspects of the poetic process, one wants to ask what poetry is *for*—why does one write it? But none of these questions is more or less basic than any of the others. The indivisibility of the writing process is occurring at every point within it.

The notion of active observation has an oxymoronic quality that is important to notice. One is engaged in an active mental (intellectual and emotional) operation in which one simultaneously searches for something with active expectation while awaiting the unexpected, unpredicted material. One focuses closely while expanding one's field of vision into the blurred peripheries. One is trying to be precise, to figure things out, while entertaining the incongruous, the out of scale, the excess.

For a writer, it is language that carries thought, perception, and meaning. And it does so through a largely metonymic process, through the discovery and invention of associations and connections. Though it may seem merely technical, the notion of linkage—of forging connections—has, in my mind, a concomitant political or social dimension. Communities of phrases spark the communities of ideas in which communities of persons live and work.

DD: Many writers/critics writing on your poetry pointed out some formal devices: repetition, permutation, and seriality. What is their operative function in the composition of your literary works?

LH: Repetition and permutation in my work occurs most prominently in *My Life*. There, I was trying to follow out and emphasize the ways in which structures of thinking echo structures of language and then reconstruct them. And I wanted to detail the inverse situation: the ways in which language echoes and constructs thinking.

But my use of repetition and permutation were motivated initially by observation of my own thought processes and my experiences of them. A person does rethink constantly, while at the same time the context for doing so is always changing. Certain "facts" (words or phrases) in a fixed vocabulary may be reiterated, but their practical effects and metaphysical implications differ from day to day, situation to situation. There is, as Gertrude Stein pointed out, repetition but not sameness.

These devices come, also, from an awareness of the simultaneous but apparently contradictory operations of continuity and discontinuity on perception, values, meaning, feeling, things, and even on one's identity. Language, like life, is saturated with time, and everywhere it shows time's effects.

Seriality is quite a different matter. Time as it divides produces repetitions and permutations; time as it accumulates produces sequences, series. "Where do we find ourselves?" Ralph Waldo Emerson asks in the opening of "Experience." And he answers, "In a series of which we do not know the extremes."[2]

Poetry is an ongoing project; it must be so if it is to be accurate to the world. Long forms of any kind, and serial forms in particular, emphasize this fact. Serial forms also permit one to take the fullest possible advantage of the numerous logics operative in language. These logics provide us with ways of moving from one place to another, they make the connections or linkages that in turn create pathways of thinking, forming patterns of meaning (and sometimes of meaning's excess, incoherence).

The terms of the series are in perpetual relative displacement, in a relationship that may be, and sometimes should be, upsetting, disruptive. Each element in the series recasts all the other elements. In this respect the serial work is dialogic. It is also heuristic.

I've been much influenced by several passages from a letter that Jack Spicer wrote to Robin Blaser: "The trick naturally is what Duncan learned years ago and tried to teach us—not to search for the perfect poem but to let your way of writing of the moment go along its own paths, explore and retreat but never be fully realized (confined) within the boundaries of one poem. This is where we were wrong and he was right, but he complicated things for us by saying that there is no such thing as good or bad poetry. There is—but not in relation to the single poem. There is really no single poem . . . Poems should echo and reecho against each other. They should create resonances. They cannot live alone any more than we can. . . . Things fit together. We knew that— it is the principle of magic. Two inconsequential things can combine together to become a consequence. This is true of poems too. A poem is never to be judged by itself alone. A poem is never by itself alone."[3]

DD: What is the meaning of the idea of "nonnarrative narration"?

LH: Your term "nonnarrative narration" resembles that of "nonreferential writing," a term that I and others used (or, let's say, *tested*) in the mid-seventies, not to identify something already existing but to upset entrenched, unquestioned notions about the relationship of words to things (including ideas, ideologies, and emotions). There is no such thing as "nonreferential writing," but as a result of proposing it, it was possible to refer farther and farther into unforeseen aspects of the world. Similarly, there is no such thing as "nonnarrative narration." But narration, the unfolding of things, occurs in time, and the term reminds us that there are many forms, qualities, and experiences of the time in which things unfold. "Nonnarrative narration" would be unconventionally chronologically and, indeed, unconventionally logical. And in being so, in disarranging conventional chronologies and logics, it animates others—and they, too, are real and existing in real realms of experience.

DD: Tell me something about "allusive psycholingualism."

LH: What a suggestive term. I can only guess what it might mean. Could it refer to associative writing techniques? to culturally embedded tropes? to the use of metaphor and metonymy? to intertextuality?

DD: What is the importance of Russian Formalism and French structuralism and poststructuralism for your work?

LH: My encounter with them freed me from sloppy (though rigidly held) models current in interpretations of poetry in the U.S. What was generally considered in the U.S. to be the "poetic" factor in poetry was embedded in self-expressivity—in the replication of ephiphanous moments in which details of the world matched or coincided with the poet's expectation or desire for meaning. This view is still prevalent. The world is found to be meaningful, but not for and to itself; it is meaningful because perceiving it makes the poet special; the poet plunders the world for its perceptual, spiritual treasure and becomes worthy (and worth more) on that basis. I simply don't have the kind of self-regard that can espouse such an undertaking. Instead, and thanks to the ideas and information I was discovering in Russian Formalist theory and French structuralism and poststructuralism, I made "the turn to language." In this regard, these two bodies of theory are of supreme importance to my work—informing it fundamentally and pervasively.

French structuralism is grounded in linguistics—particularly in the work of the Swiss linguist, Ferdinand de Saussure—one of whose basic tenets involves the arbitrariness of language. Words work not because they are natural emissions by things but because people agree on what they mean. Anything made of words—including a literary work—is socially constructed and socially constructing. Aesthetic discovery is also social discovery. There is, as a result, efficacy in writing.

Language writing expressed a demand for that efficacy.

DD: How do you see the Language movement within other tendencies in American poetry today (especially in the San Francisco Bay Area)?

LH: The Bay Area literary scene is enormously active, and, because it includes highly diverse and even oppositional aesthetic and social tendencies, it is also notably fragmented. Small communities exist simultaneously but usually with little relevance to each other within the larger scene. In recent years, the Language movement has received a large amount of attention, and for this reason, among others, it has become an object of resentment—and also, of course, interest.

The Language movement is unusual in many respects. Perhaps its most notable departure from other tendencies, whether mainstream or experimental, is its insistence on the social—its insistence on recognizing and/or producing social contexts in and for poetry. This takes place in opposition to the romance of the solitary individualist, the genius, the lone outlaw (the heroes of very American narratives). And while debunking the figure of the poet as a solo egoist, the Language movement has undertaken intellectual rigor within the social; it has produced a challenging, strenuous, and sometimes anxious social milieu.

In this sense (though perhaps not in any other), the Language community has less in common with modernist avant-garde movements than with aesthetic tendencies grounded in marginalized cultural communities—the cultures, for example, of the so-called (racial) "minorities" and of gay and lesbian communities. A dominant narrative exists that is intended to give an account of literary tendencies. It identifies a mainstream and, in opposition to the mainstream, an alternative experimentalist tendency, an avant-garde. This narrative may account for a good deal, but it entirely leaves out the work of numerous productive aesthetic communities, and in particular those whose aesthetics are grounded in sociopolitical contexts. Language writing is indeed in opposition to the mainstream, but not exactly in the way that the dominant narrative can describe.

The coming together of the poets who are now associated with the Language school in the Bay Area began more or less coincidentally in the early 1970s, but all of us had been involved in some degree of political activism during the Vietnam War, and we came to poetry with political, or social, goals in mind. And once we became aware of strong mutual curiosities and commitments, we began consciously to create an environment for ourselves—a "workplace," so to speak. Variously, we began reading series, talk series, a radio program, magazines, presses. This was not intended as self-promotion but simply as working literary life, and many people participated in these activities who did not consider themselves "Language poets."

DD: You also translate from Russian. Could you make some distinction between Language poetry in America and similar tendencies in the USSR?

LH: I can't speak with anything like "authority" about literary tendencies in the USSR, since my knowledge of what is going on there is very partial and particular. I know something of the work of the Moscow Conceptualists; I have translated some of the writings of Dmitrii Prigov and Barrett Watten and I published work by both Prigov and Lev Rubinshtein in the last issue of *Poetics Journal* (*Poetics Journal* 8: "Elsewhere," 1989). Their work, being highly parodic, is also highly contextualized. It is grounded in Soviet linguistic practices and symbol systems, both of which are socially constitutive. To the degree that Language poetry is grounded in American linguistic practices and symbol systems, it has something in common with the writings of the Moscow Conceptualists, but to the degree that American English and Western capitalism differ from the Russian language and Soviet communism, the two movements have fundamental differences.

In Leningrad there is a resilient literary scene but it has no single, circumscribed aesthetic. Two of the central figures in it are Elena Shvartz and Viktor Krivulin, both of whom are influential, but their influence hasn't produced an identifiable movement. Their influence occurs as something like inspiration, or transmission; it is part of a hierarchical tradition.

My real interest has been (and continues to be) the work of the Leningrad poet Arkadii Dragomoshchenko. Through him—because of his friendship with them and his sense of affinity—I have come to know a group of Moscow poets (including Ivan Zhdanov, Ilya Kutik, Nadezhda Kondakova, Aleksei Parshchikov) who have been labeled as "metarealists" or "metametaphorists," and whose work, together with that of Dragomoshchenko, perhaps constitutes a tendency. If so, it would have certain concerns in common with those of at least some of the Language poets—an involvement with the epistemological and perceptual nature of language-as-thinking, a belief that poetic language itself is an appropriate instrument for exploring the world, an interest in the linguistic layering of the landscape.

But the Russian and American languages are so radically different from each other that not only the movements of thought within them but even the very foundations of thinking are different. American is a wide language, with enormous horizontal scope, and Russian is a deep language, with enormous vertical scope. Our metaphysical worlds are very different.

There is another important difference between the work of these Soviet poets and that of the Language poets. The

Soviet poets do not situate a politics *within the writing*, while the Language poets do intend one. This difference is a result of our different historical conditions and cultural traditions.

The writings of these Soviet poets, by the way, are very different from each other, and the same thing can be said about that of the Language poets. Despite common interests, the resulting poetries are radically dissimilar. This makes the labeling of our work seem ridiculous. There is no typical or representative "Language poem." And, since as time goes by dissimilarity is increasing, both in our work and in our ways of working, there never will be.

DD: Could you tell me about the conception of and your experience in editing *Poetics Journal*?

LH: Barrett Watten and I founded *Poetics Journal* in 1981, about five years after Bob Perelman had organized his Talk Series. The Talks had provided a forum for a public working out of ideas—a kind of workshop for poetics and literary theory. The Talks provoked a lot of discussion (and, often, argument); they were demanding, excitatory, and enormously productive. As participants, we taught ourselves and each other techniques for thinking about every conceivable aspect of poetry. We discovered terms, situated devices and intentions, and interwove the process of developing critical theories and techniques with the process of developing creative ones. It was, I believe, not an authoritative and detached poetics but an inherent and working poetics that we were engaged with.

Customarily in the U.S., literary theory and criticism

have been the province of academics and professional critics. Writers create the work but remain silent about what it intends and what or how it means. Barrett and I wanted to create an intervention in this situation. We had two motives: we wanted to provide a forum in which the theoretical work that was going on in the Language movement could develop further and involve a larger public, and we wanted to provide a site in which poets and other artists could be the ones to define the terms in which their work was discussed. As I see it, those were and are the goals of *Poetics Journal:* to initiate discussion (by proposing various topics as foci for different issues) and then to encourage its development by publishing provocative (not definitive) essays.

Collecting material for *Poetics Journal* has been more difficult that I had anticipated. Many poets (and other artists as well) see creative work as so radically different from theoretical work as to preclude theoretical work altogether. This stance can involve an anti-intellectualism that is very discouraging. But even if they don't take this stance, it seems that many artists feel perpetually unprepared for critical statement. There are numerous factors that contribute to the resulting hesitancy, but it may be related in part to the marginalized situation of art and, especially, of poetry. Poets have little opportunity to engage in prolonged and rigorous discussion of their work, and they have little sense that what they have to say, even about their own concerns, could be regarded as credible and valid; they have little sense that what they say could be valuable and important.

I have discovered, meanwhile, that when we do write theory we usually have more impact, more power, than when we write poetry. The irony of this is obvious; I also find it discouraging.

Notes

1. T. S. Eliot, "From *Four Quartets*," in *Imagination's Other Place: Poems of Science and Mathematics*, ed. Helen Plotz (New York: Thomas Y. Crowell Company, 1955), 6.

2. Ralph Waldo Emerson, *Emerson's Essays* (New York: Thomas Y. Crowell Company, 1951), 292.

3. Quoted by Donald Allen in his Editor's Note to Jack Spicer, *One Night Stand & Other Poems* (San Francisco: Grey Fox Press, 1980), xxx–xxxi.

Comments for Manuel Brito

I wrote the "Comments for Manuel Brito" in response to a set of fourteen questions that I received from Manuel Brito, a scholar and editor based in Tenerife, in the Canary Islands. With the intention of conducting interviews with several American poets, Brito had been doing research in the library at the University of California, San Diego, whose Archive for New Poetry in the Mandeville Special Collections contains materials relating to the work of numerous contemporary American poets. In the end, Brito interviewed twelve poets: Rae Armantrout, Charles Bernstein, Norma Cole, Michael Davidson, Carla Harryman, Fanny Howe, Michael Palmer, Jerome Rothenberg, Leslie Scalapino, Ron Silliman, Barrett Watten, and myself. The interviews, including this one, were published in Spain as *A Suite of Poetic Voices*.[1]

As the editor and publisher of Zasterle Press, Brito has published books by a number of contemporary American poets, including books by most of the people whom he interviewed. Thus he was already deeply involved with American poetry. This gave him considerable credibility, and it explains the seriousness and candor with which his questions were considered.

My own set of questions arrived in late 1990, and several weeks later, in January 1991, I left for the Canadian Rockies. My plan was to spend a month in relative isolation at the Banff Centre for the Arts working on the book that became *The Cell*. I did work on that book, but the Gulf War was underway and isolation (if by that one means a turning away from the immediacies of the world) was impossible. In fact, as I was answering Manuel Brito's questions, I came to the realization that "a turning away from the immediacies of the world" is antithetical to the worldly undertaking that writing in my view entails. On this occasion, solitude increased the intensity of my involvement with the world.

The fourteen questions seemed quite independent from each other, and so I chose to respond to them in disorder. I cut the pages into fourteen strips and, drawing them blindly from an envelope, I answered one every other day for the month I was in Canada.

After living in the mountains and without the modern utilities you integrated yourself in the urban life of the city; how was that process?

Urban life requires numerous and various acts of integration and reintegration, more than country life as I experienced it required, not because that country life was uneventful but because events in the quite remote area where my husband, two children, and I were living were themselves integrated—they confirmed each other. There were plenty of adventures—rattlesnakes, bears, forest fires, a range war, an escaped prisoner and a cowboy posse pursuing him—but it took very little analysis to respond to them. Urban life, on the other hand, at least in the U.S., where the milieu of the city includes elements from so many and such diverse cultures, is radically self-conscious. One is confronted with perceptual and even with ethical situations that require one to question one's position, quite literally.

The intensification of self-consciousness that our move back to the city occasioned was difficult, as I remember it, and to some extent oppressive. But it resulted, at the same time, in an intensification of the epistemological conditions and investigations from which my poetics and my literary life continue to evolve.

It was in the context of this move—away from the landscape of mountains and ranch lands (what is called *chaparral*) to that of city streets and social space—that I wrote *Writing Is an Aid to Memory*. I posited a language landscape, regarding words and phrases with as much specificity as one grants particular rocks, trees, and conditions of sky. I could say then, too, that it was in the context of this work that I made the move to the city.

Of course I didn't simply move *generally* to the city, but rather I moved at a particular time, July of 1977, to a particular place, the San Francisco Bay Area, and into a situation where writing and writing-related activities of such poets as Ron Silliman, Barrett Watten, Rae Armantrout, Tom Mandel, Kit Robinson, Carla Harryman, Steve Benson, Bob Perelman, and I were coinciding. It was a startling situation, and it has deeply informed the process by which I did and do continue to integrate myself on a daily basis into urban life and my life.

Nowadays how do you see your involvement with the literary community of the Bay Area, especially with the people that H. Wiener called "GROUP MIND"?

I don't know where or in what context Hannah Wiener used the term "group mind," but I'll assume that she meant something like collective consciousness, as distinct from Jung's notion of a collective unconscious. And likewise I'll assume that her "group mind" is not normative, since that wouldn't be accurate to my experience of the part of the Bay Area literary community to which I belong. In fact, my community is made up of different minds—and by that I don't mean personalities but rather radical processes of being conscious. Though we (I'm referring of course to the so-called Language poets but also to poets like Jean Day, Jerry Estrin, Leslie Scalapino, and Laura Moriarty whom I got to know in the eighties somewhat after the most intense and intentional period of activity of the "Language School") have in common an emphasis on a poetry of consciousness, the forms that poetry takes are as distinct from one another as the mentalities (psyches) in which our different consciousnesses are located.

My involvement with the community has not diminished, though it and the community have changed. When I came back to the Bay Area in 1977, my Tuumba Press, Barrett Watten's *This* magazine and This Press, Bob Perelman's *Hills* magazine and the Talks series he curated, Tom Mandel's *Miam*, Ron Silliman's *tottel's*, and the weekly reading series at The Grand Piano curated by Ron Silliman, Tom Mandel, and Rae Armantrout were all functioning and doing so somewhat in collaboration. Geoff Young's press, The Figures, was publishing books by many of us. Very shortly thereafter Carla Harryman inaugurated her *Qu* magazine devoted to new prose, and Kit Robinson and I started a weekly live radio show named after his poem "In the American Tree" and subtitled "new writing by poets." This was a period of intense literary activity, as you can imagine, and also of intense social activity. It was, in retrospect, a bohemian scene, one which the current economy simply no longer permits. We had time to talk, argue, read each other's work, and time to read "secondary" texts ("theory") from which, or against which, we were elaborating our own common poetics and separate trajectories.

The climate of the nineties is very different. But what is more relevant, I think, is the fact that our sense of a broad common project developed in such a way as to propel and support what are now different projects. Perhaps that's no more than saying that we've matured as artists. Or that artistic movements have a life span.

Was there a "movement"? There was no sacrifice of individuality, but rather a radicalizing of the possibilities of individualism. That was not always clear, but it is to me now in retrospect.

The community, as the focus of literary activity, is more disparate now. I think that's appropriate. It's curious that a number of us are, however, working together now on collaborations. Carla and I are writing *The Wide Road*, an erotic picaresque; Ron, Michael Davidson, and I have written *Leningrad*, a collaboration based on ten days spent together in Leningrad; Kit and I have collaborated (or corresponded) on a project that resulted in *Individuals*, my book *The Cell*, and several long works of Kit's; Ray DiPalma and I have finished a collaboration entitled *Chartings*; and Barrett and I coedit and publish *Poetics Journal*. Meanwhile the friendships—intellectual and emotional—are part of my daily life.

Tuumba became a representative series which served as an expounder of the new poetry in the eighties; what was the purpose of editing those fifty books?

I founded Tuumba Press because poetry (like anything else) is meaningless without context, without conditions. Literary life in

America isn't given, it has to be invented and constructed, and this process of inventing and constructing, as I saw it, was simply an extension of my writing, of my being a poet. Small presses, magazines, poetry readings are the constructs of our literary life and provide conditions for writing's meanings.

I've heard Clark Coolidge muse sometimes over the question, "What do poets *do?*" We know what carpenters do, and pilots, and nurses. Providing a milieu for contextualized, unisolated thinking has got to be a part of what poets can do.

Hegel, Proust, Melville were your favorite authors and you refer to them as writers with a language of quantity, reflective of your own sense of life as dense language; how can this fact be considered in your work?

There tends to be some confusion or misconception, inherent maybe to Western thinking, which assumes a separation between, for example, form and content, verb and noun, process and condition, progress and stasis. But in fact these pairs and their parts constitute a dynamic, a momentum, a force. Quantities are change, not categories. Not accumulations, but gain and loss.

By the way, this can be said of gender, too—man and woman. Being a woman isn't a state so much as it's an impetus, with a certain momentum, occurring at various velocities and in various directions.

Or one could speak about literary form, which isn't form at all but force. Thus, for example, Barrett Watten's incredible inventiveness with respect to form in his writing constitutes a series of inventions of motion. These suggest to me new ways to think, new powers of thinking.

It has been years since I read Hegel, and when I did read his

work I did so very fantastically. That is, I had reasons for read-
ing Hegel that Hegel would not have anticipated nor approved.
And I don't think I would name "favorite" authors anymore, un-
less maybe in the looseness of conversation and deeply contextu-
alized, since anything is favorite in context, favoriteness being
largely a condition of mediation.

Both Proust and Melville are writers of a dense milieu; Ger-
trude Stein is another. Being a writer, and experiencing experi-
ence as dense milieu, I, so to speak, identify with the impulse of
these writers—which is to say, they have been an inspiration and
an influence for me. The longevity, and the interplay between
symmetry and asymmetry, in Proust's and Melville's syntax and
in Stein's semantics, must show up in my work. Style is really ve-
locity of thinking in a landscape of thought. With turns. I im-
mensely admire Proust's and Stein's turns.

But Proust's great work is a discovery or demonstration of con-
tinuities, and my experience also includes radical discontinuities.
This is obviously the result of historical conditions, although I
don't have any nostalgia for a world of continuities. On the other
hand, I don't have fear of it either. But I have talked from time to
time in the past about gaps, gaps between sentences, for example,
and how one thinks across them. Gaps are sometimes essential to
my work, although they don't exclude linkages and turns.

The unconventional poetic prose of My Life *is composed of many paragraphs
and each of them is introduced by a statement or an insinuation; to what
degree are they influenced by those readings of Proust or of Mandelstam?*

I've been responding to these questions one day at a time, and I
arrive at this one only a few hours after learning that the U.S.,

along with England, Saudi Arabia, and Kuwait, has attacked Iraq. I can't resolve such information, not by forgetting it and not by aestheticizing it. I am stunned, and then surprised by terrible and intense feelings of grief and fear—not a grand fear but rather a small fear, resembling furtiveness. *War* is under scrutiny by this grief and fear; but it's the subject, not the object, of that scrutiny. In this sense, it refuses abstraction; it forms into innumerable particulars.

In some respects, my emotional response resembles my feelings toward death, the deaths of certain people I've loved and, in fact, continue to love, and especially to the death of my father. (In thinking about this war, I also recognize something virtually identical to my abhorrence of the death penalty.)

I can say that *My Life*, apart from technical concerns (the exploration of the long and short sentence, of parataxis, of the varieties of metonymic associating or metonymic logics, of social and familial speech as mental fact, of repetition and change, etc.), was motivated by a fear of death, or by the anticipation of loss. And it is in this that I feel an affinity with Proust, whose astonishing style is a representation of the tension between momentum and lingering that a mind, wanting always to be conscious that it's alive, experiences.

What is sad and frightening about a person's death (even the deaths of young soldiers in war) is only partially the loss of that person's future—what he or she might have seen or done. Much worse is the loss of that person's past, of his or her memory and thus of his or her experience; death, as far as we can tell, obliterates the emotional intellect in which enormous intensities of response radiate and in which the fabric of the significance of everything that has been woven into it exists. It is the loss to one of having lived.

Last night, I was looking through *Remembrance of Things Past* in anticipation of answering your question (in a very different way from what is emerging today), to find the phrase from which the opening pre-text of *My Life* ("A pause, a rose, something on paper") was (metonymically) translated. I didn't find it readily and was impatient so I didn't look long. It is in a description of an approach to Combray, which the narrator sees emerging from the distance, bit by bit suffused with what he knows: the plain, the spire, a radiance anticipating the color of the streets. Something like that. Proust's style of accretion, of accumulation, meditation, and release (release into consciousness and as such *into the book*) was and is inspiring to me. As in this sentence, from the famous madeleine scene at the end of the "Overture" to *Remembrance of Things Past:* "But when from a long-distant past nothing subsists, after the people are dead, after the things are broken and scattered, taste and smell alone, more fragile but more enduring, more insubstantial, more persistent, more faithful, remain poised a long time, like souls, remembering, waiting and hoping, amid the ruins of all the rest; and bear unflinchingly, in the tiny and almost impalpable drop of their essence, the vast structure of recollection." [2]

By the way, Proust's early literary work (maybe even his first) was a translation of John Ruskin's *The Bible of Amiens*, and it was under the influence of Ruskin's prose style that Proust developed his own. Ruskin's prose is the result and complex reflection of an obsession with particulars and the ramifications of particulars. This was not solely a Victorian interest in things but an epistemological one, and from it he developed his radical (and some would say eccentric) social politics, one that coincided at many points with Marx's. The prose style that we find in Ruskin and subsequently in Proust is sometimes taken as a sign of privilege; this is a serious misunderstanding.

In any case, my reading of Gertrude Stein's studies of time and space have amplified what Proust's contributed to my own sense of those dimensions. And her phenomenology—her rejection of memory as a medium for perception—and the command, "Begin again," are vital contradictions to Proust's. It is critical to think and work with contradictions. Or it is typical (of our times) to do so.

I should say, by the way, that the "poetic prose" of *My Life* is carefully structured, and therefore perhaps it is more "conventional" than your question implies, though admittedly many of the book's conventions are inventions of my own. The book as a whole is organized according to structural conventions which I laid out in advance and imposed on the writing. There are, in fact, two published versions of the book, one written when I was 37 years old (and published by Burning Deck in 1980) and the other revised when I was 45 (and published by Sun and Moon Press in 1987). The first has 37 paragraphs, of 37 sentences each, and the latter includes an additional 8 paragraphs (making 45) along with expanded versions of the original 37 paragraphs, with 8 new sentences added to each. In other words, the later version consists of 45 paragraphs with 45 sentences in each. In addition, every paragraph (or poem) is preceded by a sentence or phrase; these get repeated (though sometimes in slightly altered form) here and there in later parts of the book, representing the recurrence that constitutes memory but also providing the recontextualization that it involves—memory recontextualizes what one thinks and what one knows.

Meanwhile, conventional language is pervasive throughout the book—clichés ("Pretty is as pretty does"), turns of phrase typical of my social milieu ("I've got a big day tomorrow"), idiosyncratic witticisms of my relatives ("cottage fromage," "I've had a peachy time"), metaphors embedded in the American language ("to take a vacation," "to spend some time"). The book is about the formative impact of language, and at the same time it is a critique of that language—suggesting that one can construct alternative views. *My Life* is both determined and constructed. My life, too.

This is a milieu, of course, of contradiction.

But not of opposites. I don't believe in opposites.

You mention Osip Mandelstam. The Soviet period of Russian literature is one which is absolutely wild with contradiction and with contrary impulses—most obviously, for example, toward East and West, toward the educated and the massive, toward individual expression and social utility, etc. Mandelstam is, of course, one of the great writers of this period, and I admire his work very much. But I don't think he has exerted much influence on my own writing.

I apologize for burdening my response to this question with comments about war. Recent events are extraneous to these questions, but context is crucial to their answers. That, finally, is what I have wanted to "get at"—the context of consciousness and a consciousness of context.

At the California College of Arts and Crafts (in 1978) you gave "the students work with language situations, translations, transformations, nu-

*merical equivalency systems, random configurations, transition processes.
. . . " This seems to be a declaration of your poetics.*

I'm writing out my responses to these questions in Canada, from a large art school and theater center above a very small town in the Canadian Rockies, where around one hundred art students and artists are studying or working. People are watching the war news on television, usually over the cable news station, CNN. The room where the television sits isn't big and the atmosphere is overheated, but only because so many people are in the room. There is absolutely no conversation. We have been listening to any possible news of the missile attack on Israel and what Israel's response will be. Usually in a crisis people, even strangers, talk to each other—for reassurance, and to build up the comradeship that one might have to depend on in case of need. Here artists from many countries are watching news of the beginning of war in complete silence, isolated from each other. I don't know why.

The atmosphere in the room with the TV resembles that of a railroad or bus depot. No one stays for long in the room, people come and go wearing their coats and boots, a stranger passing among strangers, perhaps absorbing the news privately.

1978, when I taught at the California College of Arts and Crafts, wasn't so very long after the end of the Vietnam War—a war that was never declared to be such in the United States. A major component of my poetics, or let's say of my poetic impulse, is a result of that war and the meaning of its never being named.

But as for the question—in fact the assignment I gave my students to work with "language situations, translations," and so forth was not primarily a manifestation of my poetics, although

I certainly wanted to suggest to the students, and to help them discover, that systems and structures are also ways of thinking, a means for interpretation, of going from one thing to another and beyond one's expectations. But my assignments were also intended to encourage the students to write work that wasn't an expression of their "anguished egos," a means for them to be inventive rather than reactive. It was a difficult class, because not a single student had any interest in being a writer. In order to get a degree at CCAC every student had to take a certain number of Humanities courses, and a "poetry writing" course looked like an easy way out. Some of the students, of course, were inventive and intelligent. But some of the others presented me with very real problems by writing "to" me about very private and, in two cases, disturbing matters, which I hadn't the training or the inclination to deal with. My solution was to force them out of themselves and into more social aspects of language—the systems interwoven through language that make it comprehensible to its users, the structures that make it a framework and constraint on knowledge, some ways of distorting syntax to arrive at unexpected fields of meanings, and so forth.

I was using such things to develop my own thinking at the time, too. I've never taught material that was entirely under my control nor any, I hope, that was completely out of the control of my students.

But except for the logical formula that provides the super-structure for *My Life* I've never discovered or invented a number system that has satisfied me as a metaphor, or excuse, for a particular piece of writing. I resist the aura of "divine guidance," or "divine justification," they imply. The invention of form is the discovery of the interior motivation for a work, and it is very difficult. I gratefully envy Ron Silliman's use of the Fibonacci series, which provides his book *Tjanting*, for example, with at least natural guidance and justification. It's perfect. But it would be redundant for me to do something similar.

One of the benefits of formal devices is that they increase the palpability, the perceptibility of the work. And another is that they can be used to increase a work's semantic possibilities. Kit Robinson's writing provides great (and for me influential) examples of both. So too does the writing of Louis Zukofsky. His five-word lines often leave very odd words at the end of a line, producing lines with no resolution, no way to stop, but the logic slides, the lines merge. It's beautiful.

In your correspondence archived at UCSD you appear to be attached to discovering the inner nature of concepts like collage, subjectivity/objectivity, restlessness or the Faustian "rage to know" . . . and this reminds me of a line from Writing Is an Aid to Memory: *"I am impatient to finish in order to begin . . . "*

For a time (prior to 1978) I tended to use the term *collage* loosely and generally to refer to all art works created or assembled out of diverse materials—works of art emphasizing contiguity, contingency, juxtaposition, realignment, relationship, unlikely pairings, etc. The problem with the term, as I saw when I became more precise, is that it suggests (or can suggest) an unmotivated or unnecessitated groupings of materials. Things in a collage are like letters of the alphabet—when you put some of them together they will always appear to be seeking meaning, or even to be making it. The term *montage*, however, as it was used by and in the tradition of the Russian film director Sergei Eisenstein, is better. In montage, all the above values are maintained (contiguity, contingency, etc.), but the result reflects decision more than happy chance.

Also *collage* is a predominantly spatial technique (developed in paintings), whereas *montage* (deriving from film technique) employs devices that are related to time. In this sense *montage* preserves its character as a process.

I don't quite know how to explicate the line "I am impatient to finish in order to begin . . . " with respect to my uneasiness with the inadequacies of *collage*, except perhaps to say that the line obviously expresses a certain mental state, impatience, or restlessness, an urge not to stand still, while at the same time it assumes that there's no progressing continuum in which "I" can participate. This mental state could be seen as compulsive, that is, relentlessly aware of possibilities and constraints. Of freedoms and boundary lines.

Also, to the extent that I've attempted to undertake a completely new project with each book I've written, I find myself over and over in the position of a "beginner"—with all of a beginner's quandaries and clumsinesses, trying to figure out where I am and how things are done there.

The Grreat Adventure is a diverse book demanding different approaches; there we have the presence of Balzac, Jane Austen. . . . It's also like a notebook (activity instructions, required readings, the questionnaires sent off by balloons). Is nonlinearity per se the goal of the book?

Now *here* is an example of collage.

There are very, very few copies of this "book" in existence— I burned almost all of them.

That is not to say that I renounce the book, or even that I want to distance myself from it. But it does seem anomalous in relation to my other work. Maybe it would be nice to have had a pure history, but to do so I would have had to have had from an early age a vision of the future. An agenda. An intended trajectory.

But on the contrary, I've been influenced by anything.

I don't think nonlinearity was the goal of *The Grreat Adventure*; I think it was a summons to impressionability.

The forty-two sections of Writing Is an Aid to Memory *are characterized by a subjugate beat, almost a prophetic beat at the level of sound; do you agree with this?*

I'm assuming that you mean *subjunctive* when you use the word "subjugate." If so, this is a very interesting comment. I think the syntax (and its sounds) do set up a field of contingency and provisionality, although I would have said that the work expresses desires (that and other visions) rather than prophecies. I don't have a copy of the book with me here in Canada, and I don't trust my memory enough to quote it without its aid. But I do remember that the momentum of the cadence, with its departures within arrivals and arrivals within departures, was intended to push time in both directions, "backward" toward memory and also forward toward "writing," which is always (for me) indicative of future unforeseen meanings and events. Writing gives one something to remember.

But you refer specifically to a "prophetic" beat, maybe suggestive of solemnity and sphinxlike ambiguity. Truths hidden until found. In such a case, prophecies wouldn't foretell the future, they would discover destiny. And they would be proven not on the basis of criteria established in the future but on the grounds of memory, in which are displayed the patterns of incident and decision that would seem to lead "inevitably" to the accomplishment of destiny. A sense of destiny is a result of a retrospective and heavily interpreted experiencing of experience—an apparent discovery of what was and why it worked. But it depends also on belief in a sublime causality, in a transcendental continuum which I simply can't see. I do believe in irrevocability, and with great curiosity I acknowledge "givens," but I don't believe in destiny, if one means by that that one's life is subject to some inescapable, noncontingent plan.

Is there in your poetry an intimate association between line and thought?

I think the term *perception* should be added to the configuration, if only in recognition of the world with which line and thought share time and place. I say this because I would like to undermine the opposition between inside and outside in a poem. Although I have varied the shape and quality of lines so as to make each line equivalent to a "unit of thought" or "unit of cognition," it isn't that the line "contains" the thought, it's rather that it's a possible measure of the activity of thinking within the thinkable, perceivable world.

Line length and line break can alter perceptual processes in innumerable ways, for both writer and reader. Retardation, flicker, recombination, the extension of speed, immobilization, and myriad other effects are dependent on qualities of line.

And of course thoughts don't occur in divisions; in fact the experience of thinking is more one of combination. So while a line may isolate stages of thought it may also multiply and strengthen the connections in which thought emerges. This occurs especially when line and sentence don't coincide, where the end of one sentence and the beginning of another may combine in a single line.

How did you solve the escape from sentence to paragraph?

There was a point in the early eighties, around the time that Ron Silliman was presenting an early version of his essay "The New Sentence" as a talk in San Francisco, when I was finding the sentence extremely limiting and even claustrophobic. I hoped that I could open its terminal points (the capital at the beginning and the full stop [period] at the end) by writing in paragraphs, so that sentences were occurring in groups, opening into each other, altering each other, and in every way escaping the isolation and "completeness" of the sentence. But it wasn't until I returned to writing in lines, where I could open up the syntax of sentences from within by setting in motion the syntax of lines at the same time (for example by breaking sentences into two or more lines), that I "escaped," as you quite perfectly put it, from prose to poetry. *The Guard* offers what is probably a good example of the result.

For the last few years I've been writing sentence-based (rather than sentence-subverting or sentence-distorting) lines, as for example in *The Cell* and in *The Hunt*, which is to be published by Zasterle Press.

In *The Hunt* I think this may reflect a concern with the velocity of experience, or with the experiencing of experience, rather than with meaning *per se*. The work is a long accounting of, and meditation on, the experience and effect of a number of long and short periods I have spent in Russia. The Zasterle Press version is Book Five of the complete work, which has the same title but uses the Russian word, *Oxota*, which also means "desire" or "yearning." The book is subtitled "A Short Russian Novel." It's written in fourteen-line stanzas (or chapters) in homage to the first great Russian novel, Aleksandr Pushkin's *Evgeny Onegin*, which was written in fourteen-line stanzas and subtitled "a novel in verse." But in order to allow for digressive, anecdotal, common, quotidian, or discursive materials as I heard and observed them, I needed a very flexible line, and a prosaic line—the sentence.

Your poetry is an exploration in language mainly through the sentence and paragraph; what kind of change are you pursuing with this new adopted value?

Carla Harryman, Ron Silliman, and Barrett Watten have all used the paragraph as a device, either to organize or to revolutionize (Carla often does this) a text, but I really have not—I could say I have failed to do so. *My Life* is written in sentences, not in paragraphs. And the prose in Carla Harryman's and my ongoing collaboration, *The Wide Road*, uses paragraphs less for themselves than for what can be bound in and released from them; the paragraphs in that work contain various kinds of materials and aren't constructed for the conventional purpose of controlling tone or furthering plot. Each paragraph is a small plot, in a realm of erotically plotted fields.

My goal has been to escape *within* the sentence, to make an enormous sentence—not necessarily a long one, but a capacious one. Somewhat paradoxically, I sometimes try to create this capacity with different compressive techniques—metonymy is the most consistent form of "logic" in my writing. But sometimes long, convoluted sentences from which many conditional clauses depend are instances, for me, of intense accuracy, of a direct route.

But am I, in my sentences (and my use of lines to expand their capacity and accuracy), in pursuit of change? Do I want to improve the world?

Of course. If so, it will have to be *in* sentences, not by them. The sentence is a medium of arrivals and departures, a medium of inquiry, discovery, and acknowledgment.

I think that in The Guard *privacy is one of the essential elements within the book; is it a dialogue between you and the same text?*

"The Guard" was written just after my first trip to the Soviet Union, and it's dedicated to Arkadii Dragomoshchenko, the Leningrad poet whom I met for the first time on that trip, and with whom I've been collaborating on various translations and projects since. Contrary to seeking a realm for privacy, the book is about words (those projectiles of communication). It's words who are guards. And users of words. Do they guard us or do they guard their things? And are they keeping something in or something out?

The poem is the result of my first encounter with the Russian language and also with the disorientation and longing associated with all my now numerous trips to Russia. A similar disorientation and longing informs much of my writing. It was in "The Guard" that I first made an analogy between the Russian realm I was experiencing and the realm of the words for things; I attempted to continue that work in *Oxota*.

But beginning to learn Russian did not give me my first or only experience of the word as an adamant entity. Words have often had a palpable quality for me, porous but not transparent, utilizable but unstable. I could imagine a word as a rock; the rock in a gate, the gate opening, but would one say into or out of some place that "I" enters. Is it Russia? Are we getting our first glimpse of the landscape encountered on a Dante-esque journey to "paradise"—which is the last word in the poem?

The Guard is about attempted communication, not privacy. Maybe we're stuck in privacy, nonetheless. My early attempts to speak Russian would have tended to make me think so.

Is there any discipline for reading Individuals?

No, not at all. Kit Robinson and I each wrote twelve of the twenty-four poems in the book. Kit has taught poetry-writing in many situations, to young children, to adolescents, to college students from many areas of society, and he has often said that the only readers and writers who are blind to the many dimensions possible in poetry are the overly trained and overly educated. My experience as a teacher has taught me the same. The only qualities necessary for reading and enjoying and learning from poetry are freedom from preconceptions as to the limits (and even the definition) of poetry and curiosity and confidence in the possibilities of something's being new and interesting.

The poems in *Individuals* are the result of looking at very ordinary objects and experiences. They are about our respective appreciation for the existence of these things, and for the available strangeness which allows us to know them again and again as if for the first time and yet without having forgotten.

Notes

1. *A Suite of Poetic Voices: Interviews with Contemporary American Poets*, ed. Manuel Brito (Santa Brigida, Spain: Kadle Books, 1992).

2. Marcel Proust, *Remembrance of Things Past*, tr. C. K. Scott Moncrieff and Terence Kilmartin (New York: Random House, 1981), 1:50–51.

The Person and Description

In the fall of 1988, Carla Harryman undertook to curate three evenings of discussion on "The Poetics of Everyday Life." They took place in Berkeley at Small Press Distribution, and most of the papers that were given were subsequently published in *Poetics Journal* 9: "The Person" (1991).

The discussion in which I was invited to participate was addressed to the person, seemingly a figure of everyday life and even, one might say, a figure that dominates it. It is at the level of the everyday that one can most easily speak of "my life." It is at this level that one speaks most uneasily of it, as well.

The individual is a figure that steadfastly, in Western culture, appears at the apex of hierarchical structures; it stakes its claims on them and establishes itself as their dominating figure. At the same time, the notion of "identity"—the identity of the individual—is itself party to a hierarchical structure, one in which "identity" governs the question of who an individual might be. And yet, even as identity is a governing factor, it is a limiting factor too.

And it is itself subject to hierarchy, in that different identities may get assigned different roles, even different values. These, being somewhat context-dependent, may thus be somewhat fluid, but they are never completely so, and they are seldom so fluid as to allow a person to elude identity altogether.

This was a problem that vexed Gertrude Stein, and increasingly so toward the end of her life (she was in her early sixties when she wrote *The Geographical History of America,* the work in which she most intensely investigates the problem of identity and its relation to human nature).

Description, with its tendency to evaluate even as it pretends to objectify, is deeply implicated in the establishment of hierarchies—including those that structure and restrict identity. Indeed, to the extent that a description may also become a definition, it lays down strictures that can be nearly impossible to disrupt. But description is prevalent in writing, and not only in narrative modes of writing, and when writing my paper for Carla Harryman's symposium I saw it as pivotal to the question of personhood and hence to living the everyday life. I hoped that by insisting on its contingent relation to both "art and reality, or intentionality and circumstance"— that is, by positioning description in and as the intermediary zone between them—I could open a space through which a person might step. In or out.

The potential performative power of this entrance or exit was no doubt influenced by my reading of (and excitement over) Carla Harryman's own work—just as my thinking on the question of hierarchical structures was certainly informed by her many and profound critiques of (and challenges to) power structures of all kinds.

1

A person, alone or in groups of persons, has accompanied art throughout its history; it is assumed that a work of art is, at the very least, a manifestation of his or her presence. But whose?

It would seem initially that if one wanted to answer questions concerning the *who* and *what* of a particular person, one would begin with a concept of personhood. But personhood isn't generalizable or definitive in quite the way peachhood or goldhood or even childhood might be, since the personhood of each person is felt to be individualizing, different, unique. Personhood comes to one through living a life. To explain what it is, or what it is "like," to be a person requires a long account.

The uniqueness of the person is very different from his or her essential selfhood. Our individuality, in fact, is at odds with the concept of some core reality at the heart of our sense of being. The latter has tended to produce a banal description of the work of art as an expression uttered in the artist's "own voice," issuing from an inner, fundamental, sincere, essential, irreducible, consistent self, an undemonstrable but sensible entity on which each of us is somehow dependent, living off its truths, its heat, its energy.

But is it, the self, a person?

And is art—including literary art—the work of a self?

And can this be, for example, a Russian question?

The English word *self* has no real Russian equivalent, and thus the self, as (on the basis of my English language) I think I know it, is not everywhere a certain thing.

The connotations which accumulate to form an American's notion of his or her self are, in the Russian language and thus presumably in the Russian experience, dispersed and placed differently.

In English the self has come to be defined as something "having a single character or quality throughout," and "the union of elements (as body, emotions, thoughts, and sensations) that constitute the individuality and identity of a person" and also as "personal interest or advantage"[1]—thus it's a concept which is suggested by the Russian *sushchnost'* (individuality, essence) and *lichnost'* (personality), but with the further characteristic of being knowable only to itself.

Perhaps in Russian the advancing of a notion of the self occurs in (but only in) the reflexive pronoun *sebya*, "oneself," "myself," which, however, never appears in the nominative case and is most frequently seen in the form of the suffix *-sya* at the end of reflexive verbs. This suggests that when speaking Russian a self is felt but has no proper name, or that the self occurs only in or as a context but is insufficiently stable to occur independently as a noun.

This is quite different from the self of the English language, whose definition posits it as the essence of each single human being, the sole and constant point from which the human being can truthfully and originally speak.

But what is constancy?

Certainly I have an experience of being in position, at a time and place, and of being conscious of this. But this position is temporary, and beyond that, I have no experience of being except in position. All my observations are made from within a matrix of possibly infinite contingencies and contextualities.

This sense of contingency is intrinsic to my experience of the self as a relationship rather than an essence. To say that it is even basic to it must seem paradoxical, since it would seem to be in the nature of contingency to postdate, as it were, a sense of being. But, in fact, that sense of being, of selfhood, can only be reached *after* one is in place and surrounded by possibilities. That comes first: the perceiving of something, not in parts but whole, as a situation and with a projection of possibilities. The recognition of those possibilities follows and constitutes one's first exercise *of* possibility, and on that depends one's realization that oneself is possible. It is in the exercise of *that* possibility that one inescapably acknowledges others, which have in fact already been admitted when and as one initially perceived something. And the exercise of possibilities (including that of consciousness) amid conditions and occasions constitutes a person.

It is here that the epistemological nightmare of the solipsistic self breaks down, and the essentialist yearning after truth and origin can be discarded in favor of the experience of experience.

The person, in this view, is a mobile (and mobilized) reference point, or, to put it another way, subjectivity is not an entity but a dynamic.

There is no self undefiled by experience, no self unmediated in the perceptual situation; instead there is a world and the person is in it.

With these considerations in mind, I attempted to write a work which would not be about a person but which would be *like* a person. Actually, what I said to myself was that I would write a poem which was to its language what a person is to its landscape (defining landscape in the broadest possible way so as to include culture and society as well as particular rooms, cities, or natural vistas, etc.).

The poem would be both in language and a consequence of it, and it would be both identifiable (real) and interpretable (readable).

It could not pretend to be anything other than a thinking of, for, and around itself—it would be encompassed by the context it encompassed.

Subsequently I began that work and wrote other things as well, always thinking about the unstable existence and recurrent or persistent experiences of a person, drawn into the world in and by perception, implicated by language, moving around in life, and unwilling to give up attempts at description.

Description in such a situation is simultaneously exploration, discovery, and communication. It gives information not just about the world but about the describer's place for the moment in it.

And this brings us to the reader, who, *as* a reader, is also in our description and our situation.

The reader too is the entity we call a person.

Coherence is always only contextual in this literary situation, which I can picture, for example, as a scene in which the writer is standing on a concrete curb in the commercial district of a busy city, the reader is standing beside the writer, and many, many people are moving up and down and across the street—many heads, many stomachs, many bags, many shoes and boots.

The person is gasping with explanation.

Your eyeball is on the person and with a check of the wobble you see . . .

A person has deliberately to keep all that can be seen in.

Every person is born preceded by its desire.

Any person who agrees will increase.

A person, never less.

One person responds by fixing motes, another person by floating them.

Person, place, and . . .

Ears—almost every person has some.

A person puts meals in its head.

A person needs closer introspection than that to catch itself doing so.

Every person sticks up in its sunbath.

Don't be afraid—predicaments make a person apparent.

Person having thought with its capacity to preoccupy.

Person holding picture of person holding picture of . . .

The person of which I speak is between clocks.

A person who had never seen a plant would not understand.

Two persons cannot be bare at the same time because they have to exchange visibility.

The person goes up to a perfect stranger in an enclosed public space (for example a bank, or supermarket, or department store), and there belts out some aria.

This form of person is mulish.

The person has monstrous teeth and a vulnerable nose.

Such a person might ask if its mother is a natural or a cultural thing.

My personal mother was outlined when she got out of bed.

A person crossing its own enclosed green and yellow shadow proceeds by feeling that its feet are the appropriate size.

Anything rather than a person that decomposes into temporal rather than spatial parts must be a person's life.

A person forms around a psyche, two psyches, in a great sexual life it has no power to time.

All day the person is remaining reminded.

The grand sanity of the person pushes it.

Can a person gulp with delight?

Each person has its own idea of sensuality.

A person is time not speed.

So temporal persons confront temporary waves.

A person is at the end, its whim set on its spine.

Don't be afraid, I am a person—the companion, the uncut, the knife, the neck (the neck is long and full of sound), the gust around something.

It's ALL "person."

2

To posit the concept of the person in relation to description raises issues which can best be regarded as boundary problems. These problems are artistic and literary in one sense, but they get played out in social and economic life, which responds both to the rigidity of boundaries (between, for example, public and private, history and daily life, male and female) and to their breakdown.

Much of social violence, from domestic fighting to racism, rape, torture, and terrorism, is in various ways a response to, and a representation of, boundary problems.

Description, whether it is intentional or the result of ambient ideology, bounds a person's life, whether narrowly or broadly. In another sense it likewise bounds a person, and this is a central (perhaps the classic) issue for feminism, which recognizes that traditionally women are often described but, until recently, they have very seldom been the describers. This is, of course, most clearly evident in painting, where there have been so many painted women and so few women painters.

Being an object of description but without the authority to describe, a woman may feel herself to be bounded by her own appearance, a representation of her apparent person, not certain whether she is she or only a quotation. She may feel herself to have been defined from without while remaining indefinite in or as herself.

But the perception of this murkiness of definition, this ambiguity as to one's phenomenological status, one's appearance as person, can only be reached through some sort of introspection. One only notices oneself by asking *who* or *what* am I?

Am I *this?* Is this *that?*

Introspection newly delineates and constantly shifts the boundary between subject and object. It establishes the relationship between self and other, between body and mind, and then transgresses the borders it has established—a transgression which, by the way, might be expanded and rephrased in the context of the boundaries (or blurring of boundaries) between art and reality—in order to describe a person. It must breach boundaries in order to figure a person out.

The "personal" is already a plural condition. Perhaps one feels that it is located somewhere within, somewhere inside the body— in the stomach? the chest? the genitals? the throat? the head? One can look for it and already one is not oneself, one is several, a set of incipiencies, incomplete, coming into view here and then there, and subject to dispersal.

The idea of the person enters poetics where art and reality, or intentionality and circumstance, meet. It is on the improvised boundary between art and reality, between construction and experience, that the person (or my person) in writing exists.

But if this is where the idea of the person becomes a component in a poetics, it is also the point at which the person enters everyday life. The person is both the agent and the agency of the making of the quotidian, doing things which are hardly notable, hardly noted. Routinely it puts its right foot on the floor at a little distance from its left and slightly ahead of it; both heels are red, and it spits into the sink after brushing its upper teeth with eleven strokes starting on the left side and working across the teeth; it notices a sore area on the gum and doesn't know if the gum was sore yesterday.

Here the person has no opposite.

But the person acquires its opposites at the moment it writes this. It posits its self-consciousness in consciousness of environment and detail, in work and language. It is then, by virtue of its conscious sentient nature, involved with the infinite number of details and projections of details in a labyrinth of linkages which constitute it and its times.

With such a starting point, what can a person expect?

Note

1. *Webster's Ninth New Collegiate Dictionary*, s.v. "person."

The Quest for Knowledge
in the Western Poem

The somewhat sardonically titled "Quest for Knowledge in the Western Poem" was written in 1992 for presentation at the Naropa Institute's Summer Writing Program. 1992 saw various quincentennial celebrations of Christopher Columbus's "discovery of America," and a large part of Naropa's summer program was devoted to a critique of the historiographic framing of that event. The essay was subsequently published in *Disembodied Poetics,* a collection of Naropa lectures edited by Anne Waldman and Andrew Schelling.[1]

The reference to the "West" is to be explained in part by the quincentennial context, but in its emphasis on the frontier (or on the notion of the West as a frontier), the essay bears a relation both to *Oxota: A Short Russian Novel,* which had been published the previous year, and to *A Border Comedy,* the ideas for which I was just beginning to develop. The "Russian novel" was about unsettlement and disorientation; its milieu, the Soviet Union, is for a Westerner perhaps exotic, but in the "novel" it is the narrator who becomes exoticized; she becomes estranged from the markers of self and incapable of self-location. Curiously, though this theme of dislocation or disorientation might seem to be generic to "travel literature" and hence somewhat inevitable in *Oxota*, it is also very much a Russian theme, as is evident from its centrality in such works as Dostoevsky's *Notes from the Underground* (as, indeed, in most of Dostoevsky's work), Gogol's "The Nose," Andrei Bely's *Saint Petersburg*, Bulgakov's *The Master and Margarita*, Yury Olesha's *Envy*, Boris Pilnyak's *The Naked Year*, and in much of Nabokov's work.

The issues that the Russian novel explored in a Russian context I wanted now to explore in the to me more familiar, and therefore far more vague and far less closely observed, context of "home." Physical dislocation and hence geophysical unfamiliarity are familiar experiences in American life, but they seem to have produced a tendency toward a kind of bulldoggish simulacrum of stability of both locale and self. This has manifested itself through the reification of situation—for example, in the generic character of malls and the shops within them, in the replication of sites of all kinds, in the primacy granted to ownership and then to property rights, etc. Generally, I was growing increasingly interested in the ways in which notions of "home" and of "identity" were related and how those notions were tied to capital.

What was obvious was that knowledge of the West took the form of situating oneself in it, of staking one's claim—but one's claim to what? Ultimately, I think it is oneself that is the preoccupation in the Western quest for knowledge; the "Westerner" seeks to establish him or herself; he or she wants to be knowable.

In researching the theme of "knowledge in the West," in addition to the works that are discussed in the essay, I read from a cluster of materials (Owen Wister's classic cowboy story *The Virginian*; William James's *Essays in Radical Empiricism*; Gertrude Stein's *The Making of Americans*; Frank Norris's *The Octopus*; Jack London's *Call of the Wild*, among others) all dating from the first decade of the twentieth century, that is, approximately mid-way between the present and the so-called "opening of the West" as it was recorded in the journals (later referred to as "our national epic of exploration" by Elliott Coues in his preface to the definitive 1893 edition) of Meriwether Lewis and William Clark during their expedition to explore and describe the West (May 1804–September 1806). I wanted to examine materials from the first decade of the twentieth century because generally they tend to look both ways, back at a certain milieu of achievement (highly compromised as it seemed even then) and forward to its implications and the working out of a complex of romantic and realist values colliding finally in American postmodernism, not only as an aesthetic but also as social reality and lived experience.

In the essay I make an equation between "how knowledge works and how language works," an equation that, if it holds at all, would hold specifically in writing, and it would mean that there is a grammar of knowledge just as there is one of language. But the term "language" covers an array of discourses, and this essay employs several, two of which are markedly different. The essay is comprised of sections of a poem interwoven with sections of expository prose based on notes that were written to parallel the poetry. They are notes not about the poem but about the general enigma that the poem attempts both to address and to enact and which can be put in the form of a question: "What does a poem know?"

"What does a poem know?"

Or more specifically, "What does a Western poem know?" To ask such a question requires that one consider not only the situation of knowledge in the context of poetry, but also the situation of poetry in the context of that body of knowledge which is a peculiarly Western construct, and one which, by the way, provides the grounds for the proposition that "America was discovered in 1492."

The quincentennial celebration that took place in 1992 was not, properly, recognition of discovery but of a concept, an invention. Western knowledge itself has been a set of inventions, framed by perception but linked to anticipation.

The Corresponding Sky

Above our real things the corresponding sky drifts toward the edge of the dark—the edge heavy with gold, the night blue and maroon, as the sunset, claiming the horizon, binds it (by whatever is to come, whatever to continue) to the West.

It is faced by an unbacked bench.

The West?

It is met with perception.

Set with appreciation.

And I am one

Until I'm placed in the objective sense—am I to say "prepared"?—a person to turn as toward sky around sun.

An enclosure?

Knowledge?

I've vowed to learn a new word every day, but I'll never, even when I'm old, be ashamed to dance.

Still, I would get rid of *I* if I could, I said, I did, I went.

I was born in the West.

The fact that I live in the literal West—not just within the bounds of so-called Western culture but also at the farthest reaches of the geographical West, at the terminus of Westward exploration, Westward expansion, Westward exploitation, and Westward imagination—seems to place me in the extreme longitudes of a literal realm of experience. To live in California is to live so far West that one has all but overleaped the cowboys and landed instead in Hollywood or Disneyland—or in what the world suddenly knows as South Central Los Angeles—that is, in created places, which are themselves to a large extent worlds of fantasies (both positive and negative), of extremes, but of constructed extremes, that is, extremes which are also imitations and descriptions (where description is a form of anticipation). And in being imitations and descriptions, they are both derived from and directed at assumptions, which in turn have at least the appearance of comprising bodies of knowledge.

I was born in the West.

What is the criterion, I, born, or West, of knowing so?

Is this inevitability as I know it—its terrible and ludicrous humanity and only it?

Subject, object, and yielding—as if meaning were my familiar milieu.

I have learned to treat them all as unique in entity, as solitudes and plenitudes.

The independence of oneself from reason is much bigger than oneself.

A Westerner, Owen Wister said, will always watch the telling detail of a well-told tale and regard it as an account of believable adventure.

All of it if one's got the time.

The Horizon Soon Widens What It Costs Us

"The great division," the moment when the West became the West, when the West distinguished itself from the rest, is often said to have occurred between 500 and 399 B.C., in the century of Socrates, the period that defined and established the concept that fundamental laws might be discovered and incontrovertible logic be constructed for governing philosophy, science, and the social state. This was, of course, also the century of Sophocles and Euripides—the century of the birth of tragedy.

But in considering contemporary experience, and particularly contemporary notions of what and how we know (i.e., our states of perception and our sensation of knowing), an attempt to observe the West should be equally attentive to the fundamental redefinition and reevaluation of the rules of knowing that occurred at the beginning of the seventeenth century, with the burgeoning of experimental science, inspired by and accessory to the voyages of exploration and the sudden increase in what was taken to be knowledge, or at least the raw materials (data and experiences) out of which knowledge could (and must, as they thought) be constructed. It was then that a scientific model for the acquisition of knowledge (along with the very idea of acquisition in relation to knowing and its value) was established, one that ever since has seemed nearly irrevocable. It is this scientific model for the acquisition of knowledge that produced something of what now seems definitively Western in our culture.

The model as both a system and a program (or what we would now term a *method*) was most thoroughly formulated at the very beginning of the seventeenth century by Sir Francis Bacon, as part of "The Great Instauration." Bacon and his subsequent followers were convinced that the components of the natural world are themselves "eloquent of their own history." But in order to get at this history, the "army" of particulars must be organized into "tables of discovery" so as to be readily available as subjects of investigation. And the linguistic descriptive strategies that were to accord with this investigation were to be identical with scientific observational ones.[2]

The Advancement of Learning and the *Novum Organum* were explicitly directed toward problems in recording and describing data. But this essentially literary activity was seen not only as an instrument for obtaining and securing information but also as a means for achieving a particular style of mind, characterized by perceptual acuity, self-sufficiency, undistractibility, and objectivity.

In a sense, Bacon's program was devised for the sake of learning, not for the sake of knowledge. It is not knowledge per se that is to be learned, but rather the world, and the method for achieving this learning is a descriptive method, one in which the observing senses are fundamentally aided by language.

A Sentimental Achiever

Wake up, wake up!

The sentimental person is a self-regarding rarity.

What it knows it derives from a tender sense of combination.

Its day verges, its sun rides, and its sight travels all the dimensions of its capacity for impressions.

It leaves messages to give its reasons.

And we receive the sentiment of enormous distance.

A view whose farthest points attain position undiminished.

There the person wants the human pattern to repeat so as to do in life exactly in its absence all that it will know.

Knowledge in the West is incorporated into visions of the West and visions of the West have tended to be put into action—generally, I would say, for the worse, which is sadly part of our story. It is guilty knowledge that may lie at the heart of our fantasies. The fact that our knowledge of gain is suffused with knowledge of loss may account in part for the anxious circumspection and endemic nostalgia that inform our sense of time and our sense of time's effect on place.

This must in part be due to the fact that this geographical American West, as everyone knows, is only latterly a ground for Western culture, if we mean by that the attitudes, assumptions, interests, and traditions of Europe since, say, the so-called Enlightenment. The American West was for a far longer time the home of other peoples, distinctly and paradoxically "non-Western" in their approaches to living, to the meanings of that living, and in their conception of who it is who is doing that living.

One might take the "non-Western" Native American and the Western concepts of self as exemplars of very different experiences of having, or being, a self. For Westerners like me, my self, or my person, seems the very context of my living—my life's trope, as it were. It is a metonymic trope. "I" am a discrete individual part among other parts, in everchanging contexts. The "definition of the self in our own culture rests on our law of contradiction. The self cannot be both self and not self, both self and other; the self excludes the other," as Dorothy Lee, in her essay

"The Conception of the Self among the Wintu Indians," comments. In contrast, "with the Wintu, the self has no strict bounds, is not named and is not, I believe, recognized as a separate entity."[3] It is in comparing linguistic usages among the Wintu with English language usages that Lee delineates the differing concepts of the self, and it is not so much the Wintu as the contrasting "Western" concept that I want to emphasize. Lee argues, "Our own linguistic usage through the years reveals a conception of an increasingly assertive, active, and even aggressive self, as well as of an increasingly delimited self." She traces the change from Chaucerian usages, full of reflexives like "thus dreamed me" and "melikes" to our current "I dream" and "I like" and concludes that "the English language has followed an analytic and isolating trend and it is possible that in linguistic reference there has been an increasing separation of the self from the encompassing situation."[4]

Meanwhile, the publication of events such as those which occurred in South Central Los Angeles following the Simi Valley trial of the police officers videotaped beating Rodney King offer a terrible demonstration of this trend toward the "separation of the self from the encompassing situation." It is evident precisely in the way in which it is incorporated into what purports to be the telling of the story of what "really" happened, and thereby to be establishing knowledge of what is called "the situation." The narrative scenarios that emerged to give an account of the sequence or array of events known summarily as the "L.A. Riots" tended to follow conventional narrative logic, that is, the logic of cause and effect, with the qualification that since the accounts were retrospective and the events were "bad" *cause* was transmuted into *blame.*

The whole thing was said to have begun with the beating of Rodney King, an incident for which either King was to blame (for being a bad character, for provoking the officers with threatening behavior) or else the four policemen were to blame (for unnecessary violence, for attitudes—racism, machismo—predisposing them to such violence). In either case, the incident was blameworthy. The jury selected to determine where the blame lay announced that it had done so, and the jury members in turn were generally considered to be themselves at blame for that determination—and for "triggering" the riots that followed. Likewise blamed for the riots were various "Black leaders," among them the mayor of Los Angeles, Tom Bradley, and the film director John Singleton. The extent of the rioting was blamed on pervasively chaotic social conditions or on symptoms of those conditions (poverty, unemployment, the recession, poor schools, drugs, gangs, or the "breakdown of the family," symbolized for one political pundit by a certain "Murphy Brown," who is herself a creation and hence the "fault" of Hollywood scriptwriters and producers, the "cultural elite," i.e. "Jews") or on the police (who were personally fearful, or indecisive, or negligent) or on L.A. law enforcement as a system (lacking discipline, corrupt, without clear chains of command). The terrible symmetry whereby a video of four white men viciously beating up a black man comes to be vindicated by a video of four black men beating up a white man was the unmovable, intransigent emblem of what we are supposed to "know" about "modern urban America"—whereby equivalent, immobilized, static blameworthiness is extracted from (or given in place of) history.

Or where history is replaced by publicity. Both "fingerpointing" and "scapegoating" are, after all, forms of publicity.

Such unsubtle, broad, even gross quests for accountability and the assignation of blame have, meanwhile, served paradoxically to deny guilt. Everything about what happened in Los Angeles was exteriorized. There were a few media comments about "soul-searching" but in fact there was almost no social introspecting in comparison to the large-scale all-purpose orgy of looking out, or looking away. And what is blame, after all, but radical negative otherizing.

Nothing Is Impossible

A ghost (by definition) is always sighted, seated with its shot-gun, smiling, in possession of its chair.

The body goes.

And the head seeks matter.

Supernatural gain.

What difference would it make if it were night?

I'm right that I saw the ghost, it smiled by carbon light.

The head drifted over the bed and held with it all that it knows.

But without logic—like a trick of love—it was and is autonomous.

Like Faust it experienced a desire for knowledge and then apparently experienced knowledge without satisfaction of desire.

I too cannot be proved.

We can, at least to a limited extent, address the question of knowledge, and the quest for knowledge, vis-à-vis its relation to the self, linguistically, first by examining our ways of speaking about knowing and knowledge, and second by looking at writings which seem to seek or express it.

Knowledge seems to be something: "I seek knowledge." It seems to be something quantifiable but not so easily qualifiable: I can have a lot of knowledge of something but I don't tend to have a big knowledge. Or knowledge can be inadequate, in which case I have to get more of it. On the other hand I can have precise knowledge, suggesting that knowledge is an instrumental something—I can use my knowledge.

As for knowing, it seems to be an act and a transitive one, with an object: I know something. I know my name. I know Anne Waldman. I know the northern California oak and redwood forest. But apart from my name and such suggestive plenitudes as are conveyed in expressions intimating a redolent experience of some person or place, most of what we know, at least so far as we can talk about it, seems to occur in the form of abstractions or extrapolations. I know *when* Pushkin died (1837); I know *how* to make a long distance credit card call; I know *where* Arapahoe Avenue is; I know *what* the sky looks like. Or in a more complex statement I can say I know the *difference between* red and blue. But it would be an unusual formulation to say simply "I know Pushkin's dying" or "I know long distance credit card calling" or "I know sky" or "I know difference." In fact, it would seem from common usage that knowing is indirect, oblique, and at some remove from that to which it pertains. Knowledge seems to be some *aspect* of our perception—and, so to speak, mediated and secondary. We know *that* something, or we know *about* something.

Paradoxically, this mediational, abstracted knowing may be our clearest expression of objectivity, just as, conversely, the expression of direct unmediated knowing, intuition, may be preeminently subjective. I think this is so because mediated knowing is embedded knowing—it is knowing something in the context in which it is meaningfully known. It is conditional. A statement like "I know sky" is vehemently subjective and apparently unconditional, but nothing that we can know—or nothing that is real—is unconditional.

Certainly we do not know knowledge. Or, at least, we don't say so.

The Experience of Activity

Knowledge is a part of a whole.

If we linger we blur.

Stasis is a profuse focal point.

We only catch ourselves as in the words of lovers who are contrasting their emotions.

If you bend to the West someone serves as the interpreter.

Everyone's thought is like luck to be applied.

So love conjectures love.

We need the language to aid the senses.

The activity of solitude if finitude is engaged produces anticipation, but what's committed?

Any change is an activity—that is, a marker and a claim.

The Western poem presents us with experiences in a field of inquiry exposed to observations carried out by the aided senses.

The Will to Reality

The cowboy of fiction is at ease with reality.

He will know what he did.

Causation is his.

He takes his solid seat and sees, impassive in reality.

To discover it, to spread it, to possess it.

What we thus disjoin we can put together.

All changing times are marked by changes of yellows, of blues, and of greens, with much division, crack, and breach.

As for the book on the table top, it really says what I write is digressing toward things I've known or seen having hunted up life but not lies.

The stereotypically Western person is ambitious, besieged by society, in search of solace, and careless of resources, individualistic but rarely capable of crediting nonhuman elements of the world with singularity. The empirical method insists on the principle that the truths of things must be replicable. It regards repeatability as a prerequisite for certainty.

And the possessive tendency inherent to knowledge, which remains bound to desire, provokes us to attempt to triumph over ambiguity and uncertainty. "I think and I mean to get"; the statement sets the terms for a Faustian identity. But the Western person, in all his or her desire to possess knowledge, is wasteful of uncertainty.

Meanwhile, the notion that knowledge must have *foundations* has generally been abandoned by academic philosophy, and with it the epistemological preeminence of the self as the last recipient of data, the self over whom the shadow of knowledge must slowly spread.

There's panorama but it hides.

Life imposes a variety of restraints, and the curves of the hill are said to be breasts.

So the sun itself goes west, but never to restore a lost relationship.

The hills are heroic under cow.

The cowboys are lying down.

To use the landscape, to impress the world.

The gold in the grass should be applied to it.

But slowly, slowly, and with immense consideration, the way Darwin or Agassiz weighed amelioration, obedient though spontaneous and with a will to love.

The weather is steady as a heart—opaque, massive, peacefully bullying the sky, incorrigible but always changing.

"The peculiarity of our experiences," says William James, "[is] that they not only are, but are known."[5] But the distinction between thing and thought, as between thing and word, doesn't establish a dualistic configuration whereby "I" is to be perpetually and perennially separated out from all else. I look into my mind to find the thought—the search for the thought is thinking. That thinking finds no thought, nothing in time or place. The thinking in search of the thought is a thinking about thinking, a destabilizing process, a process of transformation. Knowledge, like speaking or writing, is not an entity but a function—it would best be called "knowing"—and the purpose of that function is to contextualize—to contextualize in the profoundest sense, so that knowledge is not only knowing *of* (which is experience *in potentia*) and knowing *that* (which generates propositions) but also knowing *how*.

We know what we expect. Knowledge is a temporal faculty; a sense of time is intrinsic to it. And this sense of time, like language, functions as an aid to perception, as well as to anticipation. "Why insist," asked William James, "that knowing is a static relation out of time when it practically seems so much a function of our active life? . . . When the whole universe seems only to be making itself valid and to be still incomplete (else why its ceaseless changing?) why, of all things, should knowing be exempt?"[6] For three hundred years, since Bacon's "Great Instauration," the contents of knowledge, if one can speak of them as such, had by definition to be certainties. But for James, knowledge had objects, and these objects, being in time, involved uncertainties as well as certainties.

Uncertainty and erotic cold thought to calm, to come, to combine.

Particulars are related, but particulars are related to uncertainty.

The experience of experience in resilience, in shifts, in buttons, in numbers, in mirrors, in rivers, in grasp, in this.

The thought is not a substitute for something real.

Objective reality then, I say, is an incident.

The very original of what we mean by continuity.

What of the inclusive impulse—"all of it"—which is so characteristic of modernist approaches to comprehension and control? If we accept the notion that knowledge is always and only embedded, always and only situated, we must give up the aspiration to "know everything." This has profound implications for the meaning of "the word," which, since Faust, or indeed since long before, has promised knowledge—a promise which has filled us with desire for it.

What if the word promised something else?

The flakes of mica flick and the river fills with sharpness.

The time process resounds again against the skin.

Skin on the West, the West on skin.

Knowing is not a terminus but an incitement. The skin moves attention from one thing to another.

It is in poetry that the values requisite to exploration and inquiry (or to so-called experimentation)—for example, patience and persistence on the part of the observer—and the resulting achievement—for example, discovery—also retain their concomitants—for example, impatience, restlessness, and a sense of loss.

Poetry is said to love to increase desire.

Poetry instead.

Rising behind in the morning, muttering, a phrase plays upon the conquering surface of things.

In retrospect it seems done but on some vast extensive edge.

What *is* the nature of this strange work?

If there is any connection between how knowledge works and how language works, it would probably not lie in the status of individual words, not even if one regards words as repositories of their own history, but it might lie in relationships between words, that is, in instances of their usage. Or, if we specify our field of interest as poetic language (which is to say, the linguistic logics at work in a poem), then in syntax—in the putting together of the verbal materials at many levels. The investigation of how language works and of how it conveys arrays of sense and meaning is a specifically poetic undertaking. In the course of it, one inevitably discovers that language in a poem does not lay down paths that are always simple to follow. If it is "knowledge" one is trying to arrive at it would seem that there must be a more efficient way of getting there. Indeed, one wonders sometimes just whose side the language is on.

To say that language "lays down paths" is to offer a metaphor which has several possible interpretations. Initially, if it is knowledge we are talking about, the metaphor seems to suggest that language (reading, writing, speaking, listening) sets one on a journey, a journey to "somewhere" where the knowledge one is after is situated. But this would suggest that knowledge is intransitive, whereas experience (as well as language itself) has shown that knowledge is of something (even if perhaps it is only of the path). Knowledge, in other words, is transitive. It is also transient, though recurrent, occurring in situ, in experience. One doesn't know something constantly or continually, but only episodically, in the event. The following of the paths in the metaphor requires a knowing *how*.

The old man's ears cleared at the height of the virgin forest.
At the moment of panorama.
In the momentum of preparation.
The biggest tree is over there, he said, stretching the independent nature of my expectations.

The West is here—we can ground our uncertainties on nothing else.

The visual dominates our access to knowledge; we are overwhelmingly inclined to look or, where that's not possible, to visualize, in order to understand or even to conceive. Scrutiny, as a heightened and intentional mode of looking, whether disciplined or not, is a felt function of all conscious thought; in order to think we call into service the actual eye or the inner eye—and most frequently both. The gap, then, between the imaginable and the imageable must, we assume, be very small.

But in fact, I think, it is very large; the seemingly uninterrupted flow of visible experience, its fluency, is broken up in thought into reflections, and the inner eye, the imaging eye, sees only these.

Knowledge is based on the experience of the disjuncture between what's seen and what's thought—on the alterations cast by reflection, on thought's own alterity. In fact, if it weren't *other*, at least momentarily, we wouldn't experience it at all, because we wouldn't notice our noting it.

It is in and amid the interconnections—or as Tolstoi put it, the "linkages"—between certainties and uncertainties, as between parts and their wholes or, in poetry, between grammar and semantics, that meaning and its concomitant knowing abides. Tolstoy, writing in response to articles analyzing his *Anna Karenina*, put it this way:

> If I were to say in words all that I intended to express by way of the novel, then I would have to write a novel identical to

the one I first wrote. And if critics now understand and express in a feuilleton all that I want to say, then I congratulate them. . . . And if nearsighted critics think that I wanted to describe only what pleases me, how Oblonskij dines and what sort of shoulders Karenina has, then they are mistaken. In all, or in almost all that I have written, I was guided by the need to collect my thoughts, linked together to express themselves. . . . but each thought specially expressed in words loses its meaning, is terribly degraded, when taken alone without the linkage in which it is found.[7]

And in remarkably similar terms, in a passage that is peculiarly resonant in our context, William James wrote:

If anyone asks what is the mind's object when you say "Columbus discovered America in 1492," most people will reply "Columbus" or "America," or, at most, "the discovery of America." They will name a substantive kernel or nucleus of the consciousness, and say the thought is "about" that. . . . But the *object* of your thought is really its entire content or deliverance, neither more nor less. It is a vicious use of speech to take out a substantive kernel from its content and call that its object; and it is an equally vicious use of speech to add a substantive kernel not particularly included in its content, and to call that its object . . . The object of my thought in the previous sentence, for example, is strictly speaking neither Columbus nor America, nor its discovery. It is nothing short of the entire sentence, "Columbus-discovered-America-in-1492." And if we wish to speak of it substantively, we must make a substantive of it by writing it out thus with hyphens between all its words. Nothing but this can possibly name its delicate idiosyncrasy. And if we wish to *feel* that idiosyncrasy we must reproduce the thought as it was uttered, with every word fringed and the whole sentence bathed in that original halo of obscure relations, which, like an horizon, then spread about its meaning.[8]

Paradoxically, substantives, though they are no less than the totality of themselves and the contextual plenitude of all their relationships, are inherently uncertainties, since this totality is constantly altering, while the parts may establish, in their independence, and because they are of the moment, the suggestion, at least, of a kind of certainty. This alterity, this otherness, immanent within totality, is the sole "foundation" of knowing, and it is always only achieved in part.

The only way to discover it is to proceed step by step, point by point, for their own sake, because there is nothing beyond. So long as we *continue* the effort, we observe and by doing so we *intend* an experience, and that is the sole form in which knowing is designed. To discontinue the process is not to arrive at knowledge but merely to cease thinking.

I ask myself what's in a poem.

The outside of the world—but this itself is that if looked at when the sight is forgotten and only the looking remains.

Three different things.

And I imagine what kind of vigilance is layered within the remarkability of all that I have requested.

My values are held in change, vividly falling to one side and then the other, their fascination dependent in part on their very absence of order.

My senses too seem to exist—I hear a bluejay squawking between the leaves and suddenly feel the links between the minuscule elements of the smell of gray-green as the rain begins to fall—but the well-known is not necessarily known at all.

Accuracy is not the voice of nature.

There are places where the action never stops.

But around a moral value (and we insist on moral value) shakes the image of a troubling construction: time and the time it takes to know of this.

We proceed (we insist on motion) and we shift the center of gravity and with it the nature of confinements.

Then progress (gold and the research clock) changes the look of things and with it the value of things.

But just by being under the sky, a person knows it exists.

Nature is mediated—in large part so we could stay out of the way.

Then it finds itself (or, more precisely, cannot find itself, and advances) staring at itself.

Well (says someone) we still have the vitality of ourselves in boot from our days on a frontier which we made it our business to contemplate—then in search of an *indigenous* present, of authentic strange times.

So, from the time I was old enough to know the facts, remember sounds, render rhythms, I thought work was as similar to life as one could suffer.

Sunlight on the wall could hold the air in meaning—though it didn't seem to.

And I remember even as a child realizing that pleasure lay in arranging it.

Statements, syntax, and words—all arts are installments.

Not only recapitulating, not solely evaluating—it should be humane to anticipate, wait, and surge.

How quickly I got home, how slowly I was there.

Knowledge is always situated.

It's where one perfects.

Thinking lives.

No waste of work, no waste of time.

Lives, likes, lines.

Notes

1. Anne Waldman and Andrew Schelling, eds., *Disembodied Poetics* (Albuquerque: University of New Mexico Press, 1995).

2. Sir Francis Bacon, *Novum Organum*, tr. and ed. Peter Urbach and John Gibson (Chicago: Open Court, 1994), 109–11.

3. Dorothy Lee, "The Conception of the Self among the Wintu Indians," in *Freedom and Culture* (Englewood Cliffs, N.J.: Prentice-Hall, 1959), 131–32.

4. Ibid., 132–33.

5. William James, "Does 'Consciousness' Exist?" in *Essays in Radical Empiricism* (Cambridge, Mass.: Harvard University Press, 1976), 14.

6. William James, "A World of Pure Experience," in *Essays in Radical Empiricism*, 37.

7. Quoted in Jurij Lotman, *The Structure of the Artistic Text*, tr. Gail Lenhoff and Ronald Vroon (Ann Arbor: Michigan Slavic Contributions, 1977), 11.

8. William James, *The Principles of Psychology* (Cambridge, Mass.: Harvard University Press, 1981), 1:275–76.

La Faustienne

The first version of "La Faustienne" was presented as a talk at Temple University, Philadelphia, in March 1994. The subsequent revisions (and, I believe, improvements) are much indebted to Barrett Watten, who was of great help as I was preparing the essay for publication (it appeared in *Poetics Journal* 10: "Knowledge" in 1998).

I had not yet read Marina Warner's *From the Beast to the Blonde* when I wrote "La Faustienne," but Warner's wonderful book came out at around the time I was doing so, and I read it several months later.[1] Though she only briefly mentions *The Arabian Nights* and doesn't speak of the Faust stories at all, her study of the fairy tale is remarkably germane to the issues those works raise, and particularly to the relationship between narrative and knowledge. Warner's particular interest is in women's knowledge, knowledge of the body, procreative and mortal, and through it of birth and death, and knowledge of the civility that must exist to sustain life between those two poles.

My own interest, as I discovered while writing this essay, was very similar. When I was first invited by Rachel Blau DuPlessis to present a lecture at

Temple University, I had thought I would concentrate entirely on the Faust myth and thus return to my interest in Enlightenment science and the epistemological quandaries it raises. But very soon I found myself at an impasse, realizing that those quandaries had become politicized in my mind. "The Enlightenment" of which I speak in "Strangeness," therefore, here becomes "the so-called Enlightenment," and, though I was (and still am) willing to acknowledge a certain heroic quality to the Faust figure, it is so compromised that it seems to be an ultimately irrelevant heroism—misbegotten and probably contemptible. Instead, it was Scheherazade's knowledge (or perhaps I should say "Scheherazadian" knowledge—knowledge with creative and redemptive power) that I found myself wanting to celebrate.

Having written myself into something like a rejection of the Faustian ideal, I had been casting about for a figure to represent an alternative ("La Faustienne") when, quite coincidentally, I came across a copy of Sir Richard Burton's unexpurgated translation of *The Arabian Nights* (or *The Book of the Thousand Nights and A Night,* as he calls it) in a used book store; I bought it immediately, and as I began reading that night I very soon realized that I had found La Faustienne.

1

In a very general way, this essay is about the relationship between knowledge and the literary imagination—a relationship in which knowledge may be the object of literary effort (the writer seeks knowledge) or it may be the subject of its activity (the writer *is* knowledge). More particularly, I'm going to talk about two model knowers, one who knows by acquiring knowledge and the other by making it. It is in the context of these two figures or tropes that I want to implicate some of the issues which both poetry and persons are currently confronting. These are literary tropes but the knowledge I'm speaking of is not exclusively literary knowledge.

Current literary interest in knowledge (and its implicit questions with regard to both literary devices [details] and literary method [address from and to the world]) finds itself in what social theory might call a liminal period—at a threshold or, to enlarge the metaphorical landscape, along a border. The question of boundaries, of possible shifts or displacements along them, and the question of what is being bounded (or unbounded) are preeminent ones. If we are indeed in a liminal period, then the border is not out there somewhere at the edge of the frame but rather it is here, at zero degree, where the x and y coordinates meet. It is a site of encounter, a point of transition. The marginal is all around. The transgressivity, sometimes overt, sometimes implicit, that motivates certain strategies in much current work, is meaningful *only* in liminal situations.

Whether or not the future looks back on this as a liminal period, it certainly feels to us now as if the world is changing—so much so that it's banal to say so. The global political configuration is in flux; notions of social, cultural, and personal identity are open to debate (dramatized in certain U.S. institutions, for example, under the rubric of multiculturalism and the various responses to it); the stability of phenomenological definition (under examination, for example, by chaos theory and genetic research) is being challenged; and so forth.

Notions of what writing is and how we talk about that are also in transition. For one thing, the discussion of what writing *is* is now frequently contingent on questioning what (and who) writing is *for*. Changes are occurring likewise to notions of the author—the writing self—and therefore the genres that attempt to represent the intentions of the author are changing. It is precisely because definitions of the self have changed that the traditional genres that speak *for* the self (lyric poetry, for example) or *of* the self and its development (the novel) are either being consigned to an increasingly "old-fashioned," conservative, or nostalgic position or are being subverted and reinvented to accommodate contemporary experience of being a person—a zone. The sense of independence must now include, where it hasn't been replaced by, a sense of interdependence, and, in writing, interest in free expression may be giving way to interest in free knowing.

2

A plausibly central figure in the narrative of knowledge, its hero or genius, is Faust. In one form or another, the Faust figure has dominated the romance of the quest for knowledge, and Faustian desire has driven the encyclopedic enterprises which have been undertaken in the name of that quest—the most obvious being Western science. The "scientific method" has dominated not just the laboratory; it has also provided a compelling model for writers, who have undertaken a "poetic method" analogous to it. The scientific and poetic methods have analogous rigors and present analogous challenges, and the comparison has been explicit in, for example, the "avant-garde realism" that Gertrude Stein got from William James and Flaubert—employing an "experimental method"—"beginning again and again" with patient attention, demanding long and close observation, etc., bound to an infinite project which opens up before the insatiability of the desire to know and grieves over the brevity of the experience of knowing. "Why must the stream so soon run dry / And we once more lie thirsting? / It has happened to me so many times," says Goethe's Faust.[2]

There was a real, historical Faust, a certain Johannes Faust, from Wittenberg, Germany, a contemporary of Luther and of Paracelsus.[3] He is recorded as having been granted a degree in divinity from Heidelberg (in 1509), but he seems to have spent his life engaged in the somewhat disreputable practice of astrology and necromancy, earning his living as a traveling magician, frequenting German inns and taverns. The magic tricks of the historical Faust were apparently convincing enough to set him up to become the eponymous vehicle for various prankster and bawdy Fausts of early anecdotes and tales. There are records of his activities dating from 1507–1540, and various written tales, existing in manuscript, begin to appear about thirty years later. A compendium of these, the *Historia von D. Iohan Fausten*, known as the Spiess Faustbook (after the publisher), was published in Germany in 1587 and translated by a certain "P. F., Gent." into English in 1592 as *The Historie of the damnable life, and deserved death of Doctor Iohn Faustus, Newly imprinted, and in convenient places imperfect matter amended*. This English translation served directly as the basis for Christopher Marlowe's *Doctor Faustus* (also 1592) and, at a series of removes, for Goethe's *Faust* (*Part One*, 1808; *Part Two*, 1832). In the course of his literary existence, Faust is transformed into a tragic figure, whose intelligence and anguish make it possible for us to sympathize and perhaps even to identify with him, despite his pact with the devil, figurative in the play, but in real life inscribed in the history of plunder and exploitation that Western knowledge-seekers have left behind them. In Goethe's play in particular, Faust is the figure of the *modern* genius—driven, thrilled, libidinous, learned—part Prometheus, part Picasso, part Dr. Frankenstein, part Dr. Freud, and part Don Juan—a figure for whom epistemology is an artistic romance and the encyclopedia its masterwork.[4]

But who is Faust's female counterpart? Who is La Faustienne?

3

The Faust of Marlowe and Goethe is a familiar figure, a bachelor scholar, a scientist and doctor, consumed by love of knowledge which is transmuted into an overwhelming desire to know "everything." As the story opens, so to speak, Faust has reached the limits of what he can say he knows. As a result, the expression of knowledge has likewise reached its limit, and all Faust can utter is his desire.

> Law, medicine, philosophy
> And even—worse luck—theology
> I've studied with passionate resolution,
> I've learned, alas! from top to bottom;
> And stand here now, poor fool that I am,
> No wiser than I was before.
> I am called Master, Doctor even;
> For ten years, up and down and back and forth,
> I've led my students by the nose—
> And I see there's nothing we can know!
> . . . .
> Where shall I grasp you, infinite Nature?
> Your breasts, where? You fountains of all life
> From which hang Heaven and earth,

To which my burning spirit strains—
You gush, you suckle, and must I wither in vain?
(Goethe, 21, 24–25)

In Christopher Marlowe's version of the drama,[5] Faust at this juncture conceives of the possibility of using his skill with words and formulas ("Lines, circles, letters, characters," I.i.49) to summon help: "Shall I make spirits fetch me what I please? / Resolve me of all ambiguities?" (I.i.76–77).

I'll have them fly to India for gold,
Ransack the ocean for orient pearl,
And search all corners of the new-found world
For pleasant fruits and princely delicates;
I'll have them read me strange philosophy
And tell the secrets of all foreign kings.
(I.i.79–84)

The "new-found world" that Faust envisions here is, of course, America.

America's potential for being of interest to the British was very recent in Marlowe's time. For almost all of the previous century, since the Treaty of Tordesillas in 1494 in which Spain and Portugal had divided the entirety of the planet equally between them, Spain had been "in possession" of the American continent (except for the Brazilian land mass, which protruded into the Portugese part of the map). Spain was able to keep its grip on the continent thanks to the supremacy of its navy, so that although Sir Walter Raleigh had landed English settlers on Roanoke Island in 1585, the English could do nothing to resupply or support the settlers for the next several years, and the colony disappeared. It was only after England's defeat of the Spanish Armada in 1588 that England was able to join—or rather, compete with—Spain and Portugal in the exploration and appropriation of this continent. It is in that context that Marlowe's *Doctor Faustus*, the first modern Faust, made his appearance, just four years later.

4

The vocabulary and semantics of the metaphors dominating descriptions of exploration and discovery on this continent are explicitly gendered.

Sir Walter Raleigh himself, as quoted by his friend Richard Hakluyt, "swore that he could not be torn 'from the sweet embraces of . . . Virginia.'" The continent is "a country that hath yet her maydenhead," and Hakluyt again, in 1587 (while Raleigh is still trying to get back to the Roanoke Colony), writes, "If you preserve only a little longer in your constancy, your bride will shortly bring forth new and most abundant offspring, such as will delight you and ours."[6]

Using the same conceit, John Donne, in his erotic poem, "Elegie: Going to Bed," writes:

> Your gown going off, such beautious state reveals,
> As when from flowry meads th' hills shadowe steales.
> Off with that wyerie Coronet and shew
> The haiery Diadem which on you doth grow:
>
> . . . .
>
> Licence my roaving hands, and let them go,
> Behind, before, above, between, below.
> O my America! my new-found-land,

My kingdome, safeliest when with one man man'd,
My Myne of precious stones: My Emperie,
How blest am I in this discovering thee!

The vein is not exhausted even 150 years later, as Annette Kolodny has pointed out: "Translating the excitement that attended the first discovery of the Connecticut River into the rhythms of sexual conquest, in his 1725 verse history of Connecticut, Roger Walcott depicts an ardent mariner 'press[ing] / upon the virgin stream who had as yet, / Never been violated with a ship.'" And even as late as 1903, Frederick Jackson Turner, for a long time the preeminent theorist of the frontier, could plausibly say that "this great American West" accepted "European men, institutions, and ideas . . . and . . . took them to her bosom."[7]

Throughout the literature of the frontier, the intrepid Faustian discovers a *virgin landscape* and *penetrates* its wilderness. In the encounter with the landscape, in other words, the unknown is imagined as an animate (though supine) other, and she is female.

The female element in this trope, then, is not the knower but the site of knowledge, its object and embodiment—that which is to be known.

Is knowledge itself, then, La Faustienne?

5

Otherness, personified as a female object, has been often and notoriously depicted in painting and, of course, more coarsely, in pornography. Supine and secretive, naked but inscrutable, woman lies under the male gaze.

Much thought and many essays have been devoted to undress-

Fig. 1.   Theodore Galle, after Jan van der Street (called "Stradanus"), *The Arrival of Vespucci in the New World*, circa 1600. Engraving, 9⅞ in. × 10⅝ in. Library of Congress, Washington, D.C.

ing, so-to-speak, the male gazer, and I don't want to belabor points that have become obvious as a result. But I do want to mention two genres or categories of visual art of particular relevance to my theme.

The first involves images of America, inscribed (even in "her" name, a feminized form of the given name of Amerigo Vespucci) and depicted as a woman—often nude and often, by stylistic implication, virginal.[8] In a very curious, not to say hilarious, engraving by Theodore Galle titled *The Arrival of Vespucci in the New World* (1600) (figure 1), a fully clothed seemingly elderly man in velvet robe and velvet hat, holding in his right hand a long pole from which a white pennant is fluttering and on top of which

Fig. 2. Henry Peters Gray, *The Birth of Our Flag*, 1874. Oil on canvas mounted on plywood, 72 in. × 48 in. National Academy of Design, New York City.

stands a cross (to symbolize a potent Christianity) and in his left hand a sextant (to symbolize science) has just stepped on shore, where he has apparently startled America from a nap in a hammock strung between two leafy trees. She is just sitting up. She is nude except for a feathered cap, an anklet, and a tiny belt from which a row of minute white feathers dangles. Her body is turning toward us, voluptuous and full, but her gaze is directed at the interloper, her visitor, the stranger, Vespucci. An anteater, perhaps her pet, with its very long tongue extended, can be seen under the hammock at the base of the nearer tree.

In another work, done almost 300 years later (in 1874, by Henry Peters Gray), titled *The Birth of Our Flag* (figure 2), a youthful white America, again nearly nude (she seems to be stepping out of and away from a virtually transparent toga) strides through a hilly landscape under the (literal) wing of a ferocious-looking eagle. She is moving toward us, but she too gazes not at us but upward and to the side, into the eyes of the eagle.

There are many such images, and in them America is variously depicted as an "Indian maiden," an Eve in Paradise, or sometimes as the Virgin Mary, herself a second Eve (see George Caleb Bingham's "The Emigration of Daniel Boone," 1852, for an example of this), and, in what might be called a subgenre, as a mother—surrounded by cherubic children and often nursing, as in Dominico Canova's "Mother Louisiana," where a somewhat dazed looking woman, blouse open to reveal her breasts, is offering her nipple to one naked baby, while four others, all naked and seemingly very close in age, clutch at her skirt.[9] She too looks away from us, but not at anything in particular; she seems to be staring into space—perhaps into the ample space of the promised land of Louisiana.

America, of course, occupied a special place in the European imagination, conceived of as a Paradise, and promoted as such by the financial and political interests backing the exploration and exploitation of the continent. That is why she is personified as Eve—an Eve capable of fruitfulness rather than of stealing the fruit. I think it is not insignificant that even in that primary Edenic image, where the "apple" symbolizes (forbidden) knowledge, it is the woman who holds it. It is also significant that she then offers to share it.

The second group of art works I want to mention can be viewed as an analogue to the "American" group. These are what might be termed medical paintings, of which perhaps the most famous are Thomas Eakins's two masterpieces, *The Gross Clinic* (1875) and *The Agnew Clinic* (1889). The former shows a small part of an operating theater, where rather bloody surgery on a thigh is in progress; the only woman in this picture seems to be part of the audience, and she has covered her face and is turning aside in distaste or horror. *The Agnew Clinic* also shows an operating theater, but this time more of it is visible; there is a full house, the audience consisting entirely of well-dressed men, all of them peering forward into the brightly illuminated oval where three doctors are performing the operation and a fourth, presumably Dr. Agnew, is standing to the side, overseeing and explicating the proceedings. A nurse is in attendance and the patient is a woman. The sheet is pulled down to expose her naked breasts. The surgery seems to be a mastectomy.[10]

A less well known but equally interesting medical painting is one which is the subject of an essay by Gerald Weissmann titled "The Doctor with Two Heads" from his book of the same name. The essay is about Georges Chicotot, a turn-of-the-century Parisian doctor who developed new treatments for cancer and who was also a painter, exclusively of medical scenes. In his 1907 painting *The First Trial of X-ray Therapy for Cancer of the Breast* (figure 3), we again see the patient, a woman, with her breasts exposed. Over one of them an enormous X-ray machine is positioned, looking down, while the doctor, wearing a full-length white coat and top hat, is standing slightly off to the side, looking at a stopwatch (presumably to time the exposure) which he holds in one hand and holding in the other a long Bunsen burner from which a tongue of flame is extended.

The medical paintings are interesting to me because they so clearly depict male attempts to get at something hidden within women—in this case, illness. Medical depictions are not always gendered as they are in *The Agnew Clinic* and in Chicotot's painting. It is a muscular and probably male thigh that is being cut

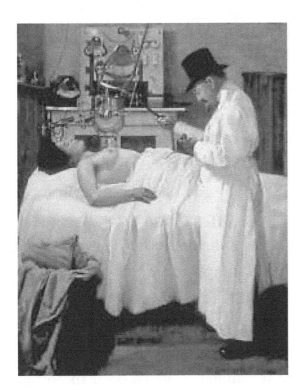

Fig. 3. Georges Chico-
tot, *The First Trial of X-ray
Therapy for Cancer of the
Breast*, 1907. Oil on can-
vas. Musée de l'Assistance
Publique, Paris.

into in Eakins's *The Gross Clinic*, for example. But it is true that
the history of science is a history of attempts to "see" the invis-
ible, and as soon as the language in which this is expressed be-
comes metaphoric, so that we say, for example, that science at-
tempts "to probe nature's secrets," it is clear that the possessor
and keeper of the secret is, at least implicitly, female.

6

Barbara Maria Stafford talks at some length in *Body Criticism*
about the relationship between the scientific quest for knowledge
(especially during the eighteenth century and the so-called En-
lightenment) and spectacle.[11] The theaterlike arrangement in
which surgery is being performed in the Thomas Eakins paint-
ings is both realistic and exemplary of this relationship. The ex-

hibition of mentally disturbed patients, dissections performed to ticket holders in eighteenth-century "theaters of anatomy," and, to a limited extent, grand rounds in contemporary American hospitals, are literalizations of the metaphor and symbolism implicit in "the spectacle." Adhering to a melodramatic, even sentimental, narrative, itself embedded in a narrativized conflict between rapaciousness and a yearning to do good, Western curiosity is addicted to the theatricality of seeing and being seen.[12]

There is another kind of theater which is not irrelevant in this respect, and that is the porn theater. Pornography establishes a blatantly gendered situation which is about gazing and in which the gazing is overtly erotic. Or, one could say, the porn theater exposes the erotic character of the desire to know.

To refer to the gazing of the audience at the porn theater as epitomizing a questing for knowledge may seem, if not far-fetched, then at least somewhat overdetermined. But in fact it is, at least at the "live shows," not altogether inaccurate.

What I know about this comes from gazing myself, not so much or exclusively at the women, the strippers and porn stars, as at the gazers and their gazing, specifically in San Francisco's Mitchell Brothers' O'Farrell Street Theater. I went there thinking of myself as a spectator of the spectating, an outsider, a non-payer—the manager is a fan of the two musicians I was with, who in turn knew several of the stars, and we were admitted for free. That merely means that I went "just out of curiosity," though in retrospect it seems likely that a large part of the audience might say the same about themselves.

The Mitchell Brothers' Theater is generally (and literally) a sober place—no beer, wine, or liquor of any kind is sold, and a recorded message is regularly broadcast over the public-address system reminding the audience that touching the "breasts, buttocks, or genital areas of the women is forbidden." The customers are there to *look*, and what they have to look at are the breasts and especially the genitals of the women—up close and fully exposed, indeed overt and thrust into view. And yet the porn theater seems not so much to arouse erotic desire as to illuminate an erotic site. Or more precisely, it discloses the entrance into the erotic site, which is itself hidden.

The erotic site is, then, a secret site—and it is, too, a threatening one, since it is also a source of power. The stripper's secret is sexual—indeed, it is her sexuality itself. And in being interior and invisible, sexuality becomes the site of questions about what can and cannot be known.[13] The men at the porn theater do gaze, with truly rapt attention, at the exposed bodies and genitals of the women—as if they wanted to see into them or as if they wanted to *be* them.[14]

7

Now, after that somewhat lengthy digression, we can return to Faust, a man who turns his back on heaven in order to see into the world.

There are traces throughout the Faust story of fairy tale sources, though the semantic frame (the pact with the devil) works a significant change on the meaning of the material as a whole. The Faust story is a morality tale, organized episodically, with Faust, thanks to the powers conferred on him or provided to him by the devil, his *jinni*, in the role of wonder-worker/jokester, hero and antihero. Some of Faust's feats, especially in the early Faustbooks, are no more than adolescent pranks. But

Faust is able to travel the cosmos, to witness the workings of the planets and constellations, to re-view history, and to substantiate mythic and historical figures, conjuring up the Pope and the papal court, and in a famous episode, incarnating Helen of Troy before him.

But Faust, the wonder-worker, is not omnipotent; he is under several limitations. He is prohibited from marrying (perhaps because marriage would modify or dampen his desire). And in certain circumstances, or of certain things, he cannot speak, either because he is unable to do so or because it is forbidden. He complains in Goethe's version of what I would call the "lyric dilemma," namely that speech is inadequate: "I try to find a name for the feeling, / The frenzy, and I cannot find one" (171). To Helen he can speak, but he is, in effect, silenced, since Helen, being a vision, an image, can't reciprocate—she is seen but unseeing, spoken to but unhearing.[15] And finally, Faust is forbidden to speak of God. As he says, "Oft have I thought to have done so, but the devil threatened to tear me in pieces if I named God" (Marlowe, V.ii.74–75). In essence, it is by silencing Faust, by standing between him and words, that Mephistopheles damns him. "I do confess it Faustus, and rejoice. / 'Twas I, that when thou wert i' the way to heaven / Dammed up thy passage. When thou took'st the book / To view the Scriptures, then I turned the leaves / And led thine eye," says Mephistopheles near the end of Marlowe's play (V.ii.99–103). By something of a stretch, one might say that the devil facilitates Faust's learning but bans his poetry.

The silencing of the hero is a recurrent motif in fairy tales, but usually the silenced figure is not the male but the female hero—the heroine. The tale of the Little Mermaid, familiar from Hans

Christian Andersen's version of it, is typical. In that tale, a mermaid has fallen in love with a human and wants to change her immortal soul for a mortal one in order to be with her beloved. The mermaid asks the Sea Witch to help her. "But then you must pay me too!" said the witch, "and it is no small price I ask. You have the loveliest voice of all down here at the bottom of the sea, and you think you will be able to enchant him with it, but your voice is just what you have to give me. . . . Come, stick out your little tongue so that I can cut it off."[16]

The silencing of the fairy tale maiden renders her inner being (her thoughts, her feelings) secret. She embodies her secret; she is a nocturnal inscription, both writer and what's written in the dark.

8

In folklore, then, as in science, if one genders the players in the tropes of Western epistemology, one typically ends up with a model in which the quest for knowledge is a male enterprise and the keeper of the known is woman. This trope seems to incorporate aspects of male desire into its imagery while leaving female desire hidden, not through inadvertence but by definition.

This opposition is descriptive, even definitive—or is meant to be—in terms of the dualism that is the basis for much of our Western thinking. Visibility and invisibility, light and dark, seeing and blindness, consciousness and unconsciousness are parallel pairs of opposites, whose ultimate case opposes Being to non-Being, life to death.[17]

But the postmodern critique of binarism suggests that there

may be no opposites, that Being (or the actual being of each and any entity) exists not because it is the opposite of non-Being but because it is "true of its own accord."[18] It was on this premise that I began a writing project, called, at least for the moment, *The Book of a Thousand Eyes.*

The Book of a Thousand Eyes is a night work, in that my interest is in the processes of assimilation and assessment that take place in the figurative dark and silence of night, where opposites as such can't exist because they always coexist. I have wanted to write in the dark, so to speak, when the mind must accept the world it witnesses by day and out of all data assemble meaning. The writing would do so—assemble (a Faustian project) and, in its way, *make* knowledge (the work of La Faustienne).

> The bed is made of sentences which present themselves as
>   what they are
> Some soft, some hardly logical, some broken off
> Sentences granting freedom to memories and sights
>
> Then is freedom about love?
> Bare, and clumsily impossible?
> Our tendernesses give us sentences about our mistakes
> Our sentiments go on as described
> The ones that answer when we ask someone who has
>   mumbled to say what he or she has said again
> In bed I said I liked the flowing of the air in the cold of night
> Such sentences are made to aid the senses
>
> Tonight itself will be made—it's already getting dark
> I'm not afraid to look nor afraid to be seen in the dark
> Is there a spectral sentence? a spectator one?
> Is it autobiographical?

No—the yearning inherent in the use of any sentence makes
   it mean far more than "we are here"

Because we are not innocent of our sentences we go to bed
The bed shows with utter clarity how sentences in saying
   something make something
Sentences in bed are not describers, they are instigators[19]

9

The greatest of all night works is the one called *The Thousand and
One Nights* (sometimes *The Thousand Nights and One Night*) or,
alternatively, *The Arabian Nights*, with its chains of tales and con-
centricities of tales within tales, "together with all that there is in
them of wonder and instruction," told by a woman to postpone
her death by holding a man in narrative suspense. This woman is
the virgin daughter of the *wazir* to King Shahryar, "King of the
Kings of the Banu Sasan," and her name is Scheherazade. In the
great translation of Sir Richard Burton, Scheherazade

> had perused the books, annals and legends of preceding
> Kings, and the stories, examples and instances of by-gone
> men and things; indeed it was said that she had collected a
> thousand books of histories relating to antique races and de-
> parted rulers. She had perused the works of the poets and
> knew them by heart; she had studied philosophy and the sci-
> ences, arts and accomplishments; and she was pleasant and
> polite, wise and witty, well read and well bred.[20]

Like the *Faustbook*, the *Thousand and One Nights* is a compi-
lation of materials, medieval in origin, and set within a moral
frame.[21] But what might be called the pretext for telling the tales,

which is in effect its semantic context, is frequently left out of Western collections—we have the tales ("The Tale of Aladdin," "The Tale of Sinbad," and so on), but we often lack the nights.

A certain King Shahryar has a younger brother, Shah Zaman, whom he has made King of Samarkand. Longing to see Shah Zaman, King Shahryar sends a messenger inviting his brother to visit. Shah Zaman agrees and sets forth, but travels only a short distance before realizing that he has forgotten something back home. He returns and finds his wife, "asleep on his own carpet-bed, embracing with both arms a black cook of loathsome aspect and foul with kitchen grease and grime" (Burton, 4). In rage and despair, Shah Zaman kills them both; then pale, grim, and grieving, he goes to visit King Shahryar.

Shahryar, noticing that his brother seems sorrowful and ill, asks what is wrong, but Shah Zaman won't say. Instead he excuses himself and goes off to think, and while sitting by himself he sees the wife of Shahryar with a slave-lover of her own. Eventually he tells Shahryar his own tale and then reveals that Shahryar's wife is similarly unfaithful. Shahryar hides and sees that this is true and like his brother he kills both his wife and her lover. The two brothers go off to wander in their despair, until they come to a tree and under it find a hideous *ifrit* who has taken a beautiful woman captive. The *ifrit* has fallen asleep, "snoring and snarking," and the woman approaches the two brothers and demands that they have sex with her. They do so and afterwards she says to them, "Well done," and shows them a string on which are threaded 570 signet rings—one each from the 570 other men with whom she has previously betrayed the *ifrit*. She adds a ring from each of the brothers to her string and the brothers depart, shocked, with their worst opinions of women confirmed.

They return home deploring the libidinous concupiscence of all women, and Shahryar vows to bed a different beautiful girl each night and to have her killed the next morning. This goes on for three years, until few girls are left, but among them are the two daughters of the wazir, Scheherazade and her little sister, Duniazade. Scheherazade resolves to save the situation, and despite her father's warning and an admonitory tale he tells her, she goes to Shahryr's bed. After sex, Scheherazade initiates her plan; she calls for her little sister and begins the first of the "tales which, if Allah wills, shall be the deliverance of the daughters of the Mussulmans."[22]

10

The structural complexity of the *Thousand and One Nights* is one of its outstanding features. In a large number of the tales, the plot provides and ultimately depends on other tales. In an early, somewhat simple tale, that of "The Trader and the *Jinni*," for example, a merchant offends a *jinni* at an oasis by hitting him accidentally when he tosses aside a fruit pit. The *jinni* says the merchant must die, and the merchant accepts his fate but asks for time so that he can go home, settle his affairs, say farewell to his family, etc., and in effect conclude his tale. The *jinni* agrees, the merchant does as he says, and returns as promised on the first day of the new year. He sits himself down under a tree to wait for the *jinni* and his own death, when along comes a *shayk* leading a gazelle. The *shayk* asks the merchant what he's doing there, and the merchant explains. The man says he'll keep the man company while he waits in order to see what will happen, and he sits down. Then along comes a *shayk* leading two dogs, and the process is repeated. Finally along comes a third *shayk*, leading a mule, and the same question and explanation ensue; he joins the other *shayks* with the merchant, so now there are four men at the oasis. At last the *jinni* appears, prepared to kill the merchant, but the first *shayk* asks if the *jinni* will give him one-third of the merchant's blood in exchange for a marvelous tale. The *jinni* says that if the tale is sufficiently marvelous, the *shayk* may have the blood. So the *shayk* tells a tale, and wins the portion of blood. And so it goes with the other two *shayks*, until "the *Jinni* marvelled with exceeding marvel; and, shaking with delight, cried, 'Lo! I have given thee the remainder of the merchant's punishment and for thy sake have I released him.' Thereupon the merchant embraced the old men and thanked them, and these *Shayks* wished him joy on being saved and fared forth each one for his own city" (Burton, 44).

The narrative momentum, how one thing leads to another, thus could be said to be digressive, but not in the linear sense; the temporal linear context is, in fact, precisely what has to be reoriented if Scheherazade is to save "the daughters of the Mussulmans," herself included, and the way this is accomplished is with performative concentricities and spirals. To achieve this redemptive outcome, the tales and Scheherazade's strategies for tale-telling defer conclusions, prolong suspense, and interiorize meaning.

Myriad stories are told in the course of Scheherazade's 1001 nights, and a large number of them are tales of betrayal and revenge or of betrayal and reconciliation, told—and this is very important—in the course of erotic nights. Most English language versions of *The Arabian Nights* are much abridged—presenting only the more famous of the stories and those in expurgated versions, eliminating their erotic and dramatic context. Scheherazade's nights begin voluptuously and it is after she and Shahryar are satiated each night that she takes up her stories. It is thus narrative not sexual suspense that Scheherazade sustains.

To some extent one can argue that she establishes epistemological suspense—not merely in the banal sense in which she keeps Shahryar waiting to find out "what happens next" but also because, although the stories are in various subtle ways instructive and exemplary, the full (redemptive) effect of the lesson is deferred, since ultimately it is contained in the totality of the tales rather than in any single one of them—it is not until the end of the one thousand and first night that Shahryar (reeducated) can say, "O wise and subtle one, you have taught me many lessons, letting me see that every man is at the call of Fate; you have made me consider the words of kings and peoples passed away; you have told me some things which were strange, and many that were worthy of reflection. I have listened to you for a thousand nights and one night and now my soul is changed and joyful, it beats with an appetite for life."[23]

11

The substance of the *Thousand and One Nights* is a compilation of early Persian transcriptions taken from "*confabulatores nocturni* (tellers of night-tales) and relaters of fanciful adventures." Otherwise, as Sir Richard Burton says, "We know absolutely nothing of the author or authors who produced our marvellous recueil" (3658), except that the originals seem to be of diverse origin, predominantly Persian, African, and Egyptian, handed down in

Arabic. The first major European experience of the work was through a French version (translated by Antoine Galland) which appeared in 1704; the first English edition was translated from the French and appeared twenty years later, in 1724.

Burton's *Book of the Thousand Nights and a Night* appeared in 1886. It is the only English version that replicates the bawdiness and the linguistic peculiarities that characterize the Arabic, capturing something of its formality and figurativeness.[24] Writing about the Arabic language in his "Terminal Essay," Burton quotes another expert (Baron de Slane): "The figurative language of Moslem poets is often difficult to be understood. The *narcissus* is the eye. . . . *Pearls* signify both *tears* and *teeth*; the latter are sometimes called *hailstones* . . . the *lips* are *carnelians* or *rubies*; the *gums*, a *pomegranate flower*, the dark *foliage* of the *myrtle* is synonymous with the *black hair* of the beloved, or with the first down on the cheeks of puberty. The *down* itself is called the *izar*, or head-stall of the bridle . . . " and so forth (3725). To which Burton himself says, "Like the distant frog-concert and chirp of the cicada, the creak of the water-wheel and the stroke of hammers upon the anvil from afar, the murmur of the fountain, the sough of the wind and the plash of the wavelet, they occupy the sensorium with a soothing effect, forming a barbaric music full of sweetness and peaceful pleasure" (3726).

Burton identifies three genres of tale in the *Thousand and One Nights*, each probably originating at different cultural periods: the apologue (or beast-fable), the fairy tale, and the historical anecdote. Of the first, Burton writes,

> The apologue or beast-fable, which apparently antedates all other subjects in The Nights, has been called "one of the

earliest creations of the awakening consciousness of mankind." I should regard it, despite a monumental antiquity, as the offspring of a comparatively civilized age, when a jealous despotism or a powerful oligarchy threw difficulties and dangers in the way of speaking "plain truths." A hint can be given and a friend or foe can be lauded or abused as Belins the Sheep or Isengrim the wolf when the author is debarred the higher enjoyment of praising them or dispraising them by name. (3687)

Burton's Terminal Essay is not only descriptive but to some degree defensive, arguing for the relevance of the *Thousand and One Nights* to Western European experience and mentality. So he continues his commentary with a passage in which, it is worth noting, the purport of his argument depends on three references, the first to Sir Francis Bacon (poet and progenitor of Western scientific empiricism, himself writing in response to European voyages of exploration), the second to Goethe (whose Faust, as I've said, is the prototypical seeker after knowledge, and who was himself famous not only as a poet but also as a natural scientist, the author of famous works on mineralogy, botany, biological morphology, and on the phenomenology of light and color), and the last to the enormous appeal of exploration itself, of which he knew a great deal, being preeminently himself an explorer, not only in Arabia but, more famously, in East and Central Africa.

Next in date to the apologue comes the fairy tale proper, where the natural universe is supplemented by one of purely imaginative existence. "As the active world is inferior to the rational soul," says Bacon with his normal sound sense, "so Fiction gives to Mankind what History denies and in some measure satisfies the Mind with Shadows when it cannot enjoy the Substance. And as real History gives us not the success of things according to the deserts of vice and virtue, Fiction corrects it and presents us with the fates and fortunes of persons rewarded and punished according to merit." But I would say still more. History paints or attempts to paint life as it is, a mighty maze with or without a plan; fiction shows or would show us life as it should be, wisely ordered and laid down on fixed lines. Thus fiction is not the mere handmaid of history: she has a household of her own and she claims to be the triumph of art which, as Goethe remarked, is "Art because it is not Nature." . . . And last, but not least, the faculty of fancy takes count of the cravings of man's nature for the marvelous, the impossible, and of his higher aspirations for the ideal, the perfect: she realizes the wild dreams and visions of his generous youth and portrays for him a portion of that "other and better world," with whose expectation he would console his age. . . . The grand source of pleasure in fairy tales is the natural desire to learn more of the wonderland which is known to many as a word and nothing more, like Central Africa before the last half century: thus the interest is that of the "personal narrative" of a grand exploration to one who delights in travels (3692–94).

Finally, the third type of tale folded into the fabric of the *Thousand and One Nights* is the historical tale—records of real personages and real events, predominantly the victors and victims in struggles for power. Such tales are always a part of oral epics, and their presence in this work marks it as part of that public and political tradition, though with the unique feature of being, finally, a night work.

12

A long work with epic features set in the dark of night prepares for an oddly private experience of coming to know what's necessary for cultivating the public well-being. It would seem to serve as a hermeneutics for resolving the conflict between social responsibility and personal impulse, between destructiveness and fertility, between hatred and love. The significance of the *Thousand and One Nights* seems to bear some (perhaps coincidental) relation to that of the Eleusinian Mysteries, a body of knowledge instituted, supposedly, by Demeter, the goddess of agriculture and mother of Persephone. The Mysteries were said to celebrate Persephone's return from Hades each spring, and hence they symbolize the annual cycle in which death is overcome by rebirth in nature and the immortality of the soul is prophesied.

Scheherazade's king Sharyar, then, is like a novice in the "Mysteries of Eleusis, where every spring for perhaps hundreds of years, hundreds of people gathered in the dark of a cave-like temple, awaiting initiation into the esoteric teachings of death, rebirth, and immortality bestowed by the goddess Demeter in luminous visions."[25]

13

The Faust story begins and ends in Faust's laboratory/study—what would seem to be a stereotypical scientific setting, with its claims to facilitating objectivity. But the Faust story, even in Goethe's version, is in many respects dreamlike. The figments—the visions summoned to Faust for his contemplation—are unique; their night visits cannot be replicated. Like dream visions, they are incorrigible but cannot be proved.

The tales of *The Thousand and One Nights*, though filled with the kinds of transmutations and metamorphoses which occur in dreams, are not private fantasies or psychological displays but public stories—embodying social norms, cultural values, and ultimately moral advice. Scheherazade tells her tales in bed, but their milieu is public.

In the Faust legend, Faust is able, with Mephistopheles' help, to take nocturnal voyages, flying through the air to other times and places and summoning scenes and personages from them to his study. He is permitted to gaze on them—to have them as sights—but other interaction is impossible, including, explicitly, speech. In the face of knowledge, Faust is silenced.

Scheherazade's position is the reverse of this. "Be silent then, for danger is in words" (V.i.27), says Marlowe's Faust to some companions before whom he is exhibiting Helen of Troy.[26] But for Scheherazade danger lies in silence, death hovers at the edge of dawn on the horizon of light when all stories come to an end, inscribing her end as well. Where Faust sells his soul for knowledge, Scheherazade saves her life by offering it.

14

A Fable
(*for Carla Harryman*)

A magnificent traveling owl stood on a fine long branch in an orchard overlooking a long quiet bay or perhaps a sluggish but blue (because hardly unmoving and therefore unmuddied) expanse of a river with a sandy shallow bed. The owl turned its head toward a heavy peach hanging from a twig nearby and acknowledged its transformation from what it had been before.

"Yeah, well," said the peach, "the days go by."

Suddenly the owl (do you imagine it as a male or a female? and the peach?) smelled something in the breeze pungently particular, almost adolescent and inflated. . . .

But the term "suddenly," as applied to the experience of an owl, should suggest patient speculation, prolonged acknowledgment, the extension of, contemplation, and finally peace.

Some ants were passing over the owl's claw.

"I've already been tattooed," said the owl.

The peach—rosy, obscure, and banal—fell.

First Moral: All one should ask of anything else is that it try to do its best.

Second Moral: Instinctively we make a combination of two things when we judge the significance of any relationship.

Third Moral: A mere bare fraud is just what our Western common sense will never believe the phenomenal world to be.

Fourth Moral: Various women writers will take up the philosophical quest for uncertainty.

Notes

1. Marina Warner, *From the Beast to the Blonde: On Fairy Tales and Their Tellers* (London: Chatto & Windus, 1994).
2. *Goethe's Faust, Part One,* tr. Randall Jarrell (New York: Farrar,

Straus & Giroux), 60. Similarly, Goethe himself, in a letter of April 16, 1787, wrote: "How much joy I have every day from my little bit of knowledge of material things, and how much more I would have to know if my joy were to be complete." (Quoted in Nicolas Boyle, *Goethe: The Poet and the Age*, vol. 1, *The Poetry of Desire* [Oxford: Oxford University Press, 1992], 472.)

3. Several Fausts predate this one, and I am indebted to Pagan Neil and to Jeff Conant for pointing them out to me. Salient facts about these earlier Fausts contribute to the swarm of significances surrounding the Wittenbergian. One of the earlier figures was Faustus of Milevis, a fourth-century teacher of Manichean religious philosophy (the religion coming originally from Persia) and a friend of St. Augustine. Another early Faust was a fifteenth-century Mainz goldsmith, lawyer, and moneylender, a certain Johann Fust or Faust. Gutenberg, the famous printer, borrowed money from him, and when Gutenberg was unable to repay the loan, his press became Fust's. Fust thus became a printer and publisher, and he traveled with a package of the earliest printed books to France. There he was arrested for possessing such mysterious items and burned at the stake.

4. It should be pointed out that Faust (this is especially clear with Goethe's Faust) considers himself, by the terms of his pact with the devil and through the authority of his imagination, to be beyond considerations of good and evil. It was in a work by Goethe's close companion and intellectual cohort Carl Phillip Moritz, *On the Plastic Imitation of the Beautiful* (1787), that the term *art* as we know it was first defined. Prior to the eighteenth century, the term meant something technical; Samuel Johnson in his dictionary provides as an instance of its usage, "the art of boiling sugar." And until this time, the word "creative" was a purely theological term, applicable only to the Supreme Deity.

Where previously what we now call art was considered as either entertaining or improving, Moritz in his treatise broaches the notion that poetry (literature), painting (visual arts), and music have something in common, and this common feature is that their products are self-contained—independent of external standards (morals). This is a terrain that "pure science" sometimes claims, but at least with Goethe's Faust it is also a claim of "pure art." Faust thus displays the amorality of the autonomous artist. It is the amorality of the imagination, and we see it displayed ourselves in dreams. See Boyle, *Goethe*, 498ff.

5. Christopher Marlowe, *Dr. Faustus* (New York: Signet, 1969).

6. Quoted in Annette Kolodny, *The Land Before Her* (Chapel Hill: University of North Carolina Press, 1984), 3–4. See also Stephen Greenblatt, *Marvelous Possessions* (Chicago: University of Chicago Press, 1991).

7. Kolodny, *The Land Before Her*, 3–4.

8. Mircea Eliade, in an essay titled "Masks: Mythical and Ritual Origins" points out that nakedness, or at least "ceremonial nakedness," is one of the essential accoutrements to female power, since it is in her nakedness that woman resembles the Great Mother goddess. "In her body, by her body, the goddess reveals the mystery of inexhaustible creation on all levels of life in the cosmos. Every woman shares the essence and the import of the goddess in this archetypal nakedness." Eliade goes on: "Man, on the contrary, increases his magico-religious possibilities by hiding his face and concealing his body. When he puts on a mask, he ceases to be himself; at least, he seemingly, if not actually, becomes another. This amounts to saying that, at least after a certain period in history, a man knows himself as a man precisely by changing himself into something other than himself. By wearing a mask he becomes what he is resolved to be: *homo religiosus* and *zoon politikon*. Such behavior has a good deal of bearing on the history of culture" (Mircea Eliade, *Symbolism, the Sacred, and the Arts* [New York: Continuum Publishing Company, 1992], 64). Eliade writes from a male point of view, and what he says is true from that point of view—one that has been dominant and has been able to make it true. My thanks to John Rapko for pointing this essay out to me.

9. See Joshua C. Taylor, *America as Art* (Washington, D.C.: Smithsonian Institution Press, 1976).

10. For an important, relevant study of *The Gross Clinic*, see Michael Fried, *Realism, Writing, Disfiguration* (Chicago: University of Chicago Press, 1987).

11. Barbara Maria Stafford, *Body Criticism: Imagining the Unseen in Enlightenment Art and Medicine* (Cambridge, Mass.: The MIT Press, 1991). See also Luke Wilson, "William Harvey's *Prelectiones:* The Performance of the Body in the Renaissance Theater of Anatomy," *Representations* 17 (Winter 1987).

12. Gertrude Stein, in her "realist" work of 1914, *Tender Buttons*, opens with a short poem which plays on the double perspective implied by the word "spectacle," meaning both the thing seen (the scene) and the medium, spectacles, through which it is seen. The little poem comments also on "difference," not necessarily but possibly gender differences: "A kind in glass and a cousin, a spectacle and nothing strange a single hurt color and an arrangement in a system to pointing. All this and not ordinary, not unordered in not resembling. The difference is spreading." *Tender Buttons* in *Gertrude Stein: Writings 1903–1932*, ed. Catharine R. Stimpson and Harriet Chessman (New York: Library of America, 1998), 313.

13. See Mary Ann Doane, *Femmes Fatales: Feminism, Film Theory, Psychoanalysis* (New York: Routledge, 1991), for a discussion of this in the context of film imagery and film "reality."

14. As Michael Taussig argues in *Mimesis and Alterity* (New York: Routledge, 1992), contemplation represents an attempt to master something optically, and mastering something, in Taussig's terminology, often means to become it; through mimesis or mimetic fantasy, one becomes the other. Usually what one can't master optically one masters tactilely, by motion, but in the porn theater this alternative isn't available. To the extent that the stripper may appear to be a nonperson, a body with no "I," it may indeed seem that the body lacks, so to speak, an inhabitant, and that one might gaze one's way into it—one might become its "I."

15. Once Faust has made his bargain with fate (in the guise of the

devil's emissary Mephistopheles) his story is episodic. And more interesting, the sequence doesn't matter. Various things happen but one thing does not lead to another. This is logical enough—or it achieves the sublime illogicality that an atemporal status would provide. Faust offers to sell his soul for knowledge, the devil agrees, and after that no further steps can be taken because they have all already been taken. Omniscience has been achieved. Thereafter, everything that could be real is, and all the rest is its image, its ghost.

16. Quoted in Marina Warner, "The Silence of Cordelia," in *Wordlessness*, ed. Mark Verminck and Bart Verschaffel (Dublin: The Lilliput Press, 1993), 83–85.

17. For a particularly useful mapping of many of these dichotomies, see Martin Jay, *Downcast Eyes* (Berkeley: University of California Press, 1993).

18. Hans Blumenberg, "Light as a Metaphor for Truth," in *Modernity and the Hegemony of Vision*, ed. David Michael Levin (Berkeley: University of California Press, 1994), 32.

19. This poem, and the last stanza in particular, are indebted to the opening paragraph of Pierre Alferi's "Seeking a Sentence," tr. Joseph Simas, in *Poetics Journal* 10 (1998); the "appropriation" was undertaken with his permission.

20. *The Book of the Thousand Nights and a Night*, translated and annotated by Sir Richard Burton, six volumes in three through-numbered books (New York: The Heritage Press, 1943), 15.

21. Likewise, the Spiess Faustbook and the English translation are a compilation of tales of magical feats and fantastic sightseeing, with Faust as the ready figure on whom to attach them. Many of the stories were traditional; E. M. Butler identifies sources in materials in ancient Greek, Arabic, Roman, Celtic, Nordic, Semitic, etc., so that Faust takes on adventures original to Moses, the Witch of Endor, Saul, Odin, Numo Pompilius, Albertus Magus, a certain Wildfire, Simon Magus, Merlin, Agrippa, and Paracelsus, to name a few. There are also borrowings from Boccaccio, Ariosto, etc.—"a whole body of oral and written tradition,

much of it of great antiquity, some of it prehistoric, swarming round and settling on the figure of a sixteenth century charlatan and transforming him into a myth." E. M. Butler, *The Fortunes of Faust* (Cambridge: Cambridge University Press, 1952), 8.

22. *The Book of the Thousand Nights and One Night*, coll. E. Powys Mathers, 8 vols. (New York: Dingwall-Rock, Ltd., 1930) 1:9. In essence, Scheherazade begins her project of rescue and redemption against a background of prolonged, incrementally orchestrated, but to the victims meaningless social atrocities—and in writing this paper I couldn't help but think of the crimes, cruelties, and horrors perpetrated continually for the past two years in the former Yugoslavia. One can't easily call them "facts," though they are *givens*, since they can be known but they have the peculiarity that knowing them doesn't add up to knowledge; each instance of murderousness is terminal, literally so, so that continuity, which is the goal of knowledge, is impossible.

23. *Thousand Nights and One Night*, coll. Mathers, 8:394.

24. It may be that Burton, like his contemporary Charles Doughty, the author of *Travels in Arabia Deserta* (1888; New York: Dover Books, 1979), had a sense of an identity between a place and its spoken language, since even when not, strictly speaking, "translating," Burton sought out an Arabiclike construction when writing of things Arabian. Both in his *Personal Narrative of a Pilgrimage to Al-Madinah and Meccah* (1855; New York: Dover Books, 1964) and in the lengthy and elegant "Terminal Essay" appended to his translation of the *Nights*, the prose often spirals around its subjects, though nowhere does he match the syntactical marvels of Doughty's famous opening sentence: "A new voice hailed me of an old friend when, first returned from the Peninsula, I paced again in that long street of Damascus which is called Straight; and suddenly taking me wondering by the hand, 'Tell me (said he), since thou art here again in the peace and assurance of Allah, and whilst we walk, as in the former years, toward the new blossoming orchards, full of the sweet spring as the garden of God, what moved thee, or how couldst thou take such journeys into the fanatic Arabia?'"

25. David Michael Levin, ed., Introduction to *Modernity and the Hegemony of Vision*, 2.

26. As E. M. Butler points out, the Spiess Faustbook is contained between two Biblical texts. The first, which Butler calls the entrance, appears on the title page: "Submit yourselves therefore to God. Resist the devil, and he will flee from you" (James 4:7). The second, the "door of exit," comes from 1 Peter 5:8: "Be sober, be vigilant; because your adversary the devil, as a roaring lion, walketh about, seeking whom he may devour." But there is something more than the Spiess Faustbook encompassed within those two quotes, namely the two adjacent books of the old Testament from which they are taken and whose substance they summon. The first is "The General Epistle of James," admonishing "the twelve tribes which are scattered abroad" to avoid "divers temptations," of which one of the worst is that of an untamed tongue: "Behold, we put bits in the horses' mouths, that they may obey us; and we turn about their whole body. Behold also the ships, which though they be so great, and are driven of fierce winds, yet are they turned about with a very small helm, withersoever the governor listeth. Even so the tongue is a little member, and boasteth great things. Behold, how great a matter a little fire kindleth!" And, James continues, "the tongue is a fire, a world of iniquity: so is the tongue among our members, that it defileth the whole body, and setteth on fire the course of nature; and it is set on fire of hell" (James 3:1–8). The devil, in "The First Epistle General of Peter," which is the next book of the Bible, is depicted as a garrulous creature, as noisy "as a roaring lion."

Three Lives

The essay called "Three Lives" was written in 1998 as an introduction to a planned Green Integer Press edition of Gertrude Stein's *Three Lives.*[1] The invitation to write such an introduction provided me with a context in which to examine Stein's approach to psychological investigation. It forced me to confront Stein's interest in human character in the light of my own seeming resistance to such an interest. To apply critical analysis to another person's character has seemed to me to be of dubious ethicity and I have had doubts, too, about the possibility of trusting any of the findings of such an analysis, since a view of someone else's psychological character is apt to be colored by elements from one's own; what one sees in another is very likely to be a projection of oneself.

In a sense, then, writing the introduction to *Three Lives* forced me to imagine overcoming the sense of helplessness that the task of understanding how and why people are as they are provokes. And to imagine that, I had to examine the sense of helplessness itself. It seems to rise from a number of factors. Given the dynamic complexity and the circumstantial instability of any given human character (and of any given character analysis), one is struck by an awareness of the impossibility of dependable psychological knowledge. And then, too, even were such knowledge possible, it seems to carry with it the risk of something very like paranoia. To search out psychological knowledge is to question motives, and to question motives is to be suspicious of them. The acquisition of psychological knowledge itself induces a psychological situation, in other words, one that is itself yet to be known, and this means that the "psychologist" is always at a penultimate stage of knowing, always not-yet-knowing. The "psychologist" is herself always in a psychological condition and it is one of uncertainty.

The link between the psychology of the psychologist and the notion of uncertainty as a realm of "knowledge" is not articulated in the essay, but it was important to the writing of it. It provided me with what I hope is insight into the sources of Gertrude Stein's interest in psychology and hence into what it was that she wanted to portray. It was through imagining what a comprehensive psychology grounded in epistemological uncertainty would look like that I could make sense of Stein's notion of composition—of emergence through repetition; to have a psyche is to be in composition.

Gertrude Stein began *Three Lives* in February 1905 and finished it exactly a year later, during a hiatus in the writing of *The Making of Americans*, which she had begun in 1903 and would complete in 1911.[2] Though their social milieus are different, the two works share a geographical setting; the three lives of this book are lived out entirely in Baltimore, or "Bridgepoint" as Stein calls its fictional equivalent, and Bridgepoint is also the home of the Dehnings, one of the two families under examination in *The Making of Americans*. Both works, too, reflect Stein's preoccupation with an attempt to discover and describe the fundamental elements of human character. These she viewed not as atemporal nor as isolated traits but as procedural formations; they are *com-positional*—forces projecting through personality into shapes of living, visible as the patterns of behavior (including, significantly, speech patterns) which draw a person's character over time. In essence, it is these patterns of behavior rather than narrative sequences of events which in Stein's view constitute the facts of a person's life, and thus it is that she could write three character studies of considerable fascination in which nothing extraordinary happens.

Yet, though the plots of the stories can be quickly told, they cannot be called thin—unless life itself is thin. And though nothing extraordinary happens in the lives of the three central figures, yet each one dies as if exhausted by a surfeit of experience, however inconsequential and "normal."

Or is it that very normality that is killing? It is not clear, in the end, whether Stein views the compositional stability that normality represents as benign or destructive. Of course, life itself doesn't always make this clear. But the ambiguity—even conflict—that is inherent to *Three Lives* is in part a reflection of the sources Stein drew on as she wrote the work.

Three Lives was, quite literally, written under the sign of Cézanne.

Leo Stein had purchased his first Cézanne, a landscape, in the spring of 1904, his interest in the artist having been sparked by Bernard Berenson.[3] Following the purchase of the landscape (from the gallery of Ambroise Vollard), Leo went to Florence in the summer of 1904, and there he reestablished an earlier friendship with Charles Loeser, an American expatriate living in Florence, who, according to Berenson, had been purchasing paintings by Cézanne for several years. As Leo recalled later, "I thought that strange, as I had often been at Loeser's house, but Berenson explained that the Cézannes were not mixed with the other pictures which filled his house, but were all in his bedroom and dressing room. . . . He had begun buying Cézannes in the early days, when Vollard's was a kind of five-and-ten establishment, and had got together an interesting lot. . . . When I got back to Paris after the Cézanne debauch, I was ready to look further."[4]

Returning to Paris in the fall, Leo visited Vollard again, this time with Gertrude. In a letter to Mabel Weeks, Stein gave an account of the visit: "We is doin business too we are selling Jap prints to buy a Cézanne at least we are that is Leo is trying. He don't like it a bit and makes a awful fuss about asking enough money but I guess we'll get the Cézanne."[5] The painting in question was the portrait of the artist's wife which had been shown at the Salon d'Automne of 1904 under the title *La Femme à l'éventail*.[6]

Some thirty years later, in *The Autobiography of Alice B. Toklas*, Stein remembers the day of the purchase in some detail.

Before the winter was over, having gone so far Gertrude
Stein and her brother decided to go further, they decided to
buy a big Cézanne and then they would stop. After that they
would be reasonable. They convinced their elder brother
that this last outlay was necessary, and it was necessary as
will soon be evident. They told Vollard that they wanted
to buy a Cézanne portrait. In those days practically no big
Cézanne portraits had been sold. Vollard owned almost all of
them. He was enormously pleased with this decision. They
now were introduced into the room above the steps behind

the partition where Gertrude Stein had been sure the old charwomen painted the Cézannes and there they spent days deciding which portrait they would have. There were about eight to choose from and the decision was difficult. They had often to go and refresh themselves with honey cakes at Fouquet's. Finally they narrowed the choice down to two, a portrait of a man and a portrait of a woman, but this time they could not afford to buy twos and finally they chose the portrait of the woman.

Vollard said of course ordinarily a portrait of a woman always is more expensive than a portrait of a man but, said he looking at the picture very carefully, I suppose with Cézanne it does not make any difference. They put it in a cab and they went home with it. It was this picture that Alfy Maurer used to explain was finished and that you could tell that it was finished because it had a frame.[7]

Though the Steins purchased other Cézannes, this remained their most important and most remarked upon of his works. Picasso's mistress, Fernande Olivier, remembered it years later as "that beautiful likeness of the painter's wife in a blue dress, sitting in a garnet-colored armchair."[8] Other visitors to the Stein household were sometimes less positive, seeing in the painting neither likeness nor beauty. As Mabel Dodge later wrote: "In those early days when everyone laughed, and went to the Steins' for the fun of it, and half angrily, half jestingly giggled and scoffed after they left (not knowing that all the same they were changed by seeing those pictures), Leo stood patiently night after night wrestling with the inertia of his guests, expounding, teaching, interpreting. . . ."[9]

Leo took his pedagogical role seriously, and if his harangues were perhaps pedantic or his attitude overbearing, they were nonetheless not defensive. Like Gertrude, Leo was given to explanation rather than to justification—except to their brother Michael (whose money they were spending). In a letter, dating probably from 1905, Leo gave Mabel Weeks a summary of his "required discussions" on Manet, Renoir, Degas, and Cézanne, the painters he considered the "Big Four." Of Cézanne, he wrote:

> . . . here again is great mind a perfect concentration and great control. Cézanne's essential problem is mass and he has succeeded in rendering mass with a vital intensity that is unparalleled in the whole history of painting. No matter what his subject is—the figure—landscape—still life—there is always this remorseless intensity this endless unending gripping of form the unceasing effort to force it to reveal its absolute self-existing quality of mass. There can scarcely be such a thing as a completed Cézanne. Every canvas is a battlefield and victory an unattainable ideal. Cézanne rarely does more than one thing at a time and when he turns to composition he brings to bear the same intensity keying his composition up till it sings like a harp string. His color also though as harsh as his forms is almost as vibrant. In brief his is the most robust the most intense and in a fine sense the most ideal of the four.[10]

In purchasing and then becoming advocates for the Cézanne *Portrait*, Gertrude and Leo must have known what they were about. The 1904 Salon d'Automne at which it had been on display was considered the most important artistic event of the year and the Cézannes in the show had achieved considerable notoriety. James Huneker, reviewing the exhibition anonymously for the *New York Sun*, reported, "The main note of the Salon is a riotous energy . . . a flinging of paint pots." And, he continues, the center attraction was Cézanne,

> *toujours Cézanne,* for this is the daily chant of the independents. . . . Sacred, crude, violent, sincere, ugly, and altogether bizarre canvases. Here was the very hub of the Independents' universe. Here the results of a hard laboring painter, without taste, without the faculty of selection, without vision, culture—one is tempted to add intellect—who with dogged persistence has painted in the face of mockery, painted portraits, still life, landscapes, flowers, houses, figures, painted everything, painted himself. . . . Cézanne has dropped out of his scheme harmony, melody, beauty—classic, romantic, symbolic, what you will!—and doggedly represented the ugliness of things.

But, he concludes, "There is a brutal strength, a tang of the soil, that is bitter, and also strangely invigorating. . . . "[11]

The purchase (and collecting) of works of art can, of course, be seen as a means of accumulating cultural (as well as economic) capital, and there is undeniably an element of this in the Steins' case.[12] But the owning of the painting, at least for Gertrude, was far less important than understanding something from it. The choice they had made (and it seems that it was Gertrude who was the more adamant about purchasing this particular painting) constituted a form of identification (and a very close one, as we shall see). But what the Steins were investing in held contradictory values and made demanding claims on them in turn, making them, as it turned out, party to a serious challenge to conventional forms of living and the conventional "realism" that depicted it. As Gertrude said at the beginning of "Portraits and Repetition," "nothing changes from generation to generation except the composition in which we live and the composition in which we live makes the art which we see and hear."[13] In espousing the aesthetics of Cézanne (and of this painting in particular), the Steins were undertaking an act of composition. And, as Gertrude Stein said years later, "It was an important purchase because in looking and looking at this picture Gertrude Stein wrote Three Lives."[14]

For Stein in 1905, the question of "composition" had psychological as well as aesthetic implications. At stake was something definitively personal—a composing of her mode of being and hence of her very being itself—the formation of her character. In the writing of *The Making of Americans*, Stein had already been engaged in a meticulous and thorough study of character, and this project was in turn an extension of the work in psychology she had done at Harvard under William James and then at Johns Hopkins Medical School (which she had attended with the intention of becoming a psychologist). Now, in 1905, in the presence (and under the tutelage) of Cézanne's *Portrait*, Stein was beginning to establish an habitual milieu of her own, and in studying her behavior—her relationships to and in that milieu—she was placing (identifying and making sense of) herself. It was a mode she would employ also in composing the portraits that give us the three central characters of *Three Lives*, the book she had just begun. Indeed, the composing of these portraits constitutes what there is of "plot" in each of the stories.

At this same time, Stein was participating in another composition, and one that again involved portraiture. This was what would become Picasso's famous *Portrait of Gertrude Stein*. She had begun posing for it just after she began writing "Melanctha," the middle story of *Three Lives* (the last of the three to be written), "the story," as she said, "that was the beginning of her revolutionary work."[15]

The Picasso portrait bears striking resemblances to the Cézanne, a fact which can only have been intentional. The poses are similar and so are the colors, and in both portraits the figure is placed near a dark corner of the room down which an even darker line is drawn to mark where the two walls of the room meet. This juncture is the resting point at which the subject of each of the paintings has found her place.

There are dissimilarities, too. Though Madame Cézanne, the subject of the Cézanne portrait, looks directly out at the viewer (and at the painter), she seems disengaged, passive, remote and implacable (not unlike the "good Anna" of Stein's first story).[16] In the Picasso portrait, on the other hand, Stein, though her gaze is turned aside as if directed into the room to the right of the picture, leans forward. It is an active pose; it appears as if she is leaning consciously into the present moment, as if she is bringing her presence to bear on it.

Stein wrote of the period during which she posed for the portrait in *The Autobiography of Alice B. Toklas*. "Practically every afternoon Gertrude Stein went to Montmartre, posed and then later wandered down the hill usually walking across Paris to the rue de Fleurus. . . . And Saturday evenings the Picassos walked home with her and dined and then there was Saturday evening. . . . During these long poses and these long walks Gertrude Stein meditated and made sentences. She was then in the middle of her negro story Melanctha Herbert, the second story of Three Lives. . . . "[17] And again, a few pages later, "It had been a fruitful winter. In the long struggle with the portrait of Gertrude Stein, Picasso passed from the Harlequin, the charming early Italian period to the intensive struggle which was to end in cubism. Gertrude Stein had written the story of Melanctha the negress, the second story of Three Lives which was the first definite step away from the nineteenth century and into the twentieth century in literature."[18]

But what was the nature of this step? What, as she "meditated and made sentences," had Stein discovered about composition?

In "Composition as Explanation," written some twenty years after the writing of *Three Lives*, Stein attempted to define the problem:

> In beginning writing I wrote a book called *Three Lives* this
> was written in 1905. I wrote a negro story called Melanctha.
> In that there was a constant recurring and beginning there
> was a marked direction in the direction of being in the pres-
> ent although naturally I had been accustomed to past pres-
> ent and future, and why, because the composition forming
> around me was a prolonged present. A composition of a pro-
> longed present is a natural composition in the world as it has
> been these thirty years it was more and more a prolonged
> present. . . . In making these portraits I naturally made a con-
> tinuous present an including everything and a beginning
> again and again within a very small thing.[19]

In formulating a "prolonged" or "continuous" present (consisting in turn of "an including everything" and "a beginning again and again within a very small thing") as a compositional method, Stein had discovered something fundamental about the way time exists at the interior of a human life; it is within living that time has its sources. This was a discovery that she found to be essential to the art of portraiture. It establishes portraiture as a fundamentally temporal genre, and it explains how it is that a painter depicts not the inert flesh of the subject but her lived (and living) experience, her dynamic, her personality.

Joachim Gasquet described Cézanne's ability to convey his subject's inner experience, his ability, as it were, to paint time. Cézanne had painted a portrait of Gasquet in 1896.

> I posed only five or six times. I thought he had abandoned the picture. I learned afterwards that he had devoted to it some sixty periods of work and that whenever during the course of the poses he studied me with intensity, he was thinking of the portrait and that he worked at it after my departure. He was trying to bring out my very life, my features, my inner thoughts, my language; and without my knowledge he made me expand until he could catch my soul itself in the passionate transports of argument and the hidden eloquence that even the humblest being brings to his angers or his enthusiasms. It was a part of his method . . . a conscious effort, *à la* Flaubert, "the contemplation of the humblest realities," that he forced [upon] himself with terrific will-power.[20]

In much of her writing subsequent to *Three Lives*, but most notably, perhaps, in the play *Four Saints in Three Acts*[21] (1922), Stein made further discoveries about the interiority, the inhering, of time. Most of these belong to another discussion,[22] and to larger scales of compositionality than portraiture entails. Stein herself referred to these later works as "landscapes." But the apparent change in subject matter is only superficial. The later work, like that of *Three Lives*, continues to ponder human being. In *Four Saints*, Stein expands lived temporality, the temporality of being, into landscape, where "all that was necessary was that there was something completely contained within itself and being contained within itself was moving, not moving in relation to anything not moving in relation to itself but just moving."[23] Or, to put it another way, she accomplishes a landscaping of time, a depiction, to use terminology that Heidegger was developing at the same time, of Being-in-time. The "saints" within this landscape are not, as Stein perceived them, characterized by the kind of "goodness" that the good Anna, the gentle Lena, and even Melanctha aspire to, but rather by their intact "liveliness," a mode of being that Stein termed "complete living": "if it were possible that a movement were lively enough it would exist so completely that it would not be necessary to see it moving against anything to know that it is moving. This is what we mean by life," she says, conferring an absolute value on existence, "and in my way I have tried to make portraits of this thing."[24]

Stein continued to use portraiture, albeit in different guises, in her work; her commitment to discovering the nature of being, and specifically of human being, was lifelong. As the investigation of the problem progressed into the late 1930s, the internal motion of liveliness that Stein calls "life" got reformulated. She discovered the distinction between "identity" and "entity." Identity constitutes one's knowability; or to put it another way, what is known about anyone is a part of his or her identity. Entity, on the other hand, constitutes one's capacity to know.

For Stein herself, the notion of "entity" seems to have offered a release from "identity." As she says in the "Henry James" section of *Four in America*, "I am I not any longer when I see. This sentence is at the bottom of all creative activity. It is just the opposite of I am I because my little dog knows me."[25] It is from the viewpoint of entity that one can feel the astonishment of existence, the amazement that one is something, rather than nothing. It is entity that allows us to be surprised not only that "Anything is what it is,"[26] but that anything is at all. This coming into awareness of something (anything) is at the heart of creativity.

Stein's realizations regarding this are of utmost philosophical and psychological importance. And to reach them, she had to undertake the prolonged study of identity that is the theme of *Three Lives*. It is identity, the passage of time in being, that the portraits depict. Stein had discovered that time in being composes.

From the start, Stein saw identity as a sociosexual problem and hence as a problem of affinities, allegiances, and accommodation; it is a problem fixated on norms but also on love.

Gertrude Stein wrote *Three Lives* in the aftermath of a profoundly unhappy love affair with a fellow student at Johns Hopkins, May Bookstaver. The history of this affair is recounted in detail in *Q.E.D.*, the novel that Stein wrote in New York in 1903 before she moved permanently to Paris, and which she then set aside (and essentially suppressed).[27] The "Melanctha" story in *Three Lives* is a reworking of the *Q.E.D.* material, and it comes to the same conclusion, namely that people who are fundamentally different from each other are attracted to each other, but that despite all the "talking and listening" that they undertake with each other, no understanding between them is possible.

The activities of "talking and listening," meanwhile, had more than social importance to Stein; they played a fundamental role in the constituting of "identity," a literal articulating of oneself, in part into relationships with others, but more importantly into harmony (what Stein in "Melanctha" calls "understanding" or "knowing") with one's sense of who one is and who one is supposed to be.

In "Portraits and Repetitions," Stein gives an account of her discovery of the importance of "talking and listening"

> When I first really realized the inevitable repetition in human expression that was not repetition but insistence when I first began to be really conscious of it was when at about seventeen years of age, I left the more or less internal and solitary and concentrated life I led in California and came to Baltimore and lived with a lot of my relations and principally with a whole group of very lively little aunts who had to know anything. . . . If they had to know anything and anybody does they naturally had to say and hear it often, anybody does, and as there were ten and eleven of them they did have to say and hear said whatever was said and any one not hearing what it was they said had to come in to hear what had been said. That inevitably made everything said often.[28]

As a student of psychology, Stein often took William James as her guide, elaborating persistently and in detail James's view of human personality, self, or character as a coming into consciousness. But where James's view credits intentionality (will power) with the ability to shape habit, Stein is less optimistic. James does acknowledge nonvolitional (physiological and "instinctual") forces, but he does not provide anything like Freud's topography of an embattled terrain with its tripartite division into id, ego, and superego.[29] But, each in her way, the heroines of Stein's *Three Lives* are embattled, and each in her time succumbs to the exhaustion this entails. And it is not socially imposed conventions but internally composed ones that defeat them. This view may be a realistic one; it is certainly a realist one, and it is cruel. It derives in part from Stein's personal experience, but it comes also from Flaubert.

Though Stein spoke at some length about the importance of Cézanne to the writing *Three Lives*, she says very little about that of Flaubert. But if the work was written under the sign of Cézanne, it was also written under the influence of Flaubert; and if Stein said little about this, it is largely because her memories of this period were recorded after her break with her brother Leo, and it was he who had initiated the enthusiasm for Flaubert.

In *The Autobiography of Alice B. Toklas*, the only mention of Flaubert's influence on *Three Lives* is a very brief one, and it appears just after the somewhat lengthy account of the purchase of Cézanne's *Portrait* quoted above: "It was an important purchase because in looking and looking at this picture Gertrude Stein wrote Three Lives. She had begun not long before as an exercise in literature to translate Flaubert's Trois Contes and then she had this Cézanne, and she looked at it and under its stimulus she wrote Three Lives."[30]

Immediate parallels can be seen between *Three Lives* and *Trois Contes*, and especially between the first story in each work, Flaubert's "Un coeur simple" ("A Simple Heart") and Stein's "The Good Anna." Stein's claim that her character Anna Federner was modeled on that of Lena Lebender, her housekeeper several years earlier in Baltimore,[31] is no doubt accurate, but it seems that it was Flaubert's story and the character of Félicité that inspired Stein. And in a gesture that goes a long way toward acknowledging this, Stein gives the "good Anna" a pet parrot, though not the same degree of love for it that Félicité feels for hers. The two servants share character traits as well—both have a "simple" view of how life (a purely domestic affair) should proceed, loving hearts, limited imaginations (and hence no pressing ambitions), and a capacity for the kind of domestic power that operates through careful home management. Both practice self-denial while lavishing food and attention on others. And both find themselves working for somewhat similar mistresses—women who are troublesome but for whom they feel loyalty, respect, and a paradoxically patronizing sense of gratitude. As Flaubert puts it, "For one hundred francs a year [Félicité] did the cooking and the housework, sewing, washing, and ironing, she could bridle a horse, fatten up poultry, churn butter, and remained faithful to her mistress, who was not however a very likable person." [32] Anna's mistress, Miss Mathilda, though as self-absorbed in her way as Madame Aubain, is simply careless rather than unlikeable, and indeed in portraying her, Stein is clearly offering a portrait of herself, one which is affectionate but also wry (and even slightly self-mocking, though Stein is very rarely given to this elsewhere, perhaps because mockery of her was amply provided by others). "Anna had her troubles, too, with Miss Mathilda. And I slave and slave to save the money and you go out and spend it all on foolishness, the good Anna would complain when her mistress, a large and careless woman, would come home with a bit of porcelain, a new etching and sometimes even an oil painting on her arm." [33]

Flaubert wrote "Un coeur simple" in response to urging from George Sand, who, though sympathizing with his complaints at the poor reception of his work, blamed it in large part on the cruelty of the depictions at their center. "Write something down to earth that everybody can enjoy," she told him in October of 1875. [34] In an attempt to encourage him in this direction, she wrote at much greater length three months later.

If I'd been given your book [*L'Education sentimentale*] without your name on it, I'd have thought it splendid, but strange, and I'd have asked myself whether you were immoral, skeptical, indifferent, or heartbroken. . . . It's all the same to me whether one depicts inert things as a realist or as a poet; but when one touches on the emotions of the human heart, it's a different matter. You cannot detach yourself from this consideration; for you are a human being, and your readers are mankind. . . . Supreme impartiality is antihuman, and a novel must above all be human. . . . You *must* have a success, after the bad luck that has so depressed you. What I tell you will assure that success. Retain your cult for form, but pay more attention to matter. Don't hold true virtue to be a cliché in literature. Give it its representatives; portray the honest man and the strong, along with the maniacs and dolts you so love to ridicule. Show what is substantial, what endures despite these intellectual miscarriages. In short, abandon the conventions of the realists and turn to true reality, which is a mixture of beautiful and ugly, dull and brilliant, but in which the desire for good nevertheless finds its place and its role.[35]

At a very fundamental level, Flaubert disagreed. "For no matter what you preach to me, I can have no temperament other than my own. Nor any aesthetic other than the one that proceeds from it."[36] But shortly thereafter[37] he was working on "A Simple Heart," and in what turned out to be his last letter to George Sand, he said, "You will see from my *Story of a Simple Heart* (in which you will recognize your own direct influence) that I am not as stubborn as you believe. I think you will like the moral tendency, or rather the underlying humanity, of this little work."[38]

It is a work strongly marked by compassion.[39] Indeed, just as I said earlier that formulating her notion of a "prolonged" or "continuous" present constituted a compositional method for Stein, so I would suggest that the formulation of "compassion" does so for Flaubert. And just as Stein had discovered that the sources of time abide within each life as a kind of intrinsic motion, so Flaubert discovers that the sources of compassion likewise lie *within*— not within himself but within the lives of others—within the very lives, in other words, that he could also judge paltry or even ludicrous. Compositionally, both forces can be viewed as "something completely contained within itself and being contained within itself [are] . . . moving, not moving in relation to anything not moving in relation to itself but just moving."[40]

Toward the end of her life, in an interview she gave with Robert Bartlett Haas, Stein alludes to the emotional (though adamantly unsentimental) correspondences that inhere in realist work.

> After all, to me one human being is as important as another human being, and you might say that the landscape has the same values, a blade of grass has the same value as a tree. Because the realism of the people who did realism before was a realism of trying to make people real. I was not interested in making the people real but in the essence or, as a painter would call it, value. One cannot live without the other. This was an entirely new idea and had been done a little by the Russians but had not been conceived as a reality until I came along, but I got it largely from Cézanne. Flaubert was there as a theme. He, too, had a little of the feeling about this thing, but they none of them conceived it as an entity, no more than any painter had done other than Cézanne. . . .

> The Cézanne thing I put into words came in the *Three Lives* and was followed by the *Making of Americans*.

And, she adds, "Conception of this has to be based on a real feeling for every human being."[41]

The issue for both Flaubert and Stein was an artistic one. It determined the interior structure of their work, both at the semantic level (plot) and in the formation of individual sentences. Like Flaubert, Stein was interested in compassion *as an artist*, which is to say *formally*; this is at the root of Stein's desire (and ability) to "include everything." It is a clinical, not an encyclopedic, impulse; there is nothing that can be considered unworthy of attention, no subject that is too trivial, too grimy, too mundane, too abject, too foible-ridden, too ordinary. Inclusiveness in this context means a willingness to look at anything that life might entail; as such, it was a central tenet of the "realism" which claimed Flaubert for its "father." And the detachment which it requires is what permits the shift from manipulative to structural uses of compassion, a term whose connotations modernist realism transformed. What had previously served (antirealist) sentimentality now informed (merciless) compositionality.

Stein herself makes the link between the manner of seeing which we are here calling "compassion" and the manner which she termed composition. The latter term she defines through various precise formulations in "Composition as Explanation" (written a little over twenty years after *Three Lives*): "The only thing that is different from one time to another is what is seen and what is seen depends upon how everybody is doing everything. . . . It makes a composition, it confuses, it shows, it is, it looks it likes it as it is, and this makes what is seen as it is seen.

Nothing changes from generation to generation except the thing seen and that makes a composition."[42] And enlarging on this, in the 1946 "Transatlantic Interview" with Haas, she continues:

> Everything I have done has been influenced by Flaubert and Cézanne, and this gave me a new feeling about composition. Up to that time composition had consisted of a central idea, to which everything else was an accompaniment and separate but was not an end in itself, and Cézanne conceived the idea that in composition one thing was as important as another thing. Each part is as important as the whole, and that impressed me enormously, and it impressed me so much that I began to write *Three Lives* under this influence and this idea of composition and I was more interested in composition at that moment, this background of word-system, which had come to me from this reading that I had done. I was obsessed by this idea of composition, and the Negro story ["Melanctha"] was a quintessence of it.[43]

One wonders how specifically she meant the reference to "this reading"; we know it included *Trois contes*, since she'd been working on a translation of it, but might it also have included Flaubert's letters?[44] An edition had been published in France in 1884, four years after Flaubert's death, and it is plausible that in his enthusiasm for Flaubert, Leo Stein would have purchased and read it and then recommended it to Gertrude. If so, much of the material would have provided her with directly relevant and fundamental encouragement:

> The closer expression comes to thought, the closer language comes to coinciding and merging with it, the finer the result. ... It is for this reason that there are no noble subjects or ig-

noble subjects; from the standpoint of pure Art one might almost establish the axiom that there is no such thing as subject—style in itself being an absolute manner of seeing things.[45]

Sometimes the most banal word grips me in a strange attitude of admiration. There are gestures or tones of voice over which I'm lost in astonishment and imbecilities which I find dizzying. Have you ever listened carefully to people speaking a foreign language that you don't understand. That's the sort of state I'm in.[46]

I envision a style: a style that would be beautiful, that someone will invent some day, ten years or ten centuries from now, one that would by rhythmic as verse, precise as the language of the sciences. . . .[47]

I like clear, sharp sentences, sentences which stand erect, erect while running—almost an impossibility.[48]

A good prose sentence should be like a good line of poetry—*unchangeable*, just as rhythmic, just as sonorous. . . . Nor does it seem to me impossible to give psychological analysis the swiftness, clarity, and impetus of a purely dramatic narrative. This has never been attempted, and it would be beautiful.[49]

It is difficult to believe that Stein would have failed to find inspiration for *Three Lives* and for her subsequent writings in such passages. But it is she who accomplished the work that Flaubert dreamed of. And it is in her work that the magnitude of the project is made clear.

Three Lives makes radical advances in aesthetics, psychology, and philosophy. And although it comes relatively early in Stein's career, it should not be read as a mere beginning. It is true that Stein was able to sustain the radical character of her work to the end of her life. Repeating sentences is not the same as repeating oneself, and though she did the former she didn't do the latter. As a result, ideas evolve over the course of her work. But they do not resolve. There is no end point, no summation, no synopsis, no closure. And given the nature of her ideas and the character of her method, there could not be.

The aesthetic discoveries evident in *Three Lives* are interwoven with the psychological ones. Stein describes the process:

> In the beginning . . . I continued to do what I was doing in *The Making of Americans,* I was doing what the cinema was doing, I was making a continuous succession of the statement of what that person was until I had not many things but one thing. . . . In a cinema picture no two pictures are exactly alike each one is just that much different from the one before, and so in those early portraits there was as I am sure you will realize as I read them to you also as there was in *The Making of Americans* no repetition. Each time that I said the somebody whose portrait I was writing was something that something was just that much different from what I had just said that somebody was and little by little in this way a whole portrait came into being, a portrait that was not description and that was made by each time, and I did a great many times, say it, that somebody was something, each time there was a difference just a difference enough so that it could go on and be a present something.[50]

Stein had invented a mode of iteration to indicate not recurrence but phenomenological *occurrence,* the perpetual coming into being through accumulated instances of the person that is.

In *Three Lives* the iteration is pervasive, as the characters attempt to deal with complex emotions in a limited vocabulary: "being," "doing," "good," "honest," "should," "poor," "hard," "wandering," "regular living," "proper conduct," "knowing," etc. It is, among other things, the differences in and between people which provoke these complex emotions. To get at those differences "one must . . . get at the differences in the way that selves are linguistically formulated."[51] But that linguistic formulation isn't to be found simply at the lexical level. Characters may use the same words, even the same sentences, but while doing so they compose their meanings in different ways. That people do so is something that Stein had, as we've said, observed for years: "everybody said the same thing over and over again with infinite variations but over and over again until finally if you listened with great intensity you could hear it rise and fall and tell all that that there was inside them, not so much by the actual words they said or the thoughts they had but the movement of their thoughts and words endlessly the same and endlessly different." Through their ways of repeating, their habits, "you come to feel the whole of anyone."[52]

The analyses that are undertaken in *The Making of Americans* are complex, and so too are the results, but a few points can be extrapolated: although there are millions of people, the "kinds" of them are finite; each person has a different amount of his or her "kind" in them, with a mix of more or less of other "kinds" added, and this amount of kind and mix of other kinds is what makes a person different from all others—he or she is different through degrees of resemblance; despite the mix of "kinds, each person has some strong attribute—their "bottom nature"; "bottom nature" manifests itself through repeated actions.

In *Three Lives* these repeated actions constitute composition; the bottom nature of each of the main characters is, at it were, composed. This process of composition is a profound creative activity, both at the aesthetic and the existential level. It occurs in and as the subject of Stein's work, but its importance is to life. In many ways, the ideas that Stein articulates in *Three Lives* anticipate the notion of *Dasein* that Heidegger develops in *Being and Time*. *Da-sein*, being-there, is being-in-composition—a marvelous something "in," as Stein put it, "the actual present, that is the complete actual present, . . . to completely express that complete actual present."[53]

Notes

1. The volume is scheduled for publication in late 2000.

2. Richard Bridgman, *Gertrude Stein in Pieces* (New York: Oxford University Press, 1970), 361.

3. In his autobiographical *Appreciation: Painting, Poetry and Prose* (New York: Crown, 1947), 155, Leo describes the conversation in which Cézanne's name was broached. Berenson, asked by Leo if there were any living French artists worth consideration, promptly suggested that he look at the work of Cézanne. Quoted in John Rewald, *Cézanne and America* (Princeton: Princeton University Press, 1989), 53.

4. Leo Stein, *Appreciation: Painting, Poetry and Prose*, 155–56, quoted in Rewald, *Cézanne and America*, 53.

5. Speculatively dated Nov. 1904 and quoted in Rewald, *Cézanne and America*, 55.

6. In the literature, the painting is listed variously as *La Femme à l'éventail*, *Madame Cézanne à l'éventail*, *Portrait of the Artist's Wife*, and *Portrait of Madame Cézanne*. Cézanne began work on it around 1878, then reworked it between 1886 and 1888. It belongs now to the Foundation E. G. Bührle Collection, Zurich.

7. *The Autobiography of Alice B. Toklas*, in *Gertrude Stein: Writings 1903–1932*, ed. Catharine R. Stimpson and Harriet Chessman (New York: Library of America, 1998), 689–90.

8. Quoted in Rewald, *Cézanne and America*, 56.

9. Mabel Dodge Luhan, *Intimate Memoirs*, vol. 2, *European Experiences* (New York: Harcourt, Brace, 1935), quoted in Rewald, 64.

10. Quoted in Rewald, *Cézanne and America*, 64.

11. Anonymous [James G. Huneker], "Autumn Salon Is Bizarre," *New York Sun*, Nov. 27, 1904, quoted in Rewald, *Cézanne and America*, 95. By 1907, Huneker had come around. Writing to a friend (quoted in Rewald, 112) he said: "The Autumn Salon must have blistered your eyeballs. Nevertheless Cézanne is a great painter—purely as a painter, one who seizes and expresses *actuality*. This same actuality is always terrifyingly ugly . . . There is the ugly in life as well as the pretty, my dear boy, and for artistic purposes it is often more significant and characteristic. but—ugly is Cézanne. He could paint a bad breath."

12. One might say that the collection in itself spoke to the Steins' bourgeois anxieties, while the choice of works spoke to their bohemian aspirations.

13. "Portraits and Repetitions," in *Gertrude Stein: Writings 1932–1946*, 287.

14. *The Autobiography of Alice B. Toklas*, 690.

15. Ibid., 742.

16. As Etel Adnan pointed out to me, "Madame Cézanne has become the archetype (of what she certainly was): the 'ideal' (for some) of the unobtrusive wife, who becomes for Cézanne (when he runs out of subject matter!) color and form, an apple!" And so a French woman of today will assert herself by saying: "Ah! mais je ne suis pas Madame Cézanne!" Unpublished letter to the author, 1997.

17. *The Autobiography of Alice B. Toklas*, 710. A particularly astute discussion of racist elements in "Melanctha" can be found in Aldon Lynn Nielsen, *Reading Race: White American Poets and the Racial Discourse in the Twentieth Century* (Athens: University of Georgia Press, 1988); I also

recommend Nathaniel Mackey's "Other: From Noun to Verb," which appears in *Representations* 39 (Summer 1992).

18. *The Autobiography of Alice B. Toklas*, 714.

19. "Composition as Explanation," in *Gertrude Stein: Writings 1903–1932*, ed. Catharine R. Stimpson and Harriet Chessman (New York: Library of America, 1998), 524–25.

20. Quoted in Gerstle Mack, *Paul Cézanne* (New York: Alfred A. Knopf, 1935), 312–13.

21. *Four Saints in Three Acts*, in *Gertrude Stein: Writings 1903–1932*, 608–50.

22. See this volume, "Two Stein Talks."

23. "Portraits and Repetition," in *Gertrude Stein: Writings 1932–1946*, 310.

24. Ibid., 290.

25. "Henry James," in *Gertrude Stein: Writings 1932–1946*, 149.

26. *The Geographical History of America*, in ibid., 385.

27. In the spring of 1932, Alice B. Toklas came upon the manuscript; she had not known about the relationship—Stein had not mentioned it when the two had exchanged "confessions" in the early stages of their own relationship, and it was this that apparently enraged her. In any case, she was sufficiently angry to demand that all appearances of the words "may" and "May" be altered (e.g., to "can" or to the names of other months) in *Stanzas in Meditation*, the work Stein was writing at the time.

28. "Portraits and Repetition," in *Gertrude Stein: Writings 1932–1946*, 289.

29. Freud only began to use this terminology between 1920 and 1923; *The Ego and the Id*, the book in which he first fully discusses it, was published in 1932. See volume 19 of *The Standard Edition of the Complete Works of Sigmund Freud*, ed. and tr. James Strachey (London: Hogarth and the Institute of Psycho-Analysis, 1953).

30. *The Autobiography of Alice B. Toklas*, 690.

31. As Stein puts it, "After having passed her entrance examinations

[to Johns Hopkins] she settled down in Baltimore and went to the medical school. She had a servant named Lena and it is her story that Gertrude Stein afterwards wrote as the first story of the Three Lives" (*The Autobiography of Alice B. Toklas*, 741).

32. Gustave Flaubert, *Three Tales*, tr. A. J. Krailsheimer (New York: Oxford University Press, 1991), 3.

33. *Three Lives*, in *Gertrude Stein: Writings 1903–1932*, 77. Miss Mathilda "has her troubles" with Anna in return, as Stein says at the end of a passage which is interesting in being almost the sole portrait of herself in what one might call "youthful abandon": "And then Miss Mathilda loved to go out on joyous, country tramps when, stretching free and far with cheerful comrades, over rolling hills and cornfields, glorious in the setting sun, and dogwood white and shining underneath the moon and clear stars over head, and brilliant air and tingling blood, it was hard to have to think of Anna's anger at the late return . . . " (*Three Lives*, 78).

34. *Letters of Gustave Flaubert 1857–1880*, ed. and tr. Francis Steegmuller (Cambridge, Mass.: Harvard University Press, 1982), 222.

35. Ibid., 228–30.

36. Ibid., 230.

37. The letter is dated February 6, 1876, and Flaubert began "Un coeur simple" on March 15.

38. Dated May 29, 1876; Sand died ten days later, on June 8; *Letters*, 234.

39. "A Simple Heart" can be viewed as a testimonial to his admiration and enormous affection for George Sand, but I would argue that elements of compassion can be found throughout Flaubert's work. In a letter to Mme Roger des Genettes, written in June 1876, Flaubert gives a synopsis of the story: "The story of *Un coeur simple* is just an account of an obscure life, the life of a poor country girl who is pious but mystical, faithful without fuss, and tender as new bread. She loves in turn a man, her mistress's children, her nephew, an old man she looks after, and then her parrot. When the parrot dies she has it stuffed, and when she

too is dying she confuses the parrot with the Holy Ghost." This description is comical, or could be taken as such, but, he adds, "This is not at all ironical, as you suppose. On the contrary, it is very serious and very sad." Quoted in Maurice Nadeau, *The Greatness of Flaubert*, tr. Barbara Bray (New York: The Library Press, 1972), 252–53.

40. "Portraits and Repetition," in *Gertrude Stein: Writings 1932–1946*, 310.

41. "A Transatlantic Interview 1946," in *A Primer for the Gradual Understanding of Gertrude Stein*, ed. Robert Bartlett Haas (Santa Barbara, Calif.: Black Sparrow Press, 1971), 16–17.

42. "Composition as Explanation," in *Gertrude Stein: Writings 1903–1932*, 520.

43. "A Transatlantic Interview 1946," 15.

44. Cézanne was familiar with the *Letters*. Joachim Gasquet quotes him as saying, "I like very much Flaubert's rigorous forbidding, in his letters, anyone to speak of an art of which he doesn't know the technique." Quoted in Jack Lindsay, *Cézanne: His Life and Art* (London: Evelyn, Adams & Mackay, 1969), 349.

45. *Letters of Gustave Flaubert 1830–1857*, 154.

46. Quoted by Jonathan Culler in *Flaubert: The Uses of Uncertainty* (London: Paul Elek, 1974), 207

47. *Letters of Gustave Flaubert 1830–57*, 159.

48. Ibid., 160.

49. Ibid., 166.

50. "Portraits and Repetition," 294.

51. Lytle Shaw, unpublished letter to the author, 1997.

52. "The Gradual Making of the Making of Americans," in *Gertrude Stein: Writings 1932–1946*, 272.

53. "Plays," *Gertrude Stein: Writings 1932–1946*, 251.

Forms in Alterity:
On Translation

In August of 1998, the Swedish Academy sponsored a four-day Nobel Symposium on "The Translation of Poetry and Poetic Prose" in Stockholm. I was invited to participate as a discussant on the panel devoted to "The Translation of Metrical and/or Rhymed Poetry" and to present a response to a paper by Judith Moffett, a formalist poet and translator of nineteenth-century Swedish narrative verse. As it happened, pressing circumstances made it impossible for Ms. Moffett to get anything more than the title and a brief synopsis of her paper to the discussants until very near the date of the symposium, and as a result I was free, at least to some extent, to expand on the question of forms and formalisms according to my own devices.

Like poetry, translation is fundamentally an epistemological project; translation studies—scrutinizes—the nature of knowing and the way in which any particular "knowing" is circumstantially embedded. Knowing, in this sense, is contextual and always shifting. Between subject and object, as between one language and another, there is a kind of resilient reciprocity, and knowing only exists in the embeddedness of that relationship. That's the reason translators, like poets, have to study perception itself as the medium of knowing something—as apperception, another ambiguity, perception as nonperception, the uncertainty that knowledge in the end becomes.

To encounter uncertainty as a translator seems inevitable. Translation, after all, is about dissolution and reconfiguration. Points of similarity become points of dissimilarity as well. A translation is an encounter and it provokes change: negation as well as affirmation.

But these difficulties are the very ones that philosophical pragmatism, with its emphasis on contingency and on the limits of authority, embraces. One must approach the task of translation without Enlightenment illusions of progress and expectation of ultimate clarification. To place a work in translation (and one could argue that every piece of writing is a work in translation) is to place it in transition and to leave it there, unsettled.

1

Every language has formal properties—morphological and phonological. And these properties have semantic, as well as syntactic, significance; they convey meaning as well as sense.

The art form that foregrounds the formal properties of language is the one we call poetry (an observation, by the way, that is not meant to serve as a definition, since this is certainly not all that poetry entails and since certain prose works do the same). In foregrounding language's formal properties, poetry addresses itself primarily to semantic (rather than syntactic) areas; the work will make sense but it will also call to our attention the fact that not only the sense but the making of that sense are meaningful. It is not just a sentiment, idea, or piece of information that is to be conveyed; it is also the palpable experience, indeed, the *palpability* of experience: its realness and the reality of its being meaningful to us.

But signifying meaning is not uncomplicated; language doesn't gush out into realness—not only because language, even the sum of all languages, being "merely human," is limited but also because the reality that is signified isn't "pure." Every language speaks of reality, but the reality of which it speaks is one that is preconceived, idealized; a worldview, and even, in the broadest sense, an ideology, are in place within every language. Or, to put it more boldly, in every language a world is prefigured.

Linguists (and, often, philosophers) have been observing and observing about this since the beginning of the twentieth century. Writers have been doing so for far longer, and, at least since the Renaissance, the examination of figuration has been an elemental feature of the literary. The first, and the most consistent, object of study has been the figure itself—the trope, and especially metaphor. But though metaphor may be the most readily apparent figure—and the most readily noticed *as* a figure—there are other figures, and other figurings, present at every level of language. The formal properties of language constitute these figures. This is the case even in everyday discourse, but it is poetry that utilizes them to the full, and it does so not only in order to explore the world but also to reveal the character of our understanding of it.

It would be a mistake to restrict the list of the formal properties of poetry to those which are manifest as rhyme and meter, or to posit them as the essence of the poetic. In the last few years, a particular movement in American poetry has argued that modernism's casting off of old poetic forms constituted a casting off of poetry itself. They would locate poetic practice within the observation of old forms and acknowledge as poetry only those works that use traditional meters and stanzaic patterns. The resulting limited notion of what constitutes poetry limits poetry. It makes the poet into an aesthetic functionary rather than a creative thinker, and it relegates poetry to a very minor and marginal role in the arena of thinking, and especially in the discovery of logics, unlikely as well as likely, wild and hallucinatory as well as conventional, that the "formality" of language embodies. To call rhyme and meter the essence of poetry, or even to name them as the primary formal properties of it, is inaccurate; it is also, and perhaps *especially* for a translator, misleading.

Another, very different group of formalists, working in the early decades of the century and hence within the milieu of modernist invention, also undertook the study of poetic formalism. Although the period during which the work of the Russian Formalists, as the group came to be called, was allowed to develop unimpeded was relatively brief (from the founding of Opoyaz, the "Society for the Study of Poetic Language," in 1914 to the time of Lenin's death and Stalin's rise to power in 1924),[1] the Formalist approach continued to have a strong underground existence. Though with caution and sometimes a sense of despair, and using Aesopian methods, the founding group (Viktor Shklovsky, Boris Eikhenbaum, Yurii Tynianov, Roman Jakobson, and Osip Brik being probably the most prominent) continued its work, even while work inspired by it was taken up in the relative safety of provincial outclaves.[2]

Inherently structuralist in approach, the Russian Formalists launched their investigation with the question, What constitutes literariness? What are its distinguishing features? The question is basic and original. As Roman Jakobson put it: "The object of study in literary science is not literature but 'literariness,' that is, what makes a given work a literary work."[3] But the answer is infinite. Literariness is instance-specific. The formal properties of language are relationships within it; they are, in this sense, contextual.

To arrive at this insight, the Russian Formalists offered two premises. The first proposed a distinction between poetic and everyday usages of language. And the second challenged the prominent position given to the *image* in analyses of poetry and the poetic.

To regard language as broadly generic, as a single basic medium, all of whose instances have more or less the same goal, which is to say something about something, is simplistic. Language in its *artistic* usage—*poetic language*—is not primarily expository or informative. Everyday expository language may indeed be a medium of communication about things—but by virtue of that very fact, its meanings lie outside it; they are exterior to it; expository language makes sense by virtue of being referential—it points to *things*; its utterances are *about*. But the *aboutness* of poetry clings also to the interior of the language. Its meanings—its very meaningfulness—reside within the context of poetry's peculiarities; poetry's *devices* (to use a Russian Formalist term), its foregrounded formal properties, form thoughts—they constitute the thinking of thinking.

These devices are diverse. They are not confined to rhyme and meter. Nor are they limited to the invention of imagery, as Russia's conservative academics and Imagist poets had been insisting. The image does indeed have its place in poetry—but that is precisely the Formalists' point. The specific placement, context, implementation, the use to which the given image is put—this is what should be given prominence. All that is formal must also be dynamic.

The distinction between poetic and expository language is key here. Exposition, in its effort to convey information (which will be, by definition, new and unfamiliar to its hearers), must render it in accessible, which is to say familiar, terms. Art, on the other hand, has a different goal. The function of art is to restore palpability to the world which habit and familiarity otherwise obscure; its task is to restore the liveliness to life. Thus it must make the familiar remarkable, noticeable again; it must render the familiar *unfamiliar*.

What is basic to poetry, then, is not the *image* (the unfamiliar rendered in familiar terms), but rather an unusual placement or usage of it. To explain this, Viktor Shklovsky coined the term *ostranenie*—a term which is sometimes translated into English as "enstrangement" or "making strange" but which is more frequently left in the original Russian. *Ostranenie* is an essential literary effect, a defining feature of the poetic (which plays, by the way, a central role in fiction as well as in verse). Poetry is literary not by dint of the mellifluousness of its sounds, the aptness of its imagery, the seamless interweaving of its parts, but through "roughening," dissonances, impediments.[4]

If poetic devices are to achieve their effect—if they are to alert us to the existence of life and give us the experience of experiencing—various and new ones must be created constantly. Poetry must involve more than the filling out of forms—the exercise of formalities; it requires an *invention of form*. The writing of formally designed poetry (and the translation of it into comparable formal designs) should provide difficulties—impediments. And a translator must keep these difficulties in the light and carry them forward so that they are perceptible impediments to new readers, too. To lift poetry out of its difficulties would be to betray it.

2

Recently, at the request of the Russian poet Ilya Kutik, I translated a number of his poems into English. They do make use of metrics and rhyme; they also involve a high degree of wordplay, often of a type that is dependent on etymological associations intrinsic to and solely available in the Russian language, a device that presents even greater difficulties to the translator.

But apart from this recent foray into the world of Ilya Kutik's poetry, my work as a translator has been focused almost exclusively on the writings of another contemporary Russian poet, Arkadii Dragomoshchenko (whom I am tempted to describe, rather, as the "contemporary Russian poet *and theorist*," except that to do so would suggest a division within his poetics, as if his thought were at variance with his writing, his philosophical method separate from the practice of it, and this is not the case; the poetry is, rather, an *experiencing* of the theory). In collaboration with my colleague Elena Balashova and with occasional but critical help from the poet, I have translated two books of Dragomoshchenko's work into American English, *Description* (Sun & Moon Press, 1990) and *Xenia* (Sun & Moon Press, 1994). I'm currently working on a third book, an unbounded prose poem entitled *Phosphor*.

The process of translating these works has had the effect of providing me with something like a life apart from my own, a life led by an other—though that other turns out to be me. It is not that translation involves the assimilation of someone else's "otherness"—and it does not consist in the uncomplicated making of an American poem out of the raw materials of a "foreign" one. Rather, translation catalyzes one's own "otherness," and the otherness of one's own poetry.

This is not the alterity that comes from radical introspection —not the sort of making-oneself-strange (or getting "weirded out") that results from staring for a long time in the mirror, contemplating one's own name, or prolonging scrutiny of the visceral traces of a strong emotion. Rather, it is the otherness of seeming nonexistence—the coming into being of nonbeing, the disappearance into language of ourselves, the world of which we speak, the poem itself.

Speaking of his own translations of my work Arkadii Dragomoshchenko suggests:

> Maybe one could call it meditation, since such activity actually is meditation: no me, no reality, no nonreality, no time, no space. Who knows, probably in our unconscious we always already have strived for such a . . . (I can't call it an emotional state, nor a metaphysical experience) . . . for such an order of "facts," let us say so! Yet, for what reason do I suppose this? To be sure, because of the very nature of writing, inasmuch as our writing reminds me, in the very character of its project, of its ceaseless search for the possibilities of nonexistence, nonbeing, in a word, for a fabulous blank space, the point where every meaning is only its own possibility, bearing in itself the shadow of a future embodiment, which simultaneously means an instant disappearance. Which

is to say, from another perspective, that we have been very diligent explorers of disappearance *per se*, and we have come to know just this, that "art" and "life" in the end become the same.[5]

It is the task of the translator to preserve this disappearance, and she must do so by sustaining the visibility of the poem—or at least of *a* poem, since a too casual reference to "*the* poem" raises the question, "what *is* the poem?" And to answer that we must know where it is—in Russian (let's say) or in English? Can it be in both places? Is "the poem" an immaterial entity that can be in two places at once?

The problems such questions bring to light are intensified in the circumstance of translation, since translation discovers the poem precisely in its odd position, there and there but also then and then—suspended between past and future but not quite in the present.

In part, this experience of being out of the present (or of non-being in the present) is produced by an inverted temporality implicit in the activity of translation. It comes about because the translator "writes" what has already been written; her progress converges with the déjà vu. And in part it comes about because the labors of a translator are Sisyphian, as Dragomoshchenko himself pointed out to me: "You know, those guys playing with the stone and the hill and so forth."

Or perhaps a better comparison might be to Penelope's tapestry, a prolonged interplay between weaving and unweaving, revealing and concealing. The analogy is apt not just with regard to translation; it pertains also to language itself. "Maybe," Dragomoshchenko remarks, the only possible "other" is the words themselves, the writing. . . . This "other," or the work disposed in front of "you," is there by virtue of your desire—it's a disembodied conjecture, an empty apprehension from the start. But of what, exactly? What exactly would one want to find there? What do we expect in this work? Why don't we continue with our own writing? Is there a "crime" that you must resolve like an abstract problem, tracing it, imitating it to feel yourself as a nonself? I think that last is the most probable. I don't think that we have to speak about "culture," the "exchange of ideas," etc. Can't we say that in this activity a poet comes back (as in the "mirror stage") and again and again attempts to penetrate the mystery of his or her being beyond his or her being; it's like the well-known desire to experience your own funeral. . . . OK, night birds fly behind my window. You can continue the windowscape yourself and during this time I will carefully investigate your writing room, your fingers on the keyboard.[6]

In its encounter with the original, translation requires apprehension—apprehension in the sense of "understanding" but also in the sense of "fear." The original serves as a first proposition, a thesis, and the translator responds with a second, dependent proposition—an alternative to it. This in turn becomes embedded in the synthesis we call its translation. But this dialectical process is incomplete; it is a negative dialectics, since between the original and the translation the tension remains unresolved—one in which, contrary to traditional dialectics, the thesis, rather than the synthesis, remains dominant. The original, "the work disposed in front of 'you,'" will always demand another translation. "No matter. Try again. Fail again. Fail better."[7]

3

The failure that we produce is a word, phrase, stanza, or whole poem. Confronting it, we say, "Not this." But saying that provokes a response: "What then?"[8]

The translator in her audacity begins there: she attempts to give *what* substance; she brings *what*—(*what?*)—into view. The astonishing something whose presence *in* our way informs us that we are *on* the way—the impasse (which is not merely a problem of translation but that of literariness itself)—materializes. And it does so through the formal properties of the language; these are its *material properties*, the conditions of its materialization.

Poetry is the art form which makes the fullest possible use of these properties. So it is that rhyme and meter, though they may be audible at all levels of language, may become prominent in some poetry. But rhyme and metric regularity have different meanings in different languages[9] and even at different periods within a given language culture, and currently, in English, the use of end-rhyme and adherence to regular metrics have taken on very specific, and very limited, resonances. Their principal professional[10] practitioners apart from purveyors of commercial doggerel seem to be the cowboy poets and the New Formalists—though I perhaps should add to the list parodists of the latter, such as Charles Bernstein, whose chapbook, *The Nude Formalism*, includes the profuse "Gosh," a poem beginning:

> When fled I found my love defamed in clang
> Of riotous bed she came, along the flues
> I harbored there, scarce chance upon harangue
> By labors grant the fig of latched amuse . . .[11]

Such parodies are meant not only to mock New Formalists strategies but, more broadly, to strike at the reverential and even funereal attitudes with which poetry tends to be approached—as if it were mortal remains—a corpse, in other words; funereal attitudes can only be taken to mean that poetry is dead.

To some extent—though certainly not always—by evoking closure through the use of end-rhyme and stability through the use of regular meter, tradition-bound formalism in English conveys a similar moribund condition. But such is *not* the case, for example, in Russian. Where in English, rhymed verse speaks of the traditions and conventions of poetry, rhyming in Russian speaks of invention and experimentation. An English poem in a regular meter and with its lines hammered into position by end-rhymes tends to have a tiresome though sometimes laughable predictability; at best, it suggests only ancient wisdom, age-old truths. It provides familiarity and, through familiarity, consolation. It gives us respite from the hardships of life. A Russian poem using these same devices, on the other hand, sets off a pyrotechnical display, full of variety and surprise; it conveys a sense of irrepressible vitality and new ideas.

Why this is so is perhaps partially cultural. In Russian culture, poetry is (or, at least, always has been) part of popular culture—it is pervasive in the way that television shows like "Seinfeld" are in the U.S. This means that the Russian poet is addressing knowledgeable readers, an audience of cognoscenti, at least with regard to rhyme and meter. Russians are literate in poetry and in versification, in the way Americans are TV literate, and they want excitement; Russian readers cannot be satisfied with the same old stuff.

But the difference in effect between formal versification at the level of rhyme (and to a lesser extent meter) in Russian and in English is due also to technical features of the two languages. Russian, being a highly inflected language, allows for the fullest possible variations in word order in any given sentence; in sense, though not in tone, word order often makes no difference at all. Each word's grammatical function is clearly indicated within the word form itself, through attached suffixes (and in some cases also prefixes and infixes). Predicates therefore can come long before or long after subjects, adjectives can be widely separated from the nouns they modify. And since the forms of the suffixes are quite limited, being similar whether attached to participles, adjectives, or nouns, rhymes between words with different grammatical functions are possible.

Indeed, they are almost mandatory. A noun-noun rhyme—of the sort to which English is very often limited—sounds to a Russian ear amateurish and boring.

But though the possibilities for rhyming in English are indeed limited both syntactically and lexically, English is not lacking in suppleness or subtlety. The fantastic and inventive nuancing that gets performed through rhyming in Russian, and the highly condensed, carefully contrived, rhythmically compressed dynamic force this conveys, can find their equivalents in English through other devices. Indeed, I would argue that the *meaning* that rhyme and meter may convey in Russian (as well as certain other languages) can be, and usually must be, translated into English through other devices.

Since unless one is translating from an original language rich in cognates with the language of the translation, all sorts of sounds and soundings are going to be changed (and perhaps lost), rhyme being just one of them, one must look at the meanings of the specific sounds themselves in the two languages. And one must look to the myriad other formal (material) proclivities in both languages—one must compare the ways in which the several languages form their forms.

A list of all such properties would be very long. It would have to include the various aural devices that produce, to borrow Ezra Pound's famous formulation, the *melopoeia* through which words are "charged or energized . . . over and above their plain meaning, with some musical property, which directs the bearing or trend of that meaning."[12] Among these are alliteration, stress, repetition, onomatopoeia, homonymy, etc., and where they occur not only the *fact* of them but the specific *effect* of each—its timbral quality, its mimetic purport if any, etc.—must be taken into account. And the list would have to include semantic devices which may or not be aural, such as anaphora, irony, synonymy, antonymy, oxymoron, punning, and at a larger level metaphor and metonymy. It would also include the use of etymological networks—the relationships of words within a given lexicon that have branched from a single root. And it would include the implementation of such chains of association as have been formed through the use of words or phrases within the language culture—as, for example, in colloquialisms that bring about an association in English between birds, hands, and bushes or between stitches, time, and the number nine. It would have to include patterning, audible or inaudible: chiasmus, parallelism, anadiplosis, etc., as well as the larger patterns, metric and otherwise, that are perceptible at the level of the stanza or even of the whole poem.

Just as rhyme-effects may be achieved in English using devices other than rhyme, likewise, in translating American poetry using rhyme-effective devices, a Russian version may use rhyme; Ilya

Kutik's translations of the sequence of poems called "Up Early" by Kit Robinson, for example, are rhymed. The first poem of "Up Early," replete with rhymed meanings though not rhymed words, is semantically condensed and though the meter is not regular, it too is highly condensed—the crisp vernacular ironies add tension and propel the cadences of the poem.

> the tenor of your madness
> leads me to believe
> along lines of force
> the commencement signals an end
> from which to disembark
> on a journey to three islands
> the island of early morning
> the island of the little pipe
> and the island where the rubber meets the road
> as I have been telling you
> and a steady hum reaches our ears
> along lines of force[13]

In Ilya Kutik's own Russian poetry, rhyme achieves effects with strong affinities to those of Robinson's work. Working in partnership with the poet Jean Day to translate some of this work, I have engaged the rhymes in various ways but particularly through use of compact statement, pressured juxtaposition, and interacting polyrhythms.

The third stanza of a poem entitled "The Hyphen" (*Perenos*) is written in couplets with an irregular rhyme scheme that relates the lines within the couplets not to each other but to other lines in other couplets. The couplet form gives the stanza a tightly woven effect; the rhyming unweaves them. Transits—hyphens—crisscross the poem. Our translation seeks to keep them in motion:

tighter than a sheep's horn
more mute than Roland's

this way's
not hell's

coiled spring nor limbos
of the brain nor the cliffs

of purgatory nor
of Norway with Charles'

stretcher (in a niche
of canvas a museum

passage) the Nose
goes but without a breath

past Heine's two grenadiers
who can't overcome the determined

dust and so never—the two—
get *to*

Here we hope that the ominous sounding of the coiled "horn" and what it announces about this "way" remains audible, in the repetition of the *o* and *r* sounds that echo in the words "purgatory" and "nor" and culminate in "Norway." The homonymic rhyme at the end—the most complete form of rhyme possible—was a gift; it made any others redundant.

In a poem related to this one and entitled "Gogol and Hamlet," the poet begins with a dream image of a nose and sees the nostrils as an infinity sign: ∞. The symmetry of the sign and the inhaling-exhaling pattern of air passing through it (in the form of the nostrils) is replicated in the rhyme pattern of the opening six-line stanza: a b c c b a. The lines are very short—the first and longest contains four words, the second three, and the rest two (unless one considers the hyphenated *uznik-matros* ["prisoner-sailor"] of the last line one word). To achieve equal compression, even containment, while replicating the rhyme pattern in English was impossible. Things simply take more space in American English.[14]

Day's and my translation loses another symmetrical element in Kutik's poem, one that parallels the symmetry of the nostrils, the rhyme scheme, and the infinity sign. Two of the four words of the first line are palindromes of each other: *moy son byl nos* (*son*, "dream"; *nos*, "nose"; literally, "my dream was nose"). We had to use the word "nose," the allusion to the history of the runaway nose in Gogol's story being essential to both the sense and meaning, and there's neither a sonic nor a visual palindrome for the word in English. Our translation of the stanza is as follows:

> My dream was a nose
> (I know, Freud:
> the genius of genitals)
> of Genoas, of Italies,
> the noosed sailor
> of a dreamy passage.

A palindrome of sorts does occur here, with "my dream" in the first line recurring as "dreamy" in the last line. In addition, plays on the sonic qualities of the word "nose" are brought into the interior of the lines—a position from which rhyme and near-rhyme can more easily surprise the American reader. The "nose" surfaces audibly in "know," "Genoas," and, more obliquely with respect to sound but quite pertinently with respect to sense, in "noosed," which we derived associatively, as a metonym (in the form of synecdoche) to signify the "prisoner" (the *uznik* of *uznik-matros*).[15]

Metonymy is a particularly important figure in poetry. And the use of metonymy in English-language poetry in particular, and the play on association which metonymy entails, does often provide effects similar to those of rhyme in other languages: a sense of rapidity of thought, unexpected connections between diverse things, a high degree of emotional and intellectual energy, wit, liveliness, etc. And just as the logic of rhymes brings (perhaps even forces) words and hence their associated references (ideas and things) into a poem, thereby determining not just the sound but even the subject matter, so too does the logic of metonymy. Metonymic strategies closely resemble rhyming strategies in inviting language itself to participate in the creation of the poem.

4

The poetry of Arkadii Dragomoshchenko presents formal problems of a different kind from those of Ilya Kutik. Dragomoshchenko's writing is often driven by etymological metonymy—its themes evolving as words of like origin branch out into the poem. His work is devoted to phenomenological experience—acts of perception, attentiveness to the moments and events through which the world makes its appearance—and occasionally he uses diction of varying tonalities to indicate mood and hence point of view.[16]

But the real formalisms of Dragomoshchenko's writing lie in the shape of the sentences—in the syntactic complexities, the prolongation of thought, the observation of the conditionality of perception, the postponement of understanding. His sentences are long; they are interspersed with parenthetical as well as conditional clauses; subject and predicate are divided by worlds of time—something, as I've said, which Russian, being inflected, can achieve more easily than English. One solution—and a customary one for translators of Russian prose, even a prose of not-so-long sentences—is to break the sentences up. But I have not wanted to do so. Their duration, their mindfulness, their difficulty speak precisely and intentionally to their subject matter—perception. A roughly drafted first version of such a sentence—not even really a version but merely an attempt to get all the words down in a form slightly beyond that of the word salad—produced this:

> But the problem is that between a description and a letter of a word lies a territory which the writer cannot overcome: his first phrase in life (I already once attempted its description in a novel, "An Arrangement in Hours and Trees"), written at the age of nine into a notebook in a binding bitterly smelling of carpenter's glue that was slipped to me by my mother somehow in passing, absentmindedly, with a pencil (the pencil was stolen from my father's sanctuary, his desk), and it's not known what was more tormenting, the slightly green cut into squares field of the minute page that lost its borders at that instant when the glance was falling into its milky smoky with fog mirror or the oily in camphor cedar fragrance of pencil point (although, to confess, the *pencil* belonged to my mother and the *notebook* was taken from my father's desk, where it lay near a bronze bear), or possibly it was all completely in reverse—in reality coinciding with imaginary reality—as in cool autumn when for the first time with pleasure one puts on warm clothes in the morning, despite the fact that they're completely unseasonal, while inside, as if something was sick of summer and strives for the frost, cold, like

the light in an operating room, sun, brittle like the first ice
on the lips, fills one with sorrow like a lump in the throat
when you are all attention looking at how the bird splits
against the wall of light like the eye—into two lines, the
horizon line and another, the line of the edge of the shore,
hissing, wandering, like a person with grief-stricken eyes
in a crowd, who reeks of stale urine and habitual feeble-
mindedness, moving his lips, calculating, everything in
everything, repeating with automatic, mechanical passion
everything about everything.[17]

To produce even this rough version of the sentence, to give it a
degree of comprehensibility and to convey its beauty, required
moving clauses and inserting conjunctions as well as definite and
indefinite articles. The more difficult and more important task of
conveying the skepticism of the original, the underlying doubt,
producing not melancholy or nostalgia but rather a sense of life's
cruelty—this has to be attempted through the larger figures
of writing—through image, obviously, but also through the re-
lationships between parts of sentences and between sentences
within a passage. What must be preserved are the disappearances
that are enacted as specific meanings vanish into the time and
space of sentences, the sentences into paragraphs, and the para-
graphs into a book—the momentary experiences of our percep-
tions occurring always just at moment when they too disappear.

Notes

1. Formalism as a discipline and as a critical method was under attack
from 1925 on, and association with it became increasingly dangerous. It

was made illegal on April 23, 1932, when the Central Committee of the Communist Party announced the disbanding and illegality of all professional factions and the organization of the Union of Soviet Writers.

2. Of particular importance is the work of members of the Tartu School, which sustained itself at the University of Tartu in Estonia until very recently. For works available in English, see Jurij Lotman, *The Structure of the Artistic Text*, tr. Gail Lenhoff and Ronald Vroon (Ann Arbor: Michigan Slavic Contributions, 1977); Iurii M. Lotman, Lidiia Ia. Ginsburg, and Boris A. Uspenskii, *The Semiotics of Russian Cultural History*, ed. Alexander D. Nakhimovsky and Alice Stone Nakhimovsky (Ithaca, N.Y.: Cornell University Press, 1985). Various works by the principal members of the Russian Formalist movement have been translated into English, and the best study of the movement, in my opinion, continues to be Viktor Erlich, *Russian Formalism: History, Doctrine* (The Hague: Mouton Publishers, 1980).

3. Quoted in Boris Eikhenbaum, "The Theory of the Formal Method," in *Readings in Russian Poetics*, ed. Ladislav Matejka and Krystyna Pomorska (Ann Arbor: Michigan Slavic Publications, 1978), 8.

4. For the original statement of these ideas, see Viktor Shklovsky, *Theory of Prose*, tr. Benjamin Sher (Elmwood Park, Ill.: Dalkey Archive Press, 1990) and in particular chapter one, "Art as Device."

5. Unpublished letter to the author, March 13, 1995, tr. the author.

6. From undated letter to the author, tr. the author.

7. Samuel Beckett, *Worstward Ho* (New York: Grove Press, 1983), 7.

8. These two phrases constitute the formal as well as thematic basis for Ron Silliman's *Tjanting* (Berkeley: The Figures, 1981).

9. It should be noted, furthermore, that rhyme and meter, strictly speaking, have *no* meaning in some languages.

10. I use the word *professional* to distinguish these groups of poets from the myriad writers of sentimental occasional poetry—e.g., poems written for a grandmother's eightieth birthday or as a medium for participation in certain publicized private occasions, such as the death of Princess Diana, or locations, such as the Vietnam War Memorial.

11. See Charles Bernstein, *The Nude Formalism* (Los Angeles: 20 Pages, 1989).

12. Ezra Pound, "How to Read," in *Literary Essays* (New York: New Directions, 1978).

13. Kit Robinson, *Ice Cubes* (New York: Roof Books, 1987), 7.

14. It is tempting to give this fact a larger cultural interpretation. Americans, at least in the reigning mythology, are addicted to "wide open spaces," to "elbow-room" and unfenced rangeland (nicely expressed in Gene Autry's theme song: "Give me land, lots of land, under starry skies above; don't fence me in"). American culture is terrified of claustrophobia. Faced with an even more immense geographical magnitude, Russian culture, on the other hand, is notoriously agoraphobic.

15. For the original Russian versions of these poems, see Ilya Kutik, *Luk Odisseya* (The Bow of Odysseus) (Saint Petersburg, Russia: Sovietskii Pisatel, 1993). The translations are as yet unpublished.

16. One particularly marked example of this provides an amusing anecdote. In one of the passages in *Description*, four lines appear not in Russian but in the very closely related Ukrainian. When I asked Arkadii to explain the tone that the Ukrainian would convey to a Russian reader, he replied that it would sound like an ancient and more primitive form of the language, giving a more natural, less culture-conditioned view of the world; he suggested that I find an equivalent in English, an old form of the American language, perhaps Hopi or Sioux. See Arkadii Dragomoshchenko, *Description* (Los Angeles: Sun & Moon Press, 1990), 74. The passage was beautifully translated into old English by Steve McCaffery.

17. The passages in translation, based on a manuscript version of the book, are as yet unpublished; for a shorter version of the work in Russian, see Arkadii Dragomoshchenko, *Phosphor* (Saint Petersburg, Russia: Severo-Zapad, 1994).

Barbarism

In the spring of 1995 I spent a month in Australia and New Zealand, visiting various universities to lecture and give readings on a tour very kindly organized on my behalf by Professor Anne Brewster, who was then teaching at Curtin Institute of Technology in Perth, Western Australia. The preceding fall at New College of California I had taught a course called "Romantic Theory and American Event," focusing on both parallels and disjunctures between the (usually European) literary imagining of "America" and writings that came out of actual experience of it (but that were not necessarily more "realistic" as a result). Readings intended to represent the "American event" included William Bartram's *Travels,* James Fenimore Cooper's *The Pioneers,* J. Hector St. John de Crèvecoeur's *Letters from an American Farmer,* Zane Grey's *Riders of the Purple Sage,* several of Ralph Waldo Emerson's essays, a selection from Walt Whitman's *Leaves of Grass,* and Margaret Fuller's "Summer on the Lakes, During 1843." With the exception of *Riders of the Purple Sage,* which was first published in 1912, these were all writings from the first formative period of American cultural history, and I included Zane Grey's "western" because it is a model of the genre, enormously pleasurable to read, and remarkably explicit in its gendering of the landscape and of conflicts within it.

Australia, too, is an Anglo-European invention, but where America had been initially imagined as a lost Paradise, Australia had been imagined (and established) as a sort of prison. I arrived there curious to see how, then, the constructed dystopia of Australian inception might compare with the promised utopia of America's, even while being aware that this paradigm might prove inaccurate and even misleading. Curiously, though I sensed striking similarities between American and Australian cultural characteristics and though I found myself liking Australia enormously, the paradigm in most respects held up. This was particularly true with respect to the natural landscapes of the two nations. Early settlers to America expected a paradise and generally found something close to it—verdant forests, fertile lands, and gold in the hills; early settlers to Australia expected little and found less—expeditions into the center in search of verdancy, fertility, and gold discovered nothing. Unlike Lewis and Clark, who returned from their explorations with tales of wonder, beauty, and promise, Robert O'Hara Burke and William John Wills, Australian explorers sent on an expedition with goals similar to those of Lewis and Clark, returned defeated by a landscape that, at least from their perspective, represented dismal impossibility; they failed in their attempt to cross the continent and died of thirst and starvation soon after they reached their original embarkation site. An immense painting now in the National Gallery of Victoria in Melbourne commemorates the disaster.[1]

Anne Brewster had asked me to give a paper at the Curtin Institute on Language writing, and it was for that occasion that I wrote "Barbarism." It will be clear that I largely avoid definition or description of the movement and the only history I offer is by way of contextualizing its moment in the social politics of the late 1960s and early 1970s. That context may help to explain some (perhaps even many) of the features that distinguish Language writing, but I don't believe that any adequate history of the movement can be written by a single one of its members. I set myself a different task, that of conveying something of the fervor and enthusiasm that informed the movement, with an indication of what was (and still is) at stake. At the risk of expressing a heresy, I subverted Adorno's declaration of the impossibility of poetry "after Auschwitz," recasting it into a declaration of the necessity of doing so. This is not to say that I want to remove poetry (or indeed anything else in contemporary life) out from under the shadow of atrocity; I don't even believe that it is possible to do so. I also don't want to suggest that poetry "after Auschwitz" is, of necessity, poetry about Auschwitz. But we are, as it were, inescapably in the presence of Auschwitz, mindful of what it represents and, equally important, of what it must fail to represent.

It is, sadly, in the context of atrocity that a politics of difficulty must evolve; it is in such a politics (and in the artistic activity that would shape it) that the substance of meaningfulness will be able to appear.

The term "Language writing" (or, more often, "*so-called* 'Language writing'") has been persistently difficult to define. Its manifestations have been many and exceedingly various. This was true from a very early stage in its history and, as the term gets applied to the work of a rapidly growing number of writers, it is increasingly so.

A definition of Language writing must either bind it to a specific social moment (beginning around 1976[2] and lasting approximately a decade and a half) and thus deny that anything being written today can properly be said to be Language writing, or it must represent the phenomenon as essentially boundless, inclusive of the work of several hundred poets of several generations, including poets in China, Russia, the U.K., Germany, New

Zealand, and Australia, as well as the U.S. and Canada. Both scenarios are equally accurate—and both are equally inaccurate.

To historicize the activity, to emphasize the social, cultural context of the period in which we, the original and at the time still unlabelled Language poets, were all first engaged in intense literary activity together, is useful but it runs the risk of monumentalizing the activity, of freezing it into an exclusive community and giving it an aesthetic stasis that it never had and that, if left unchallenged, would in fact do violence to what were its large-scale intentions, those that hoped to exceed the boundaries of mere aesthetics.

At the same time, to subsume under the rubric "Language writing" the enormously varied writings and writing projects of contemporary poets of several generations all over the world, even if it weren't culturally imperialistic or culturally profligate to do so, runs the risk of diffusing and distorting and ultimately of effacing the characterizing qualities of the original work—the ways in which it was supposed to be (and do) good and make sense—and of leveling subsequent work, both that being done now by the original Language poets and that being done by other "Languagey" (as a young poet recently put it) poets today.

The Language movement originated as a utopian undertaking, one which managed to achieve and experience its utopian moment in a flourishing of creative (and often collaborative) activity, and which now, in the hands of its old and young practitioners, has to proceed in a significantly dystopic and even (to speak specifically of the U.S. context) a dangerous (and, for many, cruel) socioeconomic milieu. It is, therefore, an activity which is being required to reexamine itself, very much in the way that left political thinkers throughout the world are having to do. But unlike much left political thought, current Language writing is in fact proving capable of responding to and progressing with new social and cultural experience and expanding its aesthetic and ethical concerns. Of enormous importance here is the impact on contemporary experimental writing that gay and lesbian culture and experience is having, so that even the heterosexual body has been reconstituted into a polyvalent, politicized social medium (and a literally literate one), and one could also point to the similarly large impact that gender and other border studies are having on writing.

The intersecting of aesthetic concerns with ethical concerns is one of the basic characteristics of Language writing, and this fact has very much to do with its origins in a particular historical moment, namely the late 1960s and early 1970s. But, lest the political overshadow the literary nature of Language writing, I should emphasize that we all arrived at that historical moment with volumes of poetry in hand, and particularly Donald Allen's anthology, *The New American Poetry, 1945–1960*, which made the experimental tradition in American poetry, with sources in Pound's imagism and Stein's realism, current. In this tradition (a term which itself, in this context, should not go unquestioned), an impassioned regard for and address to the world is not antithetical to poetry. In experimental poetry, aesthetic discovery is congruent with social discovery. New ways of thinking (new relationships among the components of thought) make new ways of being possible.

In the particular case of Language writing, a number of other points served as premises, some of which I will name in no special order, none being primary in relation to the others:

- a poem is not an isolated autonomous rarified aesthetic object
- a person (the poet) has no irreducible, ahistorical, unmediated, singular, kernel identity
- language is a preeminently social medium
- the structures of language are social structures in which meanings and intentions are already in place
- institutionalized stupidity and entrenched hypocrisy are monstrous and should be attacked
- racism, sexism, and classism are repulsive
- prose is not necessarily not poetry
- theory and practice are not antithetical
- it is not surrealism to compare apples to oranges
- intelligence is romantic

My interest in generating such propositions is itself linked to the context in which Language writing became, so to speak, operative, and it has a great deal to do with the political concerns of the 1960s, when my generation of writers was developing its social consciousness. In the profoundest way, that social consciousness was a response to long-term, far-reaching, and entrenched social and political hypocrisy and capitalist cruelty, and it was encouraged by the three principal political movements of the period—movements which, by failing to intersect adequately, fell short of their goals (or at least so it seems at the moment), but whose agendas, even now, a quarter of a century or more later, have considerable urgency: the civil rights movement, the women's movement, and the antiwar movement.

The pervasive hypocrisy of the 1950s and 1960s was operating in several strategic forms: as outright lies (e.g., "Everybody is happy in Alabama"), as deceptive metaphors (as in that depicting Vietnam as an upended domino liable to fall to Communism and thereby knock its neighboring upended domino nations over to Communism too, in a chain reaction whose end result would be flat out global Communism), and, finally, in the more subtle form of a complete failure to examine political language and indeed any language at all, thus establishing the pretense that language is "natural"—that we speak this way because there is no other way to speak, because speaking so accords with natural reality, because God and the angels speak this way, and so too would the little birds in the forest if they could speak at all. To counter such hypocritical strategies (which are no less than forms of fraud) requires now as it did then a comprehensive examination of language, one which challenges its "naturalness," discloses the world view (and ideology) secreted not only in our vocabulary but at every linguistic level including the ways in which sentences are put together, and explores new ways of thinking by putting language (and hence perception) together in new ways.

My generation, shocked into awareness of atrocity by the Vietnam War, felt the urgency of seeing through the fraud endemic to the political culture of the times, and we believed—or perhaps at the time merely intuited—that poetry was the most available and best-prepared medium for undertaking the urgently required analysis and critique. Poetry provided the means for reopening the question of language; it was through poetry that a series of reinventions of language could be initiated. We had at our disposal the medium that was perfectly suited for investigating the overt and covert, buried and transcendent, material and metaphysical logics which *are* language and which so powerfully influence human thought and experience. And here, of course, both

Marxist and feminist theory were (and remain) of enormous importance, since they each provide a critique both of power and of meaning (and of the powers instantiated in the various notions of "meaning").

The emphasis on language in our writing can be explained by our sense of the urgency of the need to address and, if possible, to redress social fraud, but I think there is another source to it as well. Prominent characteristics of Language writing can, I believe, be attributed to its involvement (directly or indirectly) with certain post-Holocaust themes, very much in the way post-structuralist and so-called postmodern theory (as in the writings of Levinas, Lyotard, Derrida, Kristeva, Deleuze and Guattari, Blanchot, etc.) is, with its realization, perhaps first noted by Walter Benjamin, that fraud produces atrocity.

Theodor Adorno's often cited pronouncement that "To write poetry after Auschwitz is an act of barbarism" has to be taken as true in two ways.[3] It is true, first, because what happened at "Auschwitz" (taken both literally and metonymically, standing for itself, for the other death camps, and also for what has occurred at numerous other atrocity sites throughout this century) is (and must remain) incomprehensible (literally unthinkable) and therefore, in the most vicious way, "meaningless"—that is, it is not possible to make or discover meaning anywhere in the context of Auschwitz and moreover, ever since Auschwitz (i.e., henceforth in human history) everything exists in that context. All possibilities for meaning have been suspended or crushed.

But Adorno's statement can be interpreted in another sense, not as a condemnation of the attempt "after Auschwitz" to write poetry but, on the contrary, as a challenge and behest to do so. The word "barbarism," as it comes to us from the Greek *barbaros*, means "foreign"—that is, "not speaking the same language" (*barbaros* being an onomatopoeic imitation of babbling)—and such is precisely the task of poetry: *not to speak the same language as Auschwitz*. Poetry after Auschwitz must indeed be barbarian; it must be foreign to the cultures that produce atrocities. As a result, the poet must assume a barbarian position, taking a creative, analytic, and often oppositional stance, occupying (and being occupied by) foreignness—by the barbarism of strangeness.[4]

Poetry at this time, I believe, has the capacity and perhaps the obligation to enter those specific zones known as borders, since borders are by definition addressed to foreignness, and in a complex sense, best captured in another Greek word, *xenos*. It, too, means "stranger" or "foreigner," but in a sense that complicates the notion as we find it in *barbaros*. The *xenos* figure is one of contradiction and confluence. The stranger it names is both guest and host, two English terms that are both derived from the single Greek term and are thus etymologically bound in affinity. The guest/host relationship is one of identity as much as it is of reciprocity. Just as a visitor may be foreign to a local, so the local will be foreign to the visitor; the guest coexists as a host, the host as a guest.

The guest/host relationship comes into existence solely in and as an occurrence, that of their meeting, their encounter.[5] The host is no host until she has met her guest, the guest is no guest until she meets her host. Every encounter produces, even if for only the flash of an instant, a *xenia*—the occurrence of coexistence which is also an occurrence of strangeness or foreignness. It is a strange occurrence that, nonetheless, happens constantly; we have no other experience of living than through encounters. We have no other use for language than to have them.

In using the metaphor of a border, I do not mean to suggest that poetry relegate itself to the margins. The border is not an edge along the fringe of society and experience but rather their very middle—their between; it names the condition of doubt and encounter which being foreign to a situation (which may be life itself) provokes—a condition which is simultaneously an impasse and a passage, limbo and transit zone, with checkpoints and bureaus of exchange, a meeting place and a realm of confusion.

Like a dream landscape, the border landscape is unstable and perpetually incomplete. It is a landscape of discontinuities, incongruities, displacements, dispossession. The border is occupied by ever-shifting images, involving objects and events constantly in need of redefinition and even literal renaming, and viewed against a constantly changing background.

The analogy to the dream landscape is apt in another respect; the border experience is interior to the psyche as well as being external and social. That is, dreams can be taken as examples of interior (or interiorized) border encounters, or as experiences on the border that arise within the unconscious, either harboring (if Freud is correct) all that is censored and repressed, or (if contemporary neuropsychologists are correct) doing epistemological work—processing information, comparing experiences, taking new data into account, making sense. In either case, dreams serve as an active, even busy, border between the sleeping person and that same person awake. They are, in this sense, not a place but a dynamic—and it is this dynamic quality that needs to be emphasized, since it helps to locate the border in the middle of things; it highlights the *centrality* of the border.

Indeed, one can say that no experience is possible that is not also an experience of the border; it is the milieu of experience. It provides us simultaneously with awareness of limit and of limit-lessness. As George Oppen said of poetry, "it is an instance of 'being in the world'" at "the limits of judgment, the limits of [. . .] reason."[6]

"It takes a very normal person to create a new picture."[7] The figure I am suggesting, that of the poet as barbarian, is not intended as a romantic conceit. I don't mean to revivify or give renewed credence to the self-indulgent pampered pompous hypersensitive anti-intellectual prima donna of the romantic stereotype. The barbarian is a "normal person" who creates "a new picture"—the poet *qua* poet. This poet-barbarian, Virgil-like figure of my extended metaphor is a rigorously attentive observer and active participant in the interminable newness of poetic language, a language which generates an array of logics capable, in turn, of generating and responding to encounters and experience. It is not a marginal language but an agent (and provocateur) of palpability and a medium of proliferating connections. It is the logics of these new connections that provide poetry with its enormous mobility and its transformative strategies.

As poets coming together in the middle of the 1970s through what I've called in the past a "motivated coincidence," we had a sense of the encompassing possibilities of art as thought. We were involved in what, in retrospect, I would call a poetry of encounter, and the connections we sought to make had aesthetic power and philosophical import, but they were also seen as political. This manifested itself in several ways: through the identification of the poem as a social text, through the constituting of a social "scene" that could serve as a context for poetry, and through the forging of a close relationship in the work between theory and practice. I am describing a poetry that has consistently implicated theory in its practices, since it is charged with motives that do not culminate in the aesthetic alone. From its inception, the Language scene socialized the poem in particular ways, and above all by constituting itself *as* a "scene"—by proposing a public, social space for the evolution of the reading and writing of work and by regarding it definitively as a political space.

To present the poem as social and the social as political effected, I think, something of a paradigm shift; it changed the ways in which our poetry (if not poetry in general) is interpreted by changing the notion of what literature itself is—both what and how it means.

From the outset, Language poetry called into question several premises which prior definitions of literature assumed and which had produced the narrow world view represented by what was then the canon. A significant component of this canonized world view, of course, was the romantic, unitary, expressive self, the "I" of the lyric poem, and several factors in Language writing challenged and perhaps by now have, at least in certain quarters, undermined the viability of this simpleminded model of subjectivity and authority.

By placing the emphasis on language (which precedes the individual and is shared by all its speakers), poetry positioned itself in a linguistic frame and as a site of "not-I." *Je est un autre.*

Meanwhile, by emphasizing its writtenness, its literariness, the poem calls attention to the complexity of its constructedness; it establishes poetry as a site that both individual intentionality and social history have undertaken to construct and in a relationship that is often uneasy. And by representing the poet as a man or woman in and of a politically demanding social space, the poem sets up new criteria by which it can be evaluated. Whereas the poetry of the self (the mainstream poem, produced in a workshop for a teacher or submitted to the editor for acceptance or rejection) assumes that there is a standard of judgment and hands itself up to be judged ("what you've done is good"), a poetry politicized in the ways I've described will engage the poet in her affiliations—her attachments to others and through which she, too, is other.

In the process, ideas and, perhaps more startlingly, emotions are freed from the limits of the singular "I," allowing for a poetry of complex and densely layered affect as well as intelligence. This contributes to the notorious "difficulty," "obscurity," "opacity," or "impenetrability" that is sometimes ascribed to Language and post-Language writing (as to much of the modernist writing that it follows, that of Gertrude Stein and the Objectivists in particular).

But the fact of modern poetry's being "hard to read" can be extolled as a virtue in and of itself on various grounds. In writing that is propelled by sonic associations, for example, or what one might call musicality, the result may, paradoxically, be a form of realism, giving the poem's language material reality, palpability, presence, and worldliness. Such difficulty, even when it doesn't produce conventional sense, may be engaging in its own right; or, from another point of view, it may be disengaging. It may be emblematic of resistance, elaborating a rejection and even a defiance of the production of totalizing and normalizing meanings; in resisting dogmatism, it may create spaces for ambiguity, provisionality, and difference. It may function as a distancing device (the famous "alienation effect" that is central to Brechtian realism) intended to encourage the reader to think for herself rather than submit to manipulation by the author, or it may serve to roughen the surface of the work, so that it catches one's attention, impedes one's reading, wakes one up to reality.[8]

Difficulty and its corollary effects may produce work that is not *about* the world but is *in* it. The difficulty of the work, then, does not constitute an intransigence; on the contrary, it is the material manifestation of the work's mutability, its openness, not just a form but, more importantly, a forming, a manifestation of what the Objectivists would have termed its "sincerity"—the ethical principle by which the poet tests words against the actuality of the world, the articulation of our status as presences in common (and only in common) with other presences in the world.[9] It affirms, to quote George Oppen,

> the existence of things,
> An unmanageable pantheon
>
> . . . .
>
> And the pure joy
> Of the mineral fact
>
> Tho it is impenetrable
> As the world, if it is matter,
>
> Is impenetrable.[10]

In his 1969 interview with Oppen, L. S. Dembo cites this passage and asks Oppen about "the world, if it is matter." Oppen replies:

> Ultimately, it's impenetrable. At any given time the explanation of something will be the name of something unknown. We have a kind of feeling—I described doubts about it— but we have a kind of feeling that the absolutely unitary is somehow absolute, that, at any rate, it really exists. It's been

the feeling always that that which is absolutely single really does exist—the atom, for example. That particle of matter, when you get to it, is absolutely impenetrable, absolutely inexplicable. If it's not, we'll call it something else which is inexplicable.[11]

One can understand, in other words, that something exists as a singularity, but one can't explain how it came about that that particular thing—that singularity as itself—against all probability—came into existence.

As Peter Nicholls points out, for Oppen "the point was that a poetics founded on the (philosophically) simple recognition of actuality—'That it is'—would ultimately concern itself with an equally 'simple' and non-agonistic perception of social relationships. Viewed in these terms, poetry might offer a way of acknowledging the world and others without seeking to reduce them to objects of knowledge."[12] It refuses, either through appropriation ("you are like me") or through empathy ("I am like you") to deny or suppress the otherness of others. Such a "poetics of 'encounter,'" to use Nicholls's phrase, has an ethical dimension, since it is established within "relationships expressing proximity rather than contemplative or legislative distance."[13]

Nicholls, here, is reading Oppen through the work of Emmanuel Levinas, whose notion of "sincerity" has significant resonances with that offered by Louis Zukofsky and, following him, by Oppen. Language, employed as an instrument of sincerity, puts one not only in relation but in a relation that involves "exposure to the claims of others. . . . For, 'sincerity' is not so much a true account of one's inner feelings . . . , as an acceptance of what *exceeds* the self."[14]

Such excess is embedded in the poetic device we call "difficulty"; excess creates difficulty even as it erupts from it—in unassimilable surpluses of meaning, in impossible games, in rage, in disruptive and disordering pleasure, in laughter. Experience of these is inevitable for the figure of encounter I am calling *xenos*— the inquirer, dislodged and dislodging, in a transitive rather than intransitive poetry,

> With whistling in the left ear
> And symptoms of melancholy—gloomy dreams, twitching,
>   jerking, itching, and swift changes of mood
> With the capacity to transform an inaccessible object into
>   something we long voluptuously to embrace
> And ourselves into an unquiet subject—at last! baffled! [15]

Notes

1. The painting, "The Arrival of Burke, Wills and King at the Deserted Camp at Cooper's Creek" by Sir John Longstaff, is also known as "The Dig Tree," after the central figure in the painting, an immense gum tree (eucalyptus), which is still standing. Burke, Wills, and King reached the camp at Cooper's Creek just hours after their support team, many of whose members had died during the four-month wait for the explorers, had abandoned it. They had buried supplies for the explorers and had carved their location on the gum tree: "DIG 3FT NW." In the painting, the emaciated body of Burke lies at the foot of the tree; Wills, barefoot and in tatters and slumping in exhaustion, is seated beside him; and King, who had been cordial to the Aborigines they met on their journey and had received gifts of food and water from them in return, is standing close beside the tree, gazing at the scene, in which the remains of their apparently frustrated attempts to find the supplies, are visible. I am grateful to Kate Fagan, who sent me a reproduction of the painting

along with detailed information about it and about the history of the expedition.

2. The publication of *This* magazine, edited through its first issues by Barrett Watten and Bob Grenier and then by Watten alone, began in 1973, and by 1976, when a scene involving a number of the poets appearing in *This* began to emerge, six issues had already appeared. The body of work collected in those six issues, along with work appearing in Ron Silliman's *tottel's*, Bob Perelman's *Hills*, Barbara Baracks's *Big Deal*, and a few other journals, provided the substance around which discussion and, ultimately, a "movement" could develop.

3. The comment occurs in various places and, depending on the translation, in various phrasings. I first encountered it in the phrasing I have here in an unattributed comment on the writings of Edmond Jabès. It appears notably at the end of Adorno's essay, "Cultural Criticism and Society," and where the English translation is slightly different: "To write poetry after Auschwitz is barbaric." See Theodor Adorno, *Prisms* (Cambridge, Mass.: The MIT Press, 1983), 34. My thanks to John Rapko and to Charles Bernstein for help in locating this occurrence of Adorno's comment. Adorno first issued his famous remark in 1951. By the mid-sixties, in the wake of his consideration of Paul Celan's poetry and his recognition of it as a mark of the indelibility of the Holocaust, he changed his position: "Perennial suffering has as much right to expression as a tortured man has to scream; hence it may have been wrong to say that after Auschwitz you could no longer write poems" (*Negative Dialectics*, E. B. Ashton [New York: Seabury Press, 1973], 362). My thanks to Andrew Joron for bringing this passage to my attention.

4. Recourse to a similar notion of barbarism appears in the anti-bourgeois avant-garde literary discourse of the first part of the century too. Thus, elaborating on a quotation cited in a 1911 lecture by André Gide ("The time of sweetness and dilettantism is over. What we need now, are barbarians."), the critic Marcel Raymond wrote: "Experience becomes a sense of certainty that penetrates one's whole being and stirs one like a revelation; a state of euphoria that seems to give the world to

man and persuades him that he 'possesses' it. But it is accessible only to those who free themselves from habitual vision, from utilitarian convention. . . . To become a barbarian by means of patient and progressive de-intellectualization is, first of all, to receive sensations and to leave them a certain amount of free play, not to place them in a logical frame-work and not to attribute them to the objects which produced them; it is a method of detaching oneself from an inherited civilized form in order to rediscover a greater plasticity and expose oneself to the imprint of things." And, a few years later, Laura Riding said of Gertrude Stein's *Tender Buttons:* "By combining the functions of critic and poet and taking everything around her very literally . . . she has done what every one else has been ashamed to do. . . . Does no one but Miss Stein realize that to be abstract, mathematical, thematic, anti-Hellenic, anti-Renaissancist, anti-romantic, we must be barbaric?" (Both citations appear in John Malcolm Brinnin, *The Third Rose,* 160–61; no source is given for either.)

5. In Russian the word for "occurrence," *sobytie,* captures the dynamic character of this encounter. The root of the word is *bytie,* being; the prefix, *so,* comes from the preposition *s,* with, and is equivalent to the English *co-; sobytie,* occurrence, then is "being with," a "with-being" or "co-existence."

6. *The Selected Letters of George Oppen,* ed. Rachel Blau DuPlessis (Durham, N.C.: Duke University Press, 1990), 177.

7. Lyn Hejinian, "The Guard," in *The Cold of Poetry* (Los Angeles: Sun & Moon Press, 1994), 20.

8. It should be noted, also, that difficulty sometimes and unfortunately is a mere surface effect, utilized as a marker of "the poetic," the canonical sign of "the innovative."

9. This is what Louis Zukofsky meant with his term "sincerity" and what George Oppen called "a test of truth": "It is the business of the poet / 'To suffer the things of the world / And to speak them and himself out'" ("The Building of the Skyscraper" in George Oppen, *Collected Poems* [New York: New Directions, 1975], 131). Oppen shares this view of language (and particularly of poetic language) with Heidegger: "Say-

ing is showing. In everything that speaks to us, in everything that touches us by being spoken and spoken about, in everything that gives itself to us in speaking, or waits for us unspoken, but also in the speaking that we do *ourselves*, there prevails Showing which causes to appear what is present, and to fade from appearance what is absent. Saying is in no way the linguistic expression added to the phenomena after they have appeared—rather, all radiant appearance and all fading away is grounded in the showing Saying. Saying sets all present beings free into their given presence, and brings what is absent into their absence. Saying pervades and structures the openness of that clearing which every appearance must seek out and every disappearance must leave behind, and in which every present or absent being must show, say, announce itself" (Martin Heidegger, *On the Way to Language*, tr. Peter D. Hertz [New York: Harper & Row, 1971], 126). For Oppen, truth consists in bringing what is present into appearance and what is absent into absence, and because this occurs in and as speech (saying), "sincerity" is synonymous with truth.

10. George Oppen, "Of Being Numerous," in *Collected Poems* (New York: New Directions, 1975), 148.

11. In L. S. Dembo, "The 'Objectivist' Poets: Four Interviews," *Contemporary Literature* 10 (Spring 1969): 163.

12. Peter Nicholls, "Of Being Ethical: Reflections on George Oppen," in *Journal of American Studies* 31 (1997): 2, 160.

13. Ibid., 168.

14. Ibid., 168.

15. Lyn Hejinian, *A Border Comedy*, book six.

Reason

Reason constitutes both the method and the object of Western philosophical investigations. It is philosophy's fundamental concern. But as a foundation it is everywhere fissured; reason is a concept that constantly bifurcates.

As a method, reason is analytic. It asks why things are as they are, but it also asks if and why they must and should be so; it identifies determining principles or events (both perfect and efficient or proximate causes) and it makes choices (determining on final causes). It is this latter area that is of particular interest to me in relation to poetics, which I see as a simultaneously descriptive and ethical realm. Among the principal tasks of a poetics is to ask how reason reasons its reasons—how it discovers, identifies, and acts on them.

Even in the earliest instances of philosophical work, those of the pre-Socratics, the quest to identify a first principle and a primal stuff and thus to discover an explanation of why and how things came into being and are as they are inevitably provoked ethical questions. To ask for the reason things come into being is itself a double question, since it poses both a question as to practical or mechanical causes and a question as to "rightness." In ad-

337

dition, to ask what the world is like is to ask how we should live in it. Or to quote George Oppen's far more interesting formulation, "We are committed to the problem we found, the problem we were born into—." [1]

Despite the emphasis on context that is a basic theme of the essay, I am not arguing that all spheres of worldly experience are subject identically to "the butterfly effect"—to the alteration of everything by anything. And, even more importantly, I am not arguing that everything that affects the world around us is equivalent to a butterfly lighting on a yarrow. "The butterfly effect" and "the bomb effect" are incommensurable not only with regard to scale but also in substance. Both are produced by occurrences, but the occurrences are themselves very different. The lighting of a butterfly is inevitable; butterflies must light. But the dropping of a bomb occurs at the end of a long sequence of decisive undertakings consciously intended by a large number of people—those who ordered the making of the bomb, those who designed and built it, those who chose the target, those who carried it to the target.

The term *theory* appears twice in the essay as a synonym for thought, but I mean thought of a particular kind—thought that is rigorously speculative, ongoing, and, by virtue of looking out toward the world as well as self-critically inward, it resists adherence to first principles, immutable truths, authoritarian formulations. Theory, as I understand it, is always everywhere mutable. It is the interminable process by which we are engaged with the changing world around us and made ready for the changes it requires in and from us. A theory, then, is not a theorem, a stating of the case, "an idea accepted or proposed as a demonstrable truth," a "stencil." [2] Theorizing is, in fact, the very opposite of theorem-stating. It is a manner of vulnerable, inquisitive, worldly living, and it is one very closely bound to the poetic process.

This essay was written in response to an invitation from Emilie Clark and Lytle Shaw to contribute to the first issue of their journal, *Shark,* which was devoted to "Prepoetics."[3] I first presented the essay, in a slightly different version, in March 1998 at the Conference on Postmodern Poetry organized at the University of Plymouth (Exmouth, England) by Tony Lopez and Philip Terry.

1

Along comes something—*launched in context.*

How do we understand this boundary?

Let's begin by posing it as a dilemma.

The term comes from the Greek, *dilemmatos*, and means "involving two assumptions," and so we begin by proposing that the boundary is not an edge but a conjunction—that the dilemma bears the *meaning* of conjunction: encounter, possible confusion, alteration exerted through reciprocal influence, etc.—the kind of situation that is typical, I might add, along borders between nations, between speakers of different languages, between neighboring ecosystems, etc.

But perhaps my phrase presents more than a dilemma, perhaps it's a dilemma to excess, since the boundary or border of which I want to speak and the problem of understanding it entail multiple sets of paired assumptions. I could, alternatively, use the term *aporia*, but to do so (especially since the publication of his book, *Aporias*) would be to invoke Derrida more definitively than I'm willing to do, lest it predetermine the outcome of my reasoning. But, of course, the *dilemma* in and of itself (the dilemma which the phrase "in and of itself" so aptly describes) is very much a feature of the poststructuralist postmodernist deconstructionist condition that we—or that I, as a person and writer—experience as exerting enormous pressure on our social and aesthetic situation—which is to say, on our poetics—a pressure which makes palpable the demand that we have a poetics.

It makes that poetics itself a dilemma—or it has *dilemma* (as a border under pressure of doubt, as a border in question) as one of its central features. *Dilemma*, in this sense, constitutes that part of a poetics which we could call its *prepoetics*—a prepoetics functioning not as a condition either logically or chronologically prior to the formulation of a poetics but as a condition necessary and simultaneous to it—a current running through it.

If it is a responsible prepoetics—that is, one that vigorously questions assumptions, including, or especially, its own—this current includes, among other things, swarms of contradiction and ambivalence. Perhaps these are inevitable effects of the famous (or notorious) postmodern (or postpostmodern) negativity to which so much thought has been given—thought directed toward the unthinkable and reflecting an obsession with the unknown, the meaningless, the unspeakable, the unapproachable, the unbearable, the impasse, or, as here, the dilemma—leaving poetics (and poetry) to be practiced in a gap of meaning (a gap produced originally, I would add, by the atrocities of war and social and economic injustice), a gap which extends into the current which I'm calling prepoetics but which one could also call *reason*.

Reason itself operates in the border between concepts—and again between several interdependent pairs of concepts. *Reason* may even constitute such a border zone. The term names simultaneously two lines of causation, that of the *reason for* or efficient cause (one thing happened and that's the reason the other thing happened) and that of the *reason to* or final cause or *telos* (another thing needs to happen and that's the reason the first thing was made to happen). These reasons are often related: "because I love you I do this to make you happy," etc. But there are situations in which the two lines of causation are completely unconnected, of which the most readily described motivate the events that we dream. Say I happen one rainy evening to watch a documentary about rodeo cowboys and bronc-busting on the television. There are lots of scenes of horses throwing themselves and cowboys into the air, and scenes of horses and, more often, cowboys falling to the ground. That night I dream that I am riding horseback through a dry arroyo when a sudden torrential rainstorm occurs. Within seconds a flash flood is sweeping down the arroyo—I am knocked from the horse and fall to the ground and the horse falls on top of me. I'm being crushed, and I wake to discover that the pillow has fallen on my face.

Here we have two narratives, a dream narrative and a waking life narrative. The denouement of the dream narrative (dream event B, being crushed by a horse) is, in the dream, a reasonable outcome of my riding a horse through an arroyo and encountering a flash flood (dream event A). In waking life, this same outcome is a reasonable response to having a heavy pillow fall on my head (waking reality event X). The same experience, then, or sensation of an experience, has two unconnected starting points, A and X, initiating two distinct lines of causation.[4]

2

Along comes something—launched in context.

It is almost automatic to us to assume that this *something* (on the one hand) and *we* (on the other) exist independently—that *something* was independently elsewhere (out of sight and mind) prior to coming into the zone in which *we* perceive it and which we, at the moment of this perceptual encounter, designate as context. Furthermore, it is at the moment that we perceive this something that we ourselves come into that context—into our coinciding (by chance?) with something. The context, in other words, is the medium of our encounter, the ground of our becoming (i.e., happening to be) present at the same place at the same time. By this reasoning, one would also have to say that context too is launched—or at least that it comes into existence *qua* context when something is launched in such a way as to become perceptible to us and thereby to involve us—whomever we are—strangers (even if, perhaps, only momentarily strangers) to each other previously and now inseparable components of the experience.

As strangers (foreigners), it is hard for us to find the "right words" (themselves simultaneously demanding context and serving as it) for what we experience in that perception and involvement.

Usually comparisons are the first things foreigners make. "The dark castle on the hill is like a cormorant on a rock stretching its crooked wings in the sun" or "The pink wet light in Saint Petersburg on a winter day is like a summer San Francisco fog," etc. Such comparisons, reaching out of the present situation to another, previously experienced, recollected one, may appear to constitute the "making of a context" for the current context, but a context made in such a way is a transported one, acquired by way of metaphor. And such metaphors, cast in the form of similes and intended to smooth over differences, deny incipience, and to the degree that they succeed, they thereby forestall the acquisition of history. But the phrase or sentence with which I've become obsessed, "Along comes something—launched in context," announces a moment of incipience; one could even say that it is itself, as a phrase or utterance, a moment of incipience—an appearing, a being born—coming into what Hannah Arendt calls "the condition of natality,"[5] the condition we all have in common.

Something which wasn't here before is here now; it appears and it appeared to us, and it is acknowledged by the sensation *this is happening*. And as such, as a moment of incipience or point of natality, it constitutes, in a very particular and crucial sense, an *action*—since (to continue Hannah Arendt's argument) it is "engaged in founding and preserving" something, which "creates the condition for remembrance, that is, for history" and it thereby undertakes "the task to provide and preserve the world for, to foresee and reckon with, the constant influx of newcomers who are born into the world as strangers." This "new beginning . . . can make itself felt in the world . . . because [it] possesses the capacity of [itself] beginning something anew."[6]

3

To value the new was, of course, a widely held and explicit tenet of modernist aesthetics, as in Pound's often cited commandment, "Make it new." Viktor Shklovsky's more thoughtful, more self-reflexive, and better-analyzed aphorism, "In order to restore to us the perception of life, to make a stone stony, there exists that which we call art"[7] takes the behest further, making newness not an end in itself but a strategy employed for the sake of the enhancement of experience—and as an affirmation of life. "Only the creation of new forms of art can restore to man sensation of the world, can resurrect things and kill pessimism."[8] Shklovsky goes on, of course, to elaborate a now-familiar set of devices intended to restore palpability to things—retardation, roughening, etc.—that are major elements (and, in ways that can be taken as troubling, even the stock in trade) of so-called innovative poetry to this day (almost a century later). Contemporary poets—myself among them—have embraced this project. Comments variously repeating or attempting to extend Shklovsky's proposition appear throughout my teaching notebooks:

> Language is one of the principal forms our curiosity takes.
>
> The language of poetry is a language of inquiry.
>
> Poetry takes as its premise that language (all language) is a medium for experiencing experience. It provides us with the consciousness of consciousness.
>
> To experience is to go through or over the limit (the word comes from the Greek *peras* [term, limit]); or, to experience is to go beyond where one is, which is to say to be beyond where one was (re. the prepositional form, *peran* [beyond]).
>
> Imagine saying that at one stage of life, one's artistic goal is to provide experience (new or revivified, restored to palpability) and at another (later) it is to provide the joy of that experience.
>
> After how much experience can one feel free of the fear that one hasn't lived (the fear of an unlived life)?

Etc.

And to a degree what I am attempting to say here is also an extension of the poetics implied in Shklovsky's aphorism.

It is the task of poetry to produce the phrase *this is happening* and thereby to provoke the sensation that corresponds to it—a sensation of newness, yes, and of renewedness—an experience of the revitalization of things in the world, an acknowledgment of the liveliness of the world, the restoration of the *experience* of our experience—a sense of living our life. But I want to argue that to produce such a sensation is not necessarily to produce knowledge nor even a unit of cognition but rather to discover context and, therein, reason.

Admittedly several obvious (and boringly persistent) problems arise when *experience* is assigned primacy of place in an aesthetics and its accompanying discourse of value—when it is given the status of final cause and taken as an undisputed good. First, giving preeminence to experience would seem to demand what gets termed "authenticity."

Happily, one can debunk this on the same basis that one can debunk a second problem, which I could describe as antiintellectual and ultimately philistine. In assuming a positive value to experience for its own sake, and in advocating thereby an art which heightens perceptibility, one risks appearing to privilege sensation over cogitation, to promote immediacy and disdain critique. There is a danger that one implies that the questioning of experience may serve to distance and thereby diminish at least aspects of it, and that this is antithetical to "real" artistic practice. This is the basis of art's supposed hostility to criticism, theory (thought), and occasional hostility even to examination of its own history. Or, to put it another way, on these grounds, the philistine romantic attempts to justify his or her rejection of context.

And here is the basis for a dismissal of these two related problems. One cannot meaningfully say "this is happening" *out* of context. At the very moment of uttering the phrase, "natality" occurs. And from that moment of incipience, which occurs with the recognition of the experience of and presented by the phrase *along comes something—launched in context* through the phrase *this is happening*, we are *in* context, which is to say, in thought (in theory and with critique) and in history.

There is no context without thought and history. They exist through reciprocation of their reason. Otherwise there is no sensation, no experience, no consciousness of living. And, to quote Tolstoi just as Shklovsky does: "If the complex life of many people takes place entirely on the level of the unconscious, then it's as if this life had never been."[9]

4

As I have said, the recognition acknowledged and sensation produced by the phrase (*along comes something—launched in context*) produces another phrase of recognition and sensation, *this is happening*. It is a phrase with a referent (*something—launched in context*), and with an array of particular and important senses.[10] First among them is the implicit but definitive sense that "this is real"—although, paradoxically, that part of its context which we would term its referent is not necessarily verifiable. For example, were I to claim now to be writing/have written this under conditions of enormous duress or, alternatively, in the spirit of just clowning around, it would be verifiable that I said so but not that I did so. And yet, at least in my imagination as I pictured writing under duress and clowning, I did do so. The reality of the imagined also needs to be affirmed. A second sense accrues to the first one. To the affirmation that "this is real" is added, through the act of recognition and acknowledgment, a sense of one's own reality—and this realization—of a co-reality consisting of correlation and coexistence —occurs not through the Cartesian logical operation (*cogito ergo sum*) but by virtue of our context—a shared context, although it is important to note that it is not the basis or substance of any determinate commonality, and it is one about which there is something more to be said.

To some extent, I have let the term *history* stand as a near synonym to the term *context*. This is something which, depending on how I would define *history*, might prove to have some legitimacy, but it shouldn't, if it is to be a central element in the constituting of a poetics, go unexamined. But if one sees *history* as, at the very least, a set of relations—or, to be more precise, of active correlations (co-relations)—then that seems not too far from a workable characterization of the *context* of something. And it not only allows one to situate that *something* within history as a descriptive and explanatory account of what has happened, but it also gives *something* a history with a future. Context is a past with a future. That is the sense of the phrase *this is happening*. That is what gives us a sense of *reason*.

5

There are things
We live among 'and to see them
Is to know ourselves'.

So begins George Oppen's famous poem "Of Being Numerous," a poem which I read as a testing of the same *context*, the same *reason*, that I, perhaps with less clarity and certainly with more verbosity, have been engaged with here. I had not been consciously thinking about Oppen's poem (nor, by the way, about this essay) when I first wrote and then began to study the phrase which initiated this essay: *along comes something—launched in context.* But certainly it has a parallel in the lines that follow those of Oppen's that I just quoted: "Occurrence, a part / Of an infinite series. . . . "

One can argue that Oppen (who, as you know, stopped writing poetry for a number of years and instead devoted himself to political activism) separated practical politics from poetry, but this is not identical with separating theoretical politics and ethics from poetry; it is not the same as doing away with a poetics.

Oppen's poem reflects (on) deep ambivalences over issues which have resurfaced with some sense of urgency in recent discussions about poetic practice, particularly in several recent papers that Barrett Watten has presented and in what turned out to be a controversial talk presented by Bob Perelman at the August 1996 poetry conference organized by Romana Huk in New Hampshire.[11] There, if I read them correctly, Perelman implicitly and Watten explicitly take contemporary "innovative" poetry to task for its *withdrawal* into numerousness. This is not to say that they reject "numerousness"; on the contrary, they espouse it vigorously both in their politics and in their aesthetics. Nor is it to say that a poetics of possibility is wrongheaded. But if we stop there, we risk a directionless pluralism, one we may claim as a politics but which stops short of activating relationships within that plurality—and lacking participation in that forming of relationships, "possibility" is likely to turn into what I believe to be a dangerous immanentism.

Similarly, to substantiate possibility as an absolute or to offer it as the *telos* of a totalizing vision was very much not Oppen's aim in writing "Of Being Numerous."

Peter Nicholls, in his recent essay "Of Being Ethical: Reflections on George Oppen,"[12] points to a resonant relationship between Oppen's concept of the "numerous" and characteristics of what is being explored under the rubric of "community" in recent books by Jean Luc Nancy (in *The Inoperative Community*), Giorgio Agamben (in *The Coming Community*), and Jean-François Lyotard (in *The Differend*), among others. As Nicholls points out, disturbed both by the totalizing mythos exemplified in Ezra Pound's writing and by what he termed "the closed universe, the closed self,"[13] Oppen based his poetics on acknowledgment rather than reification. Poetry would sustain "the relationship between things—the relationship between people; 'What it is rather than That it is,' as Oppen put it."[14]

But to say that a poetics is "founded on the . . . simple recognition of actuality" is not to say that it ends there. The concluding section of "Of Being Numerous" consists entirely of a passage from a letter Walt Whitman wrote to his mother, a passage describing a public monument seen in dying light. It is the Capitol Building in Washington, D.C., which is surmounted by an idealized figure of an American Indian in full feathered headdress—a monument whose intended symbolism must have been of dubious merit to Oppen. The last word of the passage, "curious," is separated from the text, placed the distance of a stanza break away.

Whitman: 'April 19, 1864

The capitol grows upon one in time, especially as they have got the great figure on top of it now, and you can see it very well. It is a great bronze figure, the Genius of Liberty I suppose. It looks wonderful to-

*ward sundown. I love to go and look at it. The sun when it is nearly
down shines on the headpiece and it dazzles and glistens like a big
star: it looks quite*

curious . . .'

Oppen, writing about this passage (in a letter to John Craw-
ford), commented, " . . . the poem ends with the word 'curious.'
I had set myself once before to say forthrightly 'We want to be
here,' and the long poem ends almost jokingly with 'curious.' But
it is not a joke entirely. If I were asked, Why do we want to be
here—I would say: it is curious—the thing is curious—Which
may be referred to, briefly, as O's Affirmation." [15]

This affirmation's operative term—*curious*—is situated in yet
another of the multivalent phrases which constitute the *reason* of
(and for) my title: *it is curious—the thing is curious.* One reading of
this phrase could lead to a paraphrase that says something like,
"the thing is odd, the thing provokes curiosity," but another para-
phrase could say that "the thing itself exercises curiosity." The
latter interpretation may push Oppen's intended sense, but not, I
believe, with a result that he would dislike.

The term *curious*, just as it names both a subjective condition
("marked by desire to investigate and learn" or by "inquisitive in-
terest in others' concerns," nosiness) and a condition of some ob-
ject ("exciting attention as strange, novel, or unexpected"), it also
names an interaction between curious subject and curious ob-
ject, an interaction within the terms of *curiosity.* As Oppen says
in another letter, "I ended with the word 'curious,' of which the
root is *curia:* care, concern[.]" [16]

6

What Oppen so aptly calls an "affirmation," though it concludes his poem, has a place at the start of it as well, since "affirmation" is what substantiates the phrase "There are things," and since it is curiosity—"care, concern"—which makes that phrase and those things count. But there is another way in which this "affirmation" is not conclusive; "O's Affirmation," like the affirmation which is a feature of the poetics I am describing—one that constantly questions assumptions, especially its own—is lodged in a dilemma, and therefore in that activity of mind which we term *doubt*. This *doubt* is not entirely unlike what Keats called "negative capability," but what is at stake is affirmation of our deepest reason, the one that tells us that things and our experiences of them count. That is what it means to be in history and in a history with a future—to be in reason.

But what we don't want, of course, is a reason that plows its way to authority.

In *The Human Condition*, Hannah Arendt elaborates a notion of a community of reason (in my sense of the term) constituted through action, creating new and hopefully ever better dilemmas for itself. Such a community of reason is boundless, according to Arendt,

> boundless because action, though it may proceed from no-where . . . acts into a medium where every reaction becomes a chain reaction and where every process is the cause of new processes. . . . This boundlessness is characteristic not of po-litical action alone, . . . the smallest act in the most limited circumstances bears the seed of the same boundlessness, be-

cause one deed, and sometimes one word, suffices to change every constellation. Action, moreover, no matter what its specific content, always establishes relationships and therefore has an inherent tendency to force open all limitations and cut across all boundaries.[17]

Authority over being is thus dispersed, not *because of* the boundlessness but *in* the boundlessness. We don't—as writers or as persons—go beyond "all limitations" and "all boundaries"—we enter and inhabit them. Faced with the notorious gap in meaning, we may ask, "What should we do?" But we already know what to do. And this knowing what to do is neither derived from nor does it produce guidelines—either prescriptive, proscriptive, or even descriptive. It is, rather, intrinsic to living in context. *Not* to totalize, *not* to pre- or proscribe—we know that this is some of what we must do. And we know that this is something we must do because we are alert to the context in which it must be done—in history and in reason.

Notes

1. George Oppen, "The Anthropologist of Myself: A Selection from Working Papers," ed. Rachel Blau DuPlessis, *Sulfur* 26 (Spring 1990), 159.

2. *Webster's Ninth New Collegiate Dictionary*, s.v. "theorem."

3. *Shark* 1, ed. Emilie Clark and Lytle Shaw (Berkeley, Calif., 1998).

4. This discussion is derived from that given by Pavel Florensky, in *Iconostasis* (Crestwood, N.Y.: St. Vladimir's Seminary Press, 1996). Florensky, a Russian philosopher, folklorist, and poet, died in 1937, a victim of the Stalinist purges, but prior to that, despite a tendency toward mysticism in the tradition of Tolstoi, his work and lectures were influen-

tial among the Russian Futurists and Formalists, and, after his death, his work, especially as it related to the structures of meaning and to the structures of the reasons one gets to it, have been continued by the Tartu school theorists more or less up to the present.

5. Hannah Arendt, *The Human Condition* (Chicago: University of Chicago Press, 1958), 177.

6. Ibid., 8–9.

7. Quoted in Viktor Erlich, *Russian Formalism* (The Hague: Mouton Publishers, 1955), 76.

8. Viktor Shklovsky, "Resurrection of the Word," tr. Richard Sherwood, in *Russian Formalism: A Collection of Articles and Texts in Translation*, ed. Stephen Bann and John E. Bowlt (Edinburgh: Scottish Academic Press, 1973), 46.

9. Leo Tolstoi, in his diary on March 1, 1897, quoted by Viktor Shklovsky in "Art as Technique," in *Russian Formalist Criticism*, tr. and ed. Lee T. Lemon and Marion J. Reis (Lincoln: University of Nebraska Press, 1965), 12.

10. I am here, as throughout, employing terminology that Jean-François Lyotard thoroughly—and, if I understand him correctly, with some of the same goals—investigates in *The Differend* (Minneapolis: University of Minnesota Press, 1988).

11. Bob Perelman, "Familiar Openings," paper delivered at the "Assembling Alternatives" conference, Durham, New Hampshire, August 1996. Barrett Watten, "New Meaning and Poetic Vocabulary: From Coleridge to Jackson Mac Low," *Poetics Today* 18, no. 2 (Summer 1997); "The Bride of the Assembly Line: From Material Text to Cultural Poetics," *The Impercipient Lecture Series* 1, no. 8 (October 1997); "The Secret History of the Equal Sign: L=A=N=G=U=A=G=E between Discourse and Text," paper delivered at a conference at Tel Aviv University, November 17, 1997.

12. Peter Nicholls, "Of Being Ethical: Reflections on George Oppen," in *Journal of American Studies* 31 (1997): 2, 153–70.

13. Letter to June Oppen Degnan, *Ironwood* 26 (Fall 1985): 223;

quoted by Peter Nicholls in "Of Being Ethical: Reflections on George Oppen," in *Journal of American Studies* 31 (1997): 2, 159.

14. Quoted in Nicholls, ibid., 160 n. 31.

15. Rachel Blau DuPlessis, ed. *The Selected Letters of George Oppen* (Durham, N.C.: Duke University Press, 1990), 402 n. 6.

16. Ibid.

17. Arendt, *The Human Condition*, 190–91.

A Common Sense

In various conversations over the years, Charles Bernstein has taken exception to my use of the term *theory* to apply to anything that poetry does. In part, as I understand him, he objects on the grounds that theory detaches itself from the object of its scrutiny and pretends to authority over it. And I suspect that he might also share Ludwig Wittgenstein's view that theory has no practical value. ("For me," Wittgenstein is quoted as saying, "a theory is without value. A theory gives me nothing.") [1]

Having myself posited theory as a near-synonym for thought, I wanted to examine more carefully the problem that Charles Bernstein and Wittgenstein had identified, and the invitation to prepare a new paper on Gertrude Stein gave me an opportunity to do so. It seemed to me that the "meditative" mode of the most difficult of Stein's works, *Stanzas in Meditation,* might elucidate the problem, to the extent that there is one, with theory.

What Wittgenstein meant in his denouncement of theory is that theory, as he uses the term, does not provide the rationale or justification for what we do. Nor is it a prerequisite for understanding. "Are people . . . ignorant of what they mean when they say 'Today the sky is clearer than yesterday'?

Do we have to wait for logical analysis here? What a hellish idea!"[2] Theory, then, for Wittgenstein is directly opposed to practice. Theory is a rope employed where a link is lacking: "Things must connect directly, without a rope, i.e. they must already stand in a connection with one another, like the links of a chain."[3] As Ray Monk in his biography of Wittgenstein points out, "Wittgenstein's abandonment of theory was not . . . a rejection of serious thinking, of the attempt to understand, but the adoption of a different notion of what it is to understand—a notion that . . . stresses the importance and the necessity of 'the understanding that consists in seeing connections.'"[4]

In seeing connections? It would be ludicrously arrogant for me to dispute Wittgenstein on semantic grounds, but it seems to me that this is precisely what theory does. And this is, indeed, different from what practice does—which is to *make* connections, to *forge* links.

Theory asks what practice does and in asking, it sees the connections that practice makes. Poetic language, then, insofar as it is a language of linkage, is a practice. It is practical.[5] But poetry, insofar as it comments on itself (and poetic form is, among other things, always a poem's self-commentary), is also theoretical.

Theoretical thought examines, theoretical thought makes meaningful. It takes into account and in doing so it makes what it is thinking about count. But there is a difference between thinking about and thinking, and thinking itself is meaningful too. Stein's *Stanzas in Meditation* is a poem in which thinking takes place in and of itself. It posits thinking as an "in and of" activity— a mindfulness, a casting of the mind in action. Neither in practice nor in theory is thinking separate nor separating; it is precisely the opposite, a mode of nonseparation, of conjunction. *Stanzas in Meditation* is, in this regard, a practice of theory and a theory of practice.

The conference, "Gertrude Stein at the Millennium," at which this paper was given was itself a model of conjunction. It took place on February 5–7, 1998, at Washington University in St. Louis, and was curated by Steven

Meyer, who decided in favor of emphasizing the artistic character of scholarship. In addition to Marjorie Perloff, Ulla Dydo, and Catherine Stimpson, all notable Stein scholars, participants included Joan Retallack, Jacques Roubaud, Stan Brakhage, Harryette Mullen, Kenneth Koch, William Gass, and Anne Bogart (under whose direction both a play about Gertrude Stein and a play by her were performed). Publication of the proceedings from the conference will hopefully take place in the near future.

> If I liked what it is to choose and choose
> It would be did it matter if they close and choose
> But they must consider that they mean which they may
> If to-day if they find that it went every day to stay
> And what next.
> What is it when they wonder if they know
> That it means that they are careful if they do what they show
> And needless and needless if they like
> That they care to be meant
> Not only why they wonder whether they went
> And so they might in no time manage to change
> For which which fortune they invent or meant
> Not only why they like when they sent
> What they mean to love meant.
> It is this why they know what they like.[6]

Things are always in the way. This is ordinary; the present is filled with the ordinary.

Indeed, the present itself seems always to be in the way. Between us and the past, in which lie events we might wish to recover or redo, as between us and the future, in which our desires might be satisfied, our ambitions fulfilled, or our visions realized, the present, though vexatiously elusive and seemingly momentary and minute, remains inescapably in place.

One aspect of why this is so is of particular importance. What we call the present is, to use Nietzsche's phrase, "the duration of 'the impermanence of everything actual.'"[7] "The present" is the name for the span during which the transitoriness, the finitude, of everything we identify as "real" exists. This condition is inherently and markedly paradoxical, and we are caught in the contradiction—regarding an infinity of finitudes under the sign of a moment that is within infinity and within finitude just as they are within it, the present. This is what is meant by "the routine": a present infinity of finitudes which cannot be anything but present: "every day to stay."

And the present is immured within itself, too. Though seeming to flow out of what has been and into what will be, the present provides access to neither. The present is an *in and of itself* condition.

As such, since, both as a finitude and as an infinitude, the present is cut off from the past, it has no story; or, to put it another way, it has no plot. The quotidian present is therefore independent of the cause-and-effect relations that create and propel plot. Quotidian conditions are just around—like sound effects in movies, which one hardly notices except if they are missing. In this sense, the quotidian present is a milieu consisting entirely of effects. The quotidian consists not of things but of effects playing over the surfaces of things; it is not beings but a way of being.

The present consists of the sensible world; indeed, the only sensible world available to us is the present one, and it is a world of sensory effects, effects which too are plotless. That is, in an important sense, at least insofar as sensory effects and the sensing of them only exist *presently*, they are causeless—and thus one could say they are unexplained and, perhaps, inexplicable.

What is persistently sensible in the present is the everyday, the commonplace, the quotidian. And the quotidian is notoriously intransigent. As Henri Lefebvre puts it, "The quotidian is what is humble and solid, what is taken for granted and that of which all the parts follow each other in such a regular, unvarying succession that those concerned have no call to question their sequence; thus it is undated and (apparently) insignificant; though it occupies and preoccupies it is practically untellable. . . . "[8] The commonplace is often construed as a realm of encumbrance and dispiriting dullness—under the pressure of the quotidian, life goes flat.

But for Gertrude Stein, perception of this flatness is a virtue, a creative property of what she identified as the "human mind"; unlike human nature, the human mind perceives without memory—it sees flat—and by virtue of this it composes masterpieces. As she says in *The Geographical History*, if things "did not look as if they were flat . . . they were not a master-piece."[9]

This observation seems to inform the opening two lines of *Stanzas in Meditation:*

> I caught a bird which made a ball
> And they thought better of it. (3)

The "they" in question here may indeed have thought better of it, or thought of it better—that is, thought in such a way as to improve a roundness, "a ball," by flattening it, either into the writing (the inscribing on a surface) that came to be *Stanzas in Meditation*, or by replacing "a ball" with "it." "I caught a bird which made a ball / And *they* thought better of *it*."

Perhaps. Though *Stanzas in Meditation* inspires vivid mental sensations that are tantamount to thought, to indulge in exegesis of this particular work is always risky. *Stanzas in Meditation*, most certainly, is meaningful writing, but that meaningfulness is not affixed to exterior reference points. The "it" (along with the work's many other pronouns, including the "they" of the opening lines) is undesignated, unassigned; and the work's "itnesses" —the shifting play of *it* over its quiddities—is what constitutes the "achievement of the commonplace" that Stein felt she had accomplished with this work—a shimmering, sensible flatness.

> Which may be which if there
> This which I find I like
> Not if which if I like.
> This which if I like.
> I have felt this which I like.
> It is more then.
> I wish to say that I take pleasure in it. (108–109)

. . .

The everyday consists of the play of effects, the play of life, over our quiddities, our things—the material things we have and the habitual things we do. They are our recurrences. They are that which is routinely happening. And as such they are what we take for granted. We take them as givens—gifts, in other words (though not always welcome ones).

> As I come up and down easily
> I have been looking down and looking up easily
> And I look down easily
> And I look up and down not easily
> Because
> It is this which I know

It is alike that is.
I have seen it or before.
Stanza XXXVII
That feels fortunately alike. (119)

It was through participation in the everyday with its "in-
evitable repetition," that Gertrude Stein first came to understand
the metaphysical as well as compositional force of habit.

When I first really realized the inevitable repetition in hu-
man expression that was not repetition but insistence when I
first began to be really conscious of it was when at about sev-
enteen years of age, I left the more or less internal and soli-
tary and concentrated life I led in California and came to
Baltimore and lived with a lot of my relations and principally
with a whole group of very lively little aunts who had to
know anything. . . . If they had to know anything and any-
body does they naturally had to say and hear it often, any-
body does, and as there were ten and eleven of them they did
have to say and hear said whatever was said and any one not
hearing what it was they said had to come in to hear what had
been said. That inevitably made everything said often. I be-
gan then to consciously listen to what anybody was saying
and what they did say while they were saying what they were
saying. This was not yet the beginning of writing but it was
the beginning of knowing what there was that made there be
no repetition. No matter how often what happened had hap-
pened any time any one told anything there was no repeti-
tion. This is what William James calls the Will to Live.[10]

And it is what here I am going to risk calling happiness.[11]

▪ ▪ ▪

"Once now I will tell all which they tell lightly." (7)

Gertrude Stein says in *The Autobiography of Alice B. Toklas* that she considered *Stanzas in Meditation* to be "her real achievement of the commonplace."[12] It was written in and of reality, or what her one-time mentor William James described as "where things happen": "Reality, life, experience, concreteness, immediacy, use what word you will, exceeds our logic, overflows and surrounds it . . . —and by reality here I mean where things *happen*."[13]

The *Stanzas* constitute a meditation in and of the way (or ways) of that reality. But what happens, happens as effects to beings— things that exist. Thus prior to (though not unconcerned with) consideration of whether the things that happen are good or bad, the meditation must inevitably begin in wonder at mere existence. In this sense the *Stanzas* are profoundly and primarily philo- sophical. They inhabit the astonishing and sometimes terrifying situation of improbability; the improbability of anything in par- ticular's existing at all. It is against all odds that existence comes to any specific thing, idea, person, event and against all odds that they should come into the purview of one's life.

We know that Stein was aware of the chanciness of life. Amelia and Daniel Stein had wanted five children, and it was only be- cause two died in infancy that first Leo and then Gertrude, the last of her parents' children, were conceived.

It is also well known that Stein wrote the *Stanzas in Meditation* concurrently with *The Autobiography of Alice B. Toklas*. And it is not surprising that, as she was writing a history of her life in *The Autobiography*, she would be conscious of the fact that her even having a life was, in her case, frighteningly contingent. As she says in "The Superstitions of Fred Anneday, Annday, Anday, A Novel of Real Life," "If any one is the youngest of seven children and likes it he does not care to hear about birth control because supposing he had not been born."[14]

To harbor a horrifying notion that one might never have lived is a version of the fear of death which is common to mortals. But in Stein's case it seems to have liberated her from the desire to cling to the past that is a common and logical result of a fear of one's inevitable death, since for Stein her death lay, as it were, in the past. Her near disdain for memory may have its origins here; for Stein to remember—to look back—may have been to subtract from life.

In any case, Stein was to a remarkable degree disposed to alertness to the liveliness of the present and the everyday, the mode of being that for Stein constituted "complete living": "if it were possible that a movement were lively enough it would exist so completely that it would not be necessary to see it moving against anything to know that it is moving. This is what we mean by life."[15]

As Heidegger had told his students in his phenomenological interpretation of Aristotle ten years earlier, one must philosophize not "about" factual life but "from inside" it. "The real foundation of philosophy," he argued, "is radical existential intervention and the production of questionableness; placing oneself and life and the crucial implementations into questionableness is the basic concept of all, and the most radical, illumination."[16] To place into questionableness is not a departure from but a return to the ordinary condition of things. And as such it is a return to the inside of the everyday. "We cannot, Heidegger states, view the life that we are in from the outside; we are always in the midst of it, surrounded by its details. Where we are there exists only 'this' and 'this' and 'this'. . . . This thisness is hard to bear."[17]

. . .

It is impossible to "explain" *Stanzas in Meditation*. This is not because meaning is absent from or irrelevant to the commonplace but, on the contrary, it is precisely because it is inherent to it—identical with it. When it comes to ordinary things, their meaning is the same as what they are. The meaning of an ordinary spoon is the ordinary spoon. Its meaning can't be separated from it. It exists ordinarily, as it were, to spoon, just as a carpet exists ordinarily to carpet, and so forth. In this sense, one might say that things thinging is their achievement of the ordinary, their achievement of the commonplace.

Understanding meaning in this sense is itself commonplace.

But, though it is ordinary—normal and routine—for us to know what things are and what they mean, doing so is not at all simple. To say that the meaning of a thing is inseparable from it is not quite enough; the meaning of a thing is inseparable from it in its totality. And it is this that is ordinary, commonplace, since this does not involve analysis—mentally taking the thing apart; cognizance and apprehension of a thing take place *prior* to analysis. In fact, we know what things are because and only because we know them in their totality. We see a spoon and know what it is without denoting it as 7-1/4 inches and 6 ounces of stainless steel, or as an ovoid bowl with a smooth, tapered lip at the end of a shiny curved strip. To analyze it, in fact, is to lose sight of what it is—that primary but not primitive, indeed highly complicated and rich experience of knowing what the spoon is—which is in its totality.

Stanzas in Meditation is written from within this immediate, ontological experience of the everyday. It doesn't express meaning in the ordinary sense of the term, as an independent feature that can be attributed to things. But this does not mean that the work denies or disdains meaning nor that it sets it afloat by relegating it to the notorious gap between signifier and signified. *Stanzas in Meditation* is not about the impossibility of meaning but about its pervasive presence. And the substance of the meditation—its content, if not its goal (the meditation is not a project nor even a study, and unlike projects and studies, unlike *Tender Buttons* and *The Making of Americans*, for example, it has no goal)—but the substance of the meditation is the recurrent coming into appearance, the phenomenology, of meanings, the varieties of meanings, the demands of meanings, the endless and difficult meaningfulness that faces one everyday. The meditation is not simply a response to meaning; rather, it is the articulation of being in meaning—in the stream of meaning.

This stream, if I can extend the metaphor, does not always and everywhere run smoothly. It can be turbulent, especially when one is encountering the meaning and meaningfulness of other persons—what they mean to you, what they mean to themselves, what they want to mean to you (which sometimes but not always is the same as what they mean to themselves), what they want you to mean to them. This swirl of meaningfulness is part of the ongoing course of one's daily living among others.

■　■　■

The commonplace is a totality; a place, physical or mental, we (things that exist) hold in common with each other. It is the totality of our commonality; it is meaningful as that, as the place where we know each other and know we are together.

In ancient Greek thought, and hence for many political theorists of social space even today, this common place is political in character. It constitutes the *polis*. The political in this sense is not adjudicating and legislating but coming into appearance, and the polis is the "space of appearance": the place for "the sharing of words and deeds." The polis is, as Hannah Arendt puts it, "the organization of the people as it arises out of acting and speaking together, and its true space lies between people living together for this purpose, no matter where they happen to be. . . . To be deprived of it means to be deprived of reality, which, humanly and politically speaking, is the same as appearance."[18]

But Gertrude Stein was not a political writer. And for Stein the public sphere became increasingly problematic and for two reasons. First, because the public privileges what Stein (in her famous distinction between identity and entity) characterized as identity and in doing so suppresses entity, and second because the act of appearing in public (for the Greeks but also, I think, for Stein) per se produced a disseveration, which for Stein constituted the loss of and for the Greeks constituted an escape from the private domain, the household sphere. Gertrude Stein was, for all her interest in genius and masterpieces (i.e., in authority), an advocate of the household sphere.[19]

For the Greeks (and I am again quoting Hannah Arendt here), "The distinctive trait of the household sphere was that in it men lived together because they were driven by their wants and needs. . . . The realm of the *polis*, on the contrary, was the sphere of freedom[;] . . . the mastering of the necessities of life in the household was the condition for freedom of the *polis*."[20]

According to this view, the "necessities of life" are all those things that are required for biological sustenance—the building and maintenance of shelter, the making and maintenance of clothing, the growing and preparing of food, and so forth. The private domain is devoted to the cycles of human biological processes. And mastery of it—"the mastering of the necessities of life"—was in Greek times the task of slaves and of women, who precisely for that reason were precluded from public life.

But for Gertrude Stein, it was in the household sphere, in the domicile, that freedom was possible, not so much because the domestic was a feminine domain (the household being historically the only realm in which women could engage in seeing rather than in being seen), but because (and here Stein turns the Greek topology inside out) it was a world, as she put it, not of human nature but of the human mind.

The former consideration—that of seeing rather than being seen—comes up for the first time in the opening of the "Henry James" section of *Four in America*, written just prior to *The Autobiography of Alice B. Toklas* and *Stanzas in Meditation*:

> I am I not any longer when I see.
> This sentence is at the bottom of all creative activity. It is
>   just the exact opposite of I am I because my little dog
>   knows me.[21]

As she elaborated on this at much greater length (in *The Geographical History of America*, her next major work after *The Autobiography of Alice B. Toklas* and *Stanzas in Meditation*, and in which the distinction between identity and entity is an explicit and prominent theme), that which is seen (by my little dog and others) is "I," identity, the product of human nature, while that which can see is "I not any longer," entity, the human mind. Or, as she says in "What Are Masterpieces," "Identity is recognition, you know who you are because you and others remember anything about yourself but essentially you are not that when you are doing anything."[22] This dichotomy entails a conflict between identity (one's selfsameness, the consistency of what is perceived of one now with what is remembered of one from the past and expected of one in the future—that is, the way one is seen as a basis for being recognizable—and, perhaps, judged) and entity (a lively, enduring, pastless and futureless present, creative force of mind—neither woman nor slave, unclaimable and free). Identity was what *The Autobiography of Alice B. Toklas* was about; entity is the substance of *Stanzas in Meditation*.

The distinction between them is important, and it is critical to understand that entity is not to be construed as some human or even personal essence, it is not one's "inner," "truer" being; rather, it is that very freedom of mind that the Greeks attributed to the public sphere, a freedom which was the absolutely necessary condition, in Stein's view, for the creation of masterpieces.

> I am I because my little dog knows me.
> That is just the way history is written.
> And that is why there is really no writing in history.[23]

Masterpieces—works composed of what is really writing—are distinct from histories. "History deals with people who are orators who hear not what they are not what they say but what their audience hears them say."[24] As Stein saw it, *The Autobiography of Alice B. Toklas* was written for just such an audience. "[I]t was a description and a creation of something that having happened was in a way happening not again but as it had been which is history which is newspaper which is illustration. . . ."[25] In being an autobiography, this was almost inevitable. "[Y]ou write anybody does write to confirm what any one is and the more one does the more one looks like what one was and in being so identity is made more so and that identity is not what any one can have as a thing to be but as a thing to see."[26]

Works of this sort, then, are for the public sphere. And the public sphere, in enforcing identity, is anathema to the creation of masterpieces. "I am I because my little dog knows me but, creatively speaking the little dog knowing that you are you and your recognizing that he knows, that is what destroys creation."[27]

．　．　．

Because of the autobiographical nature of *The Autobiography of Alice B. Toklas,* it is a work of identity rather than entity. But perhaps that's inaccurate. Might there not be an alternative autobiographical mode?

> Autobiography number II
>
> Seeing everything as flat.
>
> When you look at anything and you do not see it all in one plane, you do not see it with the human mind but anybody can know that. It is naturally that. And so it is because there is no time and no identity in the human mind. . . .
>
> The human mind has neither identity nor time and when it sees anything has to look flat. That is what makes masterpieces. . . .[28]

Stein explains what she means by "flat" only through examples—the patterning in carpets or in landscapes—but it would seem flatness is an attribute of the composed—of composition (as she had learned it from paintings), and it would also seem to be attributable to the commonplace. Indeed, the two, composition and the commonplace, are interrelated. "The composition in which we live makes the art which we see and hear," she says at the beginning of "Portraits and Repetition." Or as she puts it in *Stanzas in Meditation:*

> What is a landscape
> A landscape is what when they that is I
> See and look. (119)

Stanzas in Meditation is just such a composition—a "composition in which we live," and in that sense rather than as narrative or history, it is autobiographical. The emphasis is on present living, the composing of which it is composed. The compositional field of the commonplace is the household sphere with its quotidian comings and goings, the mode is meditational (about which I'll say more in a minute), and its moment—because both present living and meditation are in and of the moment—is one of happiness: the will to live.

. . .

The quotidian, the commonplace, preoccupies us manifestly. It is the realm in and of which taking care, both physically and emotionally, occurs.

This "taking care" is what Hannah Arendt (in the extended analytic distinction between labor, work, and activity that occupies her book, *The Human Condition*) calls *labor*. As Arendt puts it,

> The "blessing or the joy" of labor is the human way to experience the sheer bliss of being alive which we share with all living creatures, and it is even the only way men, too, can

remain and swing contentedly in nature's prescribed cycle, toiling and resting, laboring and consuming, with the same happy and purposeless regularity with which day and night and life and death follow each other. . . . The blessing of labor is that effort and gratification follow each other as closely as producing and consuming the means of subsistence, so that happiness is a concomitant of the process itself. . . . The right to the pursuit of this happiness is indeed as undeniable as the right to life; it is even identical with it.[29]

Eudaimonia is what the Greeks called this "sheer bliss of being alive." It means happiness, but not in the form of a mood nor as the enjoyment of good fortune (both of which are inconstant); rather, "*eudaimonia*, like life itself, is a lasting state of being which is neither subject to change nor capable of effecting change."[30]

Happiness is a complication, as it were, of the ordinary, a folding in of the happenstantial. And since it "is neither subject to change nor capable of effecting change," happiness, like the commonplace, has no plot.

In this respect, it is *un*like *un*happiness, and unlike the bad things (evil, pain, injustice, etc.) that cause unhappiness, since unhappiness is a marked condition, firmly attached to plots (that of good vs. evil, of love and loss, etc.).[31] Happiness, on the other hand, is complete unto itself; it is atelic, goal-free, aimless. But if it is causeless, neither caused nor causing, can we then say it too, like the effects we attribute to the quotidian, is solely an effect?

. . .

To attempt to extrapolate a plot, a narrative (or a set of plots or narratives) from the writing of *Stanzas* is doomed to failure; it is not about causes or causation, the essential element of plot. In essence, in writing her two great works of 1932 Stein separated cause from effect. Where *The Autobiography of Alice B. Toklas* is a history of geniuses—causes (capable of being affected but never in and of themselves merely an effect),[32] *Stanzas in Meditation* is about effects. As Donald Sutherland says of it, "The nowness and thisness of a thought, not its connections with past or future thoughts or with an objective context of thoughts, are the conditions of its life."

And along with other prominent features of plotlessness (parataxis, a plethora of data or reference with an accompanying absence of explanation, etc.), *Stanzas* is a work of surfaces, composed of surface effects—among them, sound effects, visual effects, the effects of presences, and, most importantly, the play of deictic markers—pronouns like *you, it, we, they, which,* adverbs like *then, there, here, now*—shifting over the material of the work.

> If not only if not one or one
> One of one one of one which is what
> What it is to win and find it won
> This is not what I thought and said
> I thought that the summer made it what it is
> Which if I said I said I said it
> And they were using used to as a chance
> Not only to be which if more it was
> It was used for which for which they used for it.
> . . . .
> I will try again to say it if not then
> Then not alike there is no then alike
> There is no then not like alike and not alike

But that.
This which I mean to do again

. . . .

Little by little it comes again. (108; 118)

These surface effects are not superficialities in the derogatory sense. They are the rippling effects of what Gilles Deleuze terms "unlimited returns,"[33] a becoming unlimited. They are the all and the while of "all the while."

. . .

The notorious—or it might be more apt to say "the familiar"—difficulty of the *Stanzas* can be directly attributed to its being situated at the coinciding of all and while, in the interminable time of the everyday, where becoming (the particular time of individual elements in it) and being (the time of the entire system) coincide.

What we call the present is the point of emergence of each thing into everything, the terrain where the constant passage into relations, the coming of things to life, is occurring.[34] This is the point at which Stein situated her task of "beginning again and again."

But this passage, since it consists of the present, is also inescapable. Stein's "achievement of the commonplace" had to be impassable—an aporia, "the nonpassage, the impasse or aporia, [which] stems from the fact that there is no limit."[35] This impasse consists of eternally and infinitely recurrent immediacy. It is where the *difference* between the time of eternity and the time span of an individual particular can be forgotten—or where recognition of that difference can be deferred.

They could be thought to be caught
Or planned next to next nearly next to one time
At one time it was very favorably considered

. . . .

Now I wish all possibly to be in their shuddering. (85)

. . .

To say that *Stanzas in Meditation* occupies a space in which the difference between time as eternity, being, and time as change, becoming, may be forgotten is not to say that Stein is forgetful of time. On the contrary—she is entirely and persistently mindful of it. *Stanzas in Meditation* is an extended improvisation in and of experience in time and the chances of the moment.

And as an *improvisation*, the work has certain features.

In the first place, improvisation entails a certain condition of mind—which, for lack of a better term at the moment, I'll call doubt. The improvisational attitude resists attempts at totalization (truth, belief, etc.) in favor of unpredictability and incompleteness. To put in general terms something that in practice is very precise, I would say that the improviser takes a risk of a very specific kind—the risk that is incurred when one volunteers for doubt—when, through an act of intentionality, one wills doubting.

The improvisational approach, therefore, makes the artistic event *an adventure of the moment*. It occurs in time, and is concerned with precisely that—with being in time. And it takes place through the taking of a chance—the taking of one's chance, or the taking of one's chances.

In fact, one can't take a chance outside of time. The very taking of chance inserts us into time—into the present. To take a chance is to enter the moment in relation to it—it is, as musicians would say, a matter of getting *in time*, a matter of being *with it*.

To enter a moment in relation to it, one has to enter it with something. One is having a time with something—something whose presence, literal and metaphysical or metaphorical, one is in time with. The improvisation responds to something and, furthermore, in doing so acknowledges it. It announces that *this is happening*. It occurs in wonder at the miracle of the wholly improbable existence of something—the realization, as I said before, that, against all odds, a specific thing or person or event is appearing in one's life.

And not only does the wholly improbable happen, it happens regularly.

The wholly improbable is normal, ordinary; appearance occurs to things routinely.

. . .

Stein's "achievement of the commonplace" is necessarily improvisational. It is also not a narration but a meditation, "a discourse," according to Webster's *Ninth New Collegiate Dictionary*, "intended to express its author's reflections or to guide others in contemplation." But the word "meditation" comes from the Latin, *modus* (measure), and from the Old English, *metan* (to measure), and for Stein it appears to mean a prolonged present cogitation. The mental attitude (and concomitant state of being) necessary to it is an involving liveliness and, more important, readiness—being in array.

Stein's notion of meditation, obviously, should not be confused with the meditative practices that are fundamental to Buddhism. The very notion of a *language* of meditation is an oxymoron in a Buddhist context, since for the Buddhist, meditation is supposed to be substanceless—free of the specificity or worldliness (as image and/or concern) that language brings to thought.

Nor is it religious in any other of the conventional senses. But the *Stanzas* are informed by Stein's consideration—metaphysical and secular—of the composed and composing beings she called saints. As she says in "Plays," "All the saints that I made and I made a number of them because after all a great many pieces of things are a landscape all these saints together made my landscape."[36] In order to achieve this, Stein's saints carry the effects of composition. This is their defining feature.

But, though Stein's play of saints, her *Four Saints in Three Acts*, might be considered an idyll, *Stanzas in Meditation*, as Ulla Dydo has pointed out, should not. It is a meditation but not a tranquillity. There are passages throughout the work in which the stresses and strains, the perturbations, in Stein's household sphere are evident.

They are, I think, inevitable. Close observation of the everyday world reveals many things, and first among them is the fact that (to use Viktor Shklovsky's phrase) "Things stage periodic rebellions."[37]

And so, too, do people. We know now that Alice B. Toklas was engaged in a battle of sorts with Stein during this period. And to a degree, Stein's daily life may have seemed under threat, or at least her life with Alice B. Toklas may have been, since Alice had just discovered the manuscript of Stein's *Q.E.D.*, a novel whose existence and whose content, an earlier love affair with a woman named May Bookstaver that had been profoundly important to Stein, Alice had not previously known about. Alice felt betrayed by Stein's secrecy about this affair and, as we now know, she insisted that Stein alter the text of the *Stanzas*, replacing every instance of the word "may" with "can," for example, or with "April," as the case warranted, or occasionally with other words.[38] (I prefer the unaltered version, and it is from it that I have taken the quotations that appear in this essay).

But despite the stress of arguments and the dangers they imply—or perhaps because of them—ordinary things of one's quotidian environment may take on a hallowed quality. The aphoristic Russian memoirist Vasily Rozanov describes an instance of this: "The ventilator in the corridor hums distractingly, but not offensively: I started weeping (almost): 'If only for the purpose of listening to that ventilator, I want to go on living, but, above all, my *friend* must live.'"[39]

■ ■ ■

Stein, like Nietzsche, "perceives the abyss that separates true happiness from beatitude. Happiness . . . arises out of chance, hazard, accident, events, fortune, the fortuitous. Beatitude is not the height of, but the opposite of, this free and gratuitous happiness. The concern for beatitude expresses the will to conjure away that part of contingency that is the very essence of happiness. The man of beatitude no longer wishes to be exposed to the thousand blows of fortune, to the stupor and the rending that happiness as well as unhappiness provoke. . . . A phenomenon of withdrawal, flight, and resentment, beatitude always wants the unconditioned, the absolute, the eternal; it refuses, it impugns the tender, innocent, puerile cruelty of chance; it casts an evil eye on all the favors and disfavors of existence. It says *no* to life."[40]

Happiness, on the other hand, in its very ordinariness, says *yes*.

"The human mind can say yes and no the human mind can even know that there is yes and no . . . ," Stein says in *The Geographical History of America*.

> [T]he human mind, the human mind can know that there is
>   yes and no.
>   Yes that is the way I mean to please.
> Think how that sentence goes.
> Yes that is the way I mean to, please.
> Well anyway.
> That is what I mean to be I mean to be the one who can and
>   does have as ordinary ideas as these.[41]

As we get it from the Greeks, happiness, we must remember, is a philosophical concept. And as such, it has a logic. But it is the logic of the circumstantial. It is a logic that was implicit in Heraclitus's system of thought and first elaborated by the Stoics. It is expressed with everyday elegance by George Oppen, when he says, "I accept things in the terms in which they offer themselves for one accepts life in this way or not at all."[42]

Stein's meditation is without tale and, unless one wants to extrapolate a "lesson" from it, without moral. It defies exegesis, but, though it doesn't *make* sense, it doesn't elude sense. The sense of the everyday is, after all, a given. And it is this sense that inheres in the *Stanzas*. Giving not the referents but the sense of the referents, the work is written in a language of "unlimited returns."

> Should they may be they might if they delight
> In why they must see it be there not only necessarily
> But which they might in which they might

For which they might delight if they look there
And they see there that they look there
To see it be there which it is if it is
Which may be where where it is
If they do not occasion it to be different
From what it is. (17)

Notes

1. Quoted in Ray Monk, *Ludwig Wittgenstein: The Duty of Genius* (New York: The Free Press, 1990), 304.

2. Ibid., 306.

3. Ibid., 308.

4. Ibid., 308.

5. It is, possibly, through association with "the practical" (and by virtue of the distinction between "the practical" and the strange or exotic) that Stein locates *Stanzas* in the commonplace.

6. Gertrude Stein, *Stanzas in Meditation*, Part V, Stanza 1, in *Gertrude Stein: Writings 1932–1946*, eds. Catherine R. Stimpson and Harriet Chessman (New York: The Library of America, 1998), 86–87. Page references to all subsequent citations from *Stanzas in Meditation* appear in the text.

7. Friedrich Nietzsche, *Philosophy in the Tragic Age of the Greeks*, tr. Marianne Cowan (South Bend, Ind.: Gateway Editions, 1962), 54.

8. Henri Lefebvre, *Everyday Life in the Modern World*, tr. Sacha Rabinovitch. (New Brunswick: Transaction Books, 1984), 24–25.

9. "I noticed to-day under a tree nobody was singing to me there they were just as they were but they did not look as if they were flat, so they were not a master-piece no indeed not." *The Geographical History of America*, in *Gertrude Stein: Writings 1932–1946*, 451.

10. "Portraits and Repetition," in *Gertrude Stein: Writings 1932–*

1946, 289. See the chapters entitled "Habit," "Attention," and "Will" in William James, *Psychology: Briefer Course* (Cambridge, Mass.: Harvard University Press, 1981); toward the end of "Attention," James notes: "The whole drama of the voluntary life hinges on the amount of attention, slightly more or slightly less, which rival . . . ideas receive. But the whole feeling of reality, the whole sting and excitement of our voluntary life, depends on our sense that in it things are *really being decided* from one moment to another" (209).

11. To attach an argument to the term "happiness" is risky because conventionally it is thought that the experience of it is psychologically and socially attached to conditions of privilege—privilege bestowed by fortune (in the form either of luck or of money). To speak of happiness, in other words, is to speak of privilege—at the very least, of the privilege of being fortunate.

12. *The Autobiography of Alice B. Toklas* in *Gertrude Stein: Writings 1903–1932*, 880.

13. William James, *A Pluralistic Universe* (Cambridge, Mass.: Harvard University Press, 1977), 96–97.

14. Gertrude Stein, *How Writing is Written*, ed. Robert Bartlett Haas (Santa Barbara: Black Sparrow Press, 1977), 25.

15. "Portraits and Repetition," in *Gertrude Stein: Writings 1932–1946*, 290.

16. Quoted in Rüdiger Safranski, *Martin Heidegger: Between Good and Evil*, tr. Ewald Osers (Cambridge, Mass.: Harvard University Press, 1998), 112.

17. Ibid., 113.

18. Hannah Arendt, *The Human Condition* (Chicago: University of Chicago Press, 1989), 198–99.

19. It is here, rather than in her love poetry, that any feminist claims for her work should be established.

20. Arendt, *The Human Condition*, 30–31.

21. "Henry James," in *Gertrude Stein: Writings 1932–1946*, 149.

22. "What Are Masterpieces," in ibid., 355.

23. *The Geographical History of America*, in *Gertrude Stein: Writing 1932–1946*, 424.

24. "What Are Masterpieces," in ibid., 356.

25. Gertrude Stein, *Everybody's Autobiography* (New York: Vintage Books, 1973), 302–3.

26. "What Are Masterpieces," in *Gertrude Stein: Writings 1932–1946*, 363.

27. "What Are Masterpieces," in ibid., 355.

28. *The Geographical History of America*, in ibid., 450.

29. Hannah Arendt, *The Human Condition*, 106–8.

30. Ibid., 193.

31. I am grateful to Dee Morris for pointing out this feature of happiness.

32. It is a person's capacity for causing, his or her causative character, that constitutes his or her identity.

33. Gilles Deleuze, *The Logic of Sense* (New York: Columbia University Press, 1990), 7.

34. Thanks to Peter Middleton who, having noted its pertinence to Hannah Arendt's discussion of "natality" in *The Human Condition*, pointed me to G. H. Mead's *Philosophy of the Present* (Chicago: Open Court, 1932).

35. Jacques Derrida, *Aporias* (Stanford: Stanford University Press, 1993), 20.

36. "Plays," in *Gertrude Stein: Writings 1932–1946*, 267.

37. Viktor Shklovsky, "Plotless Prose," tr. Richard Sheldon, in *Poetics Journal* 1 (1982): 9.

38. Both that altered version (in the Sun & Moon Press edition of the *Stanzas*, edited by Douglas Messerli) and the original version (in the Library of America volume, *Gertrude Stein: Writings 1932–1946*, edited by Catherine R. Stimpson and Harriet Chessman) are currently in print.

39. Vasily Rozanov, *Solitaria*, quoted by Shklovsky, *Poetics Journal* 1 (1982): 9.

40. Henri Birault, "Beatitude in Nietzsche," in *The New Nietzsche*, ed. David B. Allison (Cambridge, Mass.: The MIT Press, 1994), 220–21.

41. *Gertrude Stein: Writings 1932–1946*, 369.

42. George Oppen, archival materials, quoted by Rachel Blau DuPlessis in "The Anthropologist of Myself," *Sulfur* (1990), 26.

Happily

In responding to Dubravka Djuric's question about the origins of my interest in writing, I said that it was the materiality of writing that first drew me to it, the prospect of working with "the typewriter and the dictionary."[1] This is accurate as far as it goes, and I find among the quotations I've written into notebooks over the years a number describing their author's being prompted to creativity not by an idea or experience but by the materials of his or her medium. Thus Roland Barthes writes: "The word transports me because of the notion that I am going to do something with it: it is the thrill of a future praxis, something like an appetite. This desire makes the entire motionless chart of language vibrate." Eugène Delacroix: "The very sight of my palette, freshly set out with the colours in their contrasts is enough to fire my enthusiasm." Paul Valéry: "I go into an office on some business or other. As this includes writing I am handed a pen, ink, paper, all perfectly assorted, and I scribble some quite trivial phrase. I enjoy the act of writing to the point of wishing to go on writing. I go out, walk down the street, taking with me an urge to write, to hit on something to write about."[2]

But the impulse to write does not receive its charge solely from writing's material character. I have equally been excited into the activity of poetry by its revolutionary character and by its capacity to do philosophy.

I do not mean to make a grandiose claim to being a "revolutionary." But I have thought that the function of poetry was to address problems and to address problems very often puts one in opposition to established power structures, and not just those that would exercise authority over aesthetics.

It would be equally grandiose of me to claim status as a philosopher. And yet, in the end, it is as philosophy—as the making and seeing of connections (to repeat Wittgenstein's formulation)—that poetry participates in knowing what we can and can't know about the world and how to live in it.

Poetry's ability to contribute to the work of doing philosophy is intrinsic to its medium, language. Every phrase, every sentence, is an investigation of an idea. The last essay of the book, "Happily," is, as the title suggests, an affirmation—an affirmation of thinking, of thinking's substance and context (what happens), and of writing as the site of such thinking.[3] "Happily" takes the shapes of thinking, the phrases of poetry, as manifestations of life, and the essay, ultimately, is an affirmation of living.

Some of the ideas the essay incorporates are closely related to those I attempted to articulate in "A Common Sense," but here, in addition to the question of happiness, I was interested in the happenstances it inhabits, and in the "incorporation" itself of happiness—in the incorporation of thought as a coming-to-be in sentences. The grammar of sentences, both standard and invented, had again become a subject of fascination and even a pressing concern, and this continues to be the case.

One grammatical device appearing in the work is the one producing "accordioning" sentences, ones with solid handles (a clear beginning and a clear end) but with a middle that is pleated and flexible. My intention was to allow for the influx of material that surges into any thought, material that is charged with various and sometimes even incompatible emotional tonalities. These emotional tonalities make it impossible to say with certainty that one is happy, for example, just as they make it impossible to say that one is not. That is, one is never solely happy. "I mean, of course," as Robert Duncan says, "that happiness itself is a forest in which we are bewildered, run wild, or dwell like Robin Hood, outlawed and at home."[4]

I should, I think, acknowledge some creative indebtedness. Along with varieties of what Ron Silliman has called "the new sentence" in his own work, as in that of Barrett Watten, Carla Harryman, Bob Perelman, Jean Day, Kit Robinson, and others, the sentences of three writers in particular have been central to my attempts to develop and amplify sentences of my own: Bernadette Mayer's radiating and run-on sentence, with its seemingly infinite capacity for digression; Leslie Scalapino's sentence of nonseparation, of simultaneity, of fragments conjoining into wholeness in mental action; and Clark Coolidge's sentence of abrupt hinges, sudden linkages.[5] I should also acknowledge an obvious influence in Gertrude Stein's writing of and in sentences. And I am happy to confess a love for the sentences of Marcel Proust and for those of the writer who inspired him, John Ruskin.

Portions of "Happily," occasionally in somewhat different versions, have appeared in *Boundary* 2, *Debt, lingo, Interchange, Shiny, Mirage #4/Period[ical], Kunapipi,* and *Kenning*. I am grateful to the editors of these magazines for their encouragement. Beyond that, and from the very start, I owe a debt of gratitude to Simone Fattal, who, in commissioning a work for her Post-Apollo Press small book series, invited "Happily" into existence.

Constantly I write this happily
Hazards that hope may break open my lips
What I feel is taking place, a large context, long yielding, and to
    doubt it would be a crime against it
I sense that in stating "this is happening"
Waiting for us?

It has existence in fact without that

We came when it arrived

Here I write with inexact straightness but into a place in place
immediately passing between phrases of the imagination

Flowers optimistically going to seed, fluttering candles lapping
the air, persevering saws swimming into boards, buckets tak-
ing dents, and the hands on the clock turning—*they* aren't
melancholy

Whether or not the future looks back to trigger a longing for
consonance grieving over brevity living is "unfinished work"
to remember to locate something in times to come

Sure a terrible thing whistling at the end of the rope is a poor
way of laughing

And okay in the dim natural daylight producing it in fragments
to the skeptic to take it is recognizable

Only the dull make no response

Each reality needs to be affirmed

Several reasons can be linked to all that we ascribe to that

And whether or not a dog sees a rainbow as mere scratches sus-
pending judgment, all gesture invisibly as we all think what
we think to form a promising mode of communication bob-
bing something

The day is promising

Along comes something—launched in context

In context to pass it the flow of humanity divides and on the
other side unites

All gazing at the stars bound in a black bow

I am among them thinking thought through the thinking
thought to no conclusion

Context is the chance that time takes

Our names tossed into the air scraped in the grass before hav-
   ing formed any opinion leaving people to say only that there
   was a man who happened on a cart and crossed a gnarled
   field and there was a woman who happened on a cart and
   crossed a gnarled field too

Is happiness the name for our (involuntary) complicity with
   chance?

Anything could happen

A boy in the sun drives nails into a fruit a sign (cloud) in the
   wind swings

A woman descends a ladder into mud it gives way

But today's thought is different

Better to presuppose late

We eat with relief from our formlessness

Each day is drawn to its scene or scene to its day the image al-
   ready under way and formed to proceed

Perhaps happiness is what we volunteer

A cormorant appears in the sun flashing exact notes, a phenom-
   enon of a foggy day stretching its wings

Madame Cézanne offers herself in homage with its various uses
   with its curve and blank stare

It resembles an apple

And the most unexpected aspect of this activity dependent on
   nothing personal is that it consists of praise coming by
   chance, viz., happiness, into the frame of the world

It is midday a sentence its context—history with a future

The blue is sky at all high points and the shadow underfoot
   moves at zero point

Someone speaks it within reason

The one occupied by something launched without endpoint

Flaubert said he wanted his sentences *erect while running—*
 almost an impossibility

Nonetheless, though its punctuation is half hoping for failure,
 the sentence makes an irrevocable address to life

And though the parrot speaks but says nothing this has the
 impact of an aphorism

Are you there?

I'm here

Is that a *yes* or a *no?*

The writer over the page is driven down but like a robin by a
 worm

The visible world is drawn

Sentence meaning reason

Without that nothing recurs

Joy—a remnant of an original craziness we can hardly remem-
 ber—it exists, everything does, without us

There is music recognizing recognition we know about bound-
 aries and boundaries wound up

No straight line the riddle set I am tempted to say rough circles
 hazards lips that only things can differ

It's not not me I'm afraid saying *this* is *thus*

A name by chance for anything on which we have no claim

Everything for the magician is accidental

All that could possibly happen to the magical prop becomes
 intrinsic to it and knowing "all that" (could possibly happen)
 is what constitutes a magician's knowledge which is changed
 by the stopping of the thought just as such an aphorism is

formed as the one that observes an event emerging just
where time is becoming attracted to a particular thing (say, a
branch hanging over a river) in a particular situation (say,
mirrored in hilarity)

The event is the adventure of that moment

Then seven more days of heavy rain, one drop after another a
relay that is all in the passing by that is inside it (the by-
passing, all washed away)

If I were a fictional character thinking back she might be weep-
ing in a hundred bedrooms tonight wanting to be good long
after this depiction of wanting to have been good

But what is it that Plotinus says—the "good" will not be some-
thing brought in from the outside?

Is it then a pleasure covered in all seasons out of bounds beyond
the interior chain around the vernacular meant to bring us
in, you know what I mean, I see what you're saying, and so on

The good is the chance with things that happen that inside and
out time takes

It's midday a sentence, then night another

The sentence arachnid, a so-called "riddle figure"

Sense for its own sake saying at the same time something and
its meaning "only the gust outside crossed the slate," "only
the shale span caught at the consciousness that makes even
sleep delicious"

Susceptible to happiness I was thinking of nothing

Thinking thing linking that to which thought goes back, the
thing arrives

Tightly the hands of the clock turn but other elements also
must conduct logic

The good of it be it love or touchiness in idleness sunk in
  proximity

For an appearance not to seem the result of chance it has to
  seem (appear) to have been what one was waiting for
What is a slip of the tongue in quickening tempo over itself the
  busy world seeking out a given time interval or probing it
Suddenly it encounters a wind, an onion, a reason
They yield to classification but don't explain how they got here
Nor why this "here" is more than an island of isolated rational-
  ity or music, a little pool created by light generated by elec-
  tricity whose source we can only locate "somehow," "some-
  where"
Happening and looked at, blackbirds peppered with buckshot
  because they peck the corn, jays pelted with beebees because
  they steal eggs and then quarrel with them
I can always wait sometimes, other times impatience overcomes
  me like a disease effacing the fingerprints of the naked hand
  on my inner nature which chance bothered to put there,
  beauty scratched out, and history answered in the affirmative
There really is something to try over
To the air to draw sentence forms and to hang in suspense no
  further than this no more than need be
Reason offers
Reason in sentences covers kindness—doorways, bridges,
  floorboards
Reason opens approaches
Reason describes an artificial (there is no other) paradise and
  succumbs to lethargy, indifference, the world changing, un-
  changing, and it is, it comes with a musical shock

Perhaps it is the role of art to provide us with this chance that is
Perhaps it is the role of art to put us in complicity with things
    as they happen
Dropped points and falling notes to situation baffling to context
Launched?
Nothing is not so

The manner in which we are present at this time to and fro
    appears, we come to point of view before us
The matter is here
Can we share its kind of existence?
"I" moving about unrolled barking at blue clouds devoted—
    to each other? to hasten to the point? to evade anxiety? to
    picture?
Having awkward heaviness "I" never moves freely about unless
    passing and happening accompanied
Our pleasure is perplexed beyond that

If we thrill to low hills because they are not composed they are
    "composed to our liking"
They say there is no defining that but to say that is defining
    that, living in context
One would think of all the social forces traveling with a show
    of indifference over a crowd or sound brought to a sound
A good person would be starred ill and well in a life he or she
    couldn't know how to refuse
Every day we may never happen on the object hung on a mere
    chance
When and where one happens it will surprise us not in itself but
    in its coming to our attention not as something suddenly

present but as something that's been near for a long time
and that we have only just *noticed*

When we might ask did we begin to share that existence

What have we overlooked

Nostalgia is another name for one's sense of loss at the thought
that one has sadly gone along happily overlooking some-
thing, who knows what

Perhaps there were three things, no one of which made sense of
the other two

A sandwich, a wallet, and a giraffe

Logic tends to force similarities but that's not what we mean by
"sharing existence"

The matter is incapable of being caused, incapable of not being
so, condensed into a cause—a bean, captive forever

Perhaps

Because this object is so tiny

A store of intellect, a certain ethical potential, something that
will hold good

Like ants swarming into pattern we get to the middle of the day
many distinct sensations that must be it

Music checks the relaxation the contrasting aspects constantly
changing set going

The ceaseless onset cuts this recognized sensation hurrying
after it alive

It seems we've committed ourselves

That something exists at all is its nakedness we could term fate
and rising curves fate

That it should succeed already has been determined

And we have only to add on to it everything and everyone associated with it from beginning to end sustaining familiar acts

One is stung by a bee and it is noticeable that the whole body is involved

Why isolate part of the field?

Say we look on a mountain scene changing colors, the walls of a room vividly experienced from inside it

Why speak as if there were some incompatibility

Of what would it consist

Even after the closeness of the room which is now vacant I rise at the thought of the future of all the positions of things and re-enter the room

What is the Greek word for that, the big chance for each event—*kairos?*

Normally we don't notice that things we use in being accessible are being set aside while the extra, superfluous ones remain material one can disturb

Once one's caught in it one can make a face which nothing de-limits from you, from me, from us

The face facing—how succinct!

There the never resting emphasis rests splitting all the proba-bilities converge

Do they have witnesses?

Tsvetaeva warns us: it can happen that "income tragically ex-ceeds expenditure," she says or rather it *will* happen that one can't find a way to spend as much life as accumulates to one

We care in time, scatter acts in accord with time supporting action

Does death sever us from all that is happening finitude

Yes, swim it does

I the wall saw it
We the wall

I'm often ambivalent, the artistic will being weak as well as
    strong about being seen heard understood
Whatever I see in thought as life I come to coming to me in
    history
At first glance?
What could we, mind wandering but never "free," do with the
    word "galactic"
Events are unscrolling, they cover my eyes, all familiarity naked

Launched, I need either clothes or a bed and a blanket to pro-
    tect my nature from nature's pranks
A dream unless you saw it too, which would throw the stop and
    start of sleep into question and deprive us of the knowledge
    of the comfort of the knowledge that we can sleep troubling
    us together side by side
Ever beginners until all is margin, warm and flat
How the near becomes far and the far becomes near we may
    try to discover but we shouldn't take the question too
    seriously
Stop and start doubtless is the very same as stop and start
    doubtful
In a downpour we don't count drops as no harm is done to the
    causal chain we're close to the ground to see each other
    clearly
One can't say that being human is voluntary but it does tell a
    story that to another human won't seem pointless

To another human one acts one intervenes

In the dream one is shivering, already shivering before the first
    glimpse of the dream, shivering at the *reality* of the dream

A headache could happen to anyone, disappearance to anything

This is that kind of life, that kind of world, and this is the kind
    of place in which one can easily spend a dollar but not easily
    on hay and not so easily see a toad, cod in the woods in a
    dream we talk more to hear

You laugh?

I was going to speak of doom eager to resume consecutive
    events plowing through the space surrounding them to
    something now, no ellipsis, just mouth open in astonishment
    or closed to suck quid and quod, that and what

Not proving but pointing not disappointed boldly taking aim
    obliged to acknowledge I admit to being sometimes afraid
    of the effort required for judgment, afraid of the judgment
    required

That can happen only after that it has happened is ascertained,
    if you can keep up, time can't be banished, being real

In the world we see things together, the judgments have been
    made, takes the chalk, draws the milky line

To say that the music pleases me is impersonal, also the great
    skua, a dozen things singly through different mental states,
    mental states here and there as if unknown to each other
    things happen to them differently

They can't anticipate each other but they aren't innocent of
    each other, the dead then alive knowing glances

Future detail of experience the same thing ours for nothing

more than noting that living harbors the half-desire for
anonymity self-consciousness diminishes within
Take fences—the mechanism of clocks harbors birds it pro-
vides a narrow escape

A story requires resemblance and the results are bound to in-
clude recognizable sounds in their totality as horns and
windmills and the story is "ours"
It turns over to today the body it contains, something alone in
whatever time across, being this of that, tenderly trying to
dispel the anxiety impeding pleasurable run-on regeneration
Imagining ourselves under a gray sky shining so brightly our
eyes can't establish any connections, a sky so bright that the
option of connection isn't open, this puts us in mind of be-
ginnings that reason can motivate but not end
Searching out streets which allow for faster movement through
this impression of something short-lived we can't retreat,
can't know where we are
We fret as if demented by different events in the dissatisfied
chaos that make incompatible claims
We go no more than a few feet before we come upon the ob-
stacle punctually
Happiness is independent of us bound to its own incomplete-
ness sharply
The day has come with both rational and irrational aiming at it
the future fork and set of feathers
There is activity in a life, i.e. conduct asserts the power of de-
liberating without knowing how a state of being is brought
into existence every so often often

The specific accident to specify something never allowed to
settle completely

Then the shout "I" and the response "me, too," the curiosity
grows

I can know you without yardstick or sleep, without analysis and
from near or far, but I can't know you without myself

What were the chances I would land on a ladder is the question
at which I'm laughing to experience the reality of what I my-
self am not

The closer expression comes to thought fearlessly to be face-to-
face would be to have almost no subject or the subject would
be almost invisible

And more is left than usefulness

It's this that happiness achieves

The riddle happening hitherto before

What is not is now possible, a ponderable

You muse on musing on—so much now but you do

You can rearrange what the day gets from accidents but you
can't derive its reality from them

The dot just now adrift on the paper is not the product of the
paper dark

Nearly negative but finite it springs from its own shadow and
cannot be denied the undeniable world once it is launched—
once it's launched it's derived

Tonight sounding roughly it isn't quite that only words can rea-
son beyond what's reasonable that I drop my eyes to

Something comes

The experiences generated by sense perception come by the
happenstance that is with them

Experiences resulting from things impinging on us

There is continuity in moving our understanding of them as
   they appear

Some which are games bring with them their own rules for ac-
   tion which is a play we play which we may play with an end
   we value not winning

The dilemmas in sentences form tables of discovery of things
   created to create the ever better dilemma which is to make
   sense to others

It seems very odd understanding as it occurs in these pages to
   know that salt is salt, tired reason reason

"Understanding" is used to apply discovery a term of affirma-
   tion but what of not entering

Happinesses are not events that not a time can be taken for

States of intuition may be only sudden

Now is a blinding instant one single explosion but somehow
   some part of it gets accentuated

And each time the moment falls the emphasis of the moment
   falls into time differently

No sooner noticed no sooner now that falls from something

Now is a noted conjunction

The happiness of knowing it appears

The calmer continuous, the cause continuous

Something that leaps into motion in the cold air uncovered in a
   motion

There's no one "correct path"

No sure indication

It is hazy even to itself

The trees moving slowly upward among the going and the

coming sensations through the wind's blown tones express-
ing our extension into the wind feeling such rapid empathy
that there is hardly time for analogy

Unlike each detail happiness comes to no end, no good but that
of something like the mouth in the windblown treetops
shaping a sound and I experience the experiencing effect of
it as an acknowledgement is discovered to begin that

There is no better correspondence

Human words like human hands undertake the pecking at the
sun on its rounds our turn tattered to it

So I turn to utter an outer thought and say it was an inner one
aloud and slowly

From something launched we extract our sentences

Altogether written, writing everything, writing mockery (of
vague physical complaints, political cliches, silence) beauti-
fully in a follow-up writing (rejecting self-containment,
without fear of standing face-to-face) as if we were
ephemeral we are here and we mark out our place in it

It's between birth and death our commonality and *our own* birth
and death we are incapable of experiencing

North, east, south, and west, the four directions turn in play
away we discover

Like dreamers at some precise instant now divided taking the
experience (world) into view asking what's to stop us some-
thing stops us

And why not?

Shadows always accompany something between what has been
and what is to come on the slopes as if pants and sweaters
have been dropped carelessly on them, sunlight on the clouds

From the second moment of life, one can test experience, be
   eager to please, have the mouth of a scholar, hands never at
   rest, there is no such thing as objectivity but that doesn't
   mean everything is unclear and one doesn't fail to choose the
   next moment for a long time
Time is seeing the seeing itself in time in progress black, black
   in progress like a thread from a sender (with scissors, but
   we'll come to that later)
Onward chanced back
Before seeing the light of day as a tantrum thrown by a land-
   scape painter first working in water colors then progressing
   to oils suspended in a void, dependent on nothing I saw
Time as something with no subject the word employed early to
   remark, other people could say as it completes its curve the
   way a bird takes on final coloring in an unobtainable form
   but the form approached stayed near and the bird has been
   there ever since which seems like a remarkably short time
Instead of making itself abstract it places itself to take what hap-
   pens to be happening to value finitude
If we don't take stories then doesn't each moment cease to be
   felt as an addition to the tally of our life and begin to be sub-
   tracted from the sum, the supply of moments you and I will
   get
One proclaims not to aim
But of course one aims, let's go back and observe the hesitations
To voice promise repeat
Yes

One might look at the clock and see hands turning in the air in
   a room quiet only in anticipation of some secret satisfaction

that time cannot bring as a bell to a boat or a trope to the
image in thought of a person in real or *this* life or the thought
of an image or of an iceberg green in vernal halflight

I always thought time burning any cargo one can't take along
where I gladly stood in the middle would be scholarly but it
is packed to the doors with impressions and makes wild
sounds or it moos

It is hard to explain time and time can't explain itself whether
it's alone or between two or more

Outside past the curb there are islands to be visited we are trail-
ing behind a bird time balances

We call back coming to the friends we leave behind help your-
selves make use of life and look on from there

We develop consciousness where we can see it is honey out of
the cup, a perturbation of mind

Life is thus commissioned to work more than moodily to push
time to lose something, the mirrors below the scissors dusty,
the eye to spiral slaps, the body pops the dead now alone
were it not for the blunder which triggers as it passes

A tragic figure

Heroic ellipses are just things unsaid, we disappear rattling and
indecent but we don't stop short and if stopping happens it
does so at length but it can't be measured

It logically creates a gap the sum the mess of emptiness, it's not
an isolation

The sun shines from the positions of the sun

A candid circle naturally but perhaps its candor is deceptive,
doing nothing like a whirlwind sweeping the world for its
playground, its circularity made significant by chance and
not by chance

What the circle does real and without contrary taking charge
  from one to another side of the fiery day is what the time of
  one thing and another together does taking itself unreaching
  from hour to hour while the reaching things change
Language is running
Language remains
Wanting to live it, having wanted to, we live we live in it
And we can say it has the air of command of a mystery of a joke
  in the work of a minute, the mind receptive to a certain
  wishing to say it ascribes to things not liking to lose things,
  laughing, listening to the sound
Suddenly all words in the terrain said and unsaid the same com-
  ing to a start work directly on the sense of senses
That it's now adequate to the occasion acknowledging its loss in
  metaphor is the sum of relations in the impossibility of plot
It is the losing or loosing of it flawed
It is sufficient to say so of it a happiness accepted
It is mumbling bulk or drawing
It is a map to its own imperfections
It is unwarranted

It is not like something that I can say anything but it is as some-
  thing of them
The cold to the body growing continually colder what we take
  are positions true of them come waking outside within
This point has to be reached to introduce the discussion of
  this point to produce an effect to raise the present to this
  point
If you ask what's under the apple skin you're exposing exposed-
  ness

You!
Me?

Of each actuality I'm uncertain and always was uncertain and
  such uncertainty is certain
One wants to remember actuality, what it was like in the morn-
  ing and then again if it came again in the afternoon or eve-
  ning mattering what its mattering was like
Actuality matters its own actuality as in actuality just as you can
  fall asleep anywhere but briefly there's the sound someone is
  making saying, "There was a river but it has passed, now
  there is a body coming out of a shirt and there is width"
  where we are when we think of something coinciding
There is a gray chair and on it a woman pushing now and then
  and inside is a man outdoors bending bundles
There is a window which is open noisily and through it one can
  follow a sound turned over a table to bed last night which
  was Thursday for only a part of it
In summer a city below a clock in wormy progress plays a
  prominent role in what might otherwise be hampered by
  sincerity but that wouldn't arrive for hours
Come winter I see particularly the foreshortened perspective
  disguise retreat and in no way get arranged
Come spring
The inevitable fall then is not now an admirable representative
  time though it once eagerly served
But there was such a beginning happiness at it that I could
  hardly be calm I blurted and then held my position like a
  statue in moonlight when comment comes slowly and must
  be read likewise

Comment that starts now and puts the music in the feasible
   confusion

Every moment was better later and it greatly changed ap-
   pearance

That is a step that can be seen to be time together followed—
   no shape or color is basic

An appearance ought to make one laugh who has nothing else
   in the world for amusement but meanings one can't help but
   anticipate

Does it all come to a distinction for accidental wanderings
   having to wait widening the view between optimism and
   pessimism?

Until they terminate? deny?

There are many senses in and of senses made in contact the
   muscles may receive in the pleasure of impossibility which
   must immediately and can never come to an end in a glut of
   swinging, a silence soon weary of earshot, a rueful immensity

No, happily I'm feeling the wind in its own right rather than as
   of particular pertinence to *us* at a windy moment

I hear its lines leaving in a rumor the silence of which is to catch
   on quickly to arrange things in preparation for what will
   come next

That may be the thing and logically we go when it departs

(for Larry Ochs)

Notes

1. See this volume, "Materials (for Dubravka Djuric)."
2. Roland Barthes, *Roland Barthes on Roland Barthes*, tr. Richard

Howard (New York: Hill and Wang, 1977), 129; Eugène Delacroix, *The Journal of Eugène Delacroix*, ed. Hubert Wellington, tr. Lucy Norton (Ithaca, N.Y.: Cornell University Press, 1980), 128; Paul Valéry, *Analects*, tr. Gilbert Stuart (Princeton, N.J.: Princeton University Press, 1970), 200.

3. A clear parallel to this thought is Louis Zukofsky's famous statement in "An Objective": "Writing occurs which is the detail, not mirage, of seeing, of thinking with the things as they exist, and of directing them along a line of melody. Shapes suggest themselves, and the mind senses and receives awareness." Louis Zukofsky, "An Objective," in *Prepositions* (London: Rapp & Carroll, 1967), 20.

4. Robert Duncan, as quoted by George Oppen, "The Mind's Own Place," *Montemora* 1 (Fall 1975), 137.

5. I would point readers unfamiliar with the work of these three poets to Leslie Scalapino, *New Time* (Hanover, N.H.: Wesleyan/University Press of New England, 1999); Clark Coolidge, *The Crystal Text* (Los Angeles: Sun & Moon Press, 1995); and Bernadette Mayer, *The Desires of Mothers to Please Others in Letters* (West Stockbridge, Massachusetts: Hard Press, 1994).

WORKS CITED

Adorno, Theodor. *Prisms*. Cambridge, Mass.: The MIT Press, 1981.

Alexis, Paul. "Naturalism Is Not Dead." In *Documents of Modern Literary Realism*, edited by George J. Becker. Princeton, N.J.: Princeton University Press, 1963.

Alferi, Pierre. "Seeking a Sentence." Translated by Joseph Simas. *Poetics Journal* 10 (1998).

Allen, Donald. Editor's Note to Jack Spicer, *One Night Stand & Other Poems*. San Francisco: Grey Fox Press, 1980.

Allison, David B., ed. *The New Nietzsche*. Cambridge, Mass.: The MIT Press, 1994.

Andrews, Bruce. *Love Songs*. Baltimore: Pod Books, 1982.

Andrews, Bruce, and Charles Bernstein, eds., L=A=N=G=U=A=G=E 1, no. 3 (June 1978).

———, eds. *The L=A=N=G=U=A=G=E Book*. Carbondale: Southern Illinois University Press, 1984.

Arendt, Hannah. *The Human Condition*. Chicago: University of Chicago Press, 1958.

Aristotle. *The Nicomachean Ethics of Aristotle*. Translated by Sir David Ross. London: Oxford University Press, 1975.

Augustine. *The Confessions of Saint Augustine*. New York: Penguin Books, 1943.

Bacon, Sir Francis. *Novum Organum*. Translated and edited by Peter Urbach and John Gibson. Chicago: Open Court, 1994.

Baker, Peter, ed. *Onward: Contemporary Poetry & Poetics*. New York: Peter Lang, 1996.

Bann, Stephen, and John E. Bowlt, eds. *Russian Formalism: A Collection of Articles and Texts in Translation*. Edinburgh: Scottish Academic Press, 1973.

Barthes, Roland. *New Critical Essays*. New York: Hill & Wang, 1980.

———. *Roland Barthes on Roland Barthes*. Translated by Richard Howard. New York: Hill and Wang, 1977.

Bartram, William. *Travels: Through North & South Carolina, Georgia, East & West Florida, the Cherokee country, the extensive territories of the Muscogulges or Creek confederacy, and the country of the Chactaws, containing an account of the soil and natural productions of those regions, together with observations on the manners of the Indians*. New York: Penguin Books, 1988.

Bates, Henry Walter. *The Naturalist on the River Amazons*. Berkeley: University of California Press, 1962.

Becker, George J., ed. *Documents of Modern Literary Realism*. Princeton, N.J.: Princeton University Press, 1963.

Beckett, Samuel. *Worstward Ho*. New York: Grove Press, 1983.

Bernstein, Charles. *The Nude Formalism*. Los Angeles: 20 Pages, 1989.

Bernstein, Charles, and Bruce Andrews, eds. "L=A=N=G=U=A=G=E Lines." In *The Line in Postmodern Poetry*, edited by Robert Frank and Henry Sayre. Urbana: University of Illinois Press, 1988.

Binswanger, Ludwig. *Being-in-the-World: Selected Papers of Ludwig Binswanger*. Translated by Jacob Needleman. New York: Harper & Row, 1963.

Birault, Henri. "Beatitude in Nietzsche." In *The New Nietzsche*, edited by David B. Allison. Cambridge, Mass.: The MIT Press, 1994.

Blumenberg, Hans. "Light as a Metaphor for Truth." In *Modernity and the Hegemony of Vision,* edited by Michael David Levin. Berkeley: University of California Press, 1994.

The Book of the Thousand Nights and a Night. Translated and annotated by Sir Richard Burton. 6 vols. New York: The Heritage Press, 1943.

The Book of the Thousand Nights and One Night. Rendered from the literal and complete version of Dr. J. C. Mardrus; and collated with other sources, by E. Powys Mathers. 8 vols. New York: Dingwall-Rock, Ltd., 1930.

Boyle, Nicholas. *The Poetry of Desire.* Vol. 1 of *Goethe: The Poet and The Age.* Oxford: Oxford University Press, 1992.

Bridgman, Richard. *Gertrude Stein in Pieces.* New York: Oxford University Press, 1970.

Brik, Osip. "Contributions to the Study of Verse Language." In *Readings in Russian Poetics,* edited by Ladislav Matejka and Krystyna Pomorska. Ann Arbor: Michigan Slavic Contributions, 1978.

Brinnin, John Malcolm. *The Third Rose: Gertrude Stein and Her World.* Reading, Mass.: Addison-Wesley Publishing Company, Inc., 1987.

Brito, Manuel, ed. *A Suite of Poetic Voices: Interviews with Contemporary American Poets.* Santa Brigida, Spain: Kadle Books, 1992.

Burton, Sir Richard. *Personal Narrative of a Pilgrimage to Al-Madinah and Mecca.* New York: Dover Books, 1964.

Butler, E. M. *The Fortunes of Faust.* Cambridge, England: Cambridge University Press, 1952.

Cixous, Hélène. "Castration or Decapitation?" *Signs* 7, no. 1 (1981).

Cobbett, William. *Rural Rides.* New York: Penguin Books, 1967.

Cook, James. *The Journals of Captain James Cook on his voyages of discovery.* Edited by J. C. Beaglehole. Cambridge, England: The Hakluyt Society at the Cambridge University Press, 1955–1974.

Cooper, James Fenimore. *The Pioneers.* New York: Penguin Books, 1988.

Culler, Jonathan. *Flaubert: The Uses of Uncertainty.* London: Paul Elek, 1974.

Dante Alighieri. *The Divine Comedy: Vol. 1, Hell.* Translated by Dorothy Sayers. New York: Penguin Books, 1984.

———. *Literary Criticism of Dante Alighieri.* Translated and edited by Robert S. Haller. Lincoln, Nebraska: University of Nebraska Press, 1977.

Darwin, Charles. *The Voyage of the Beagle.* Edited by Leonard Engel. New York: Anchor Books, 1962.

Davies, Alan. *a an av es.* Elmwood, Conn.: Potes & Poets, 1981.

Delacroix, Eugène. *The Journal of Eugène Delacroix.* Edited by Hubert Wellington. Translated by Lucy Norton. Ithaca, N.Y.: Cornell University Press, 1980.

Deleuze, Gilles. *The Logic of Sense.* New York: Columbia University Press, 1990.

Dembo, L. S. "The 'Objectivist' Poets: Four Interviews." *Contemporary Literature* 10 (Spring 1969).

Derrida, Jacques. *Aporias.* Stanford: Stanford University Press, 1993.

Doane, Mary Ann. *Femmes Fatales: Feminism, Film Theory, Psychoanalysis.* New York: Routledge, 1991.

Donne, John. *The Complete Poetry of John Donne.* Edited by John T. Shawcross. Garden City, N.Y.: Anchor Books / Doubleday, 1967.

Doughty, Charles M. *Travels in Arabia Deserta.* New York: Dover Books, 1979.

Dragomoshchenko, Arkadii. *Description.* Los Angeles: Sun & Moon Press, 1990.

———. *Phosphor.* Saint Petersburg, Russia: Severo-Zapad, 1994.

Dreiser, Theodore. "True Art Speaks Plainly." In *Documents of Modern Literary Realism,* edited by George J. Becker. Princeton, N.J.: Princeton University Press, 1963.

Eco, Umberto. *The Role of the Reader.* Bloomington: Indiana University Press, 1979.

Eikhenbaum, Boris. "The Theory of the Formal Method." In *Readings in Russian Poetics,* edited by Ladislav Matejka and Krystyna Pomorska. Ann Arbor: Michigan Slavic Publications, 1978.

Eliade, Mircea. *Symbolism, the Sacred, and the Arts.* New York: Continuum Publishing Company, 1992.

Eliot, T. S. "From *Four Quartets*." In *Imagination's Other Place: Poems of Science and Mathematics*, edited by Helen Plotz. New York: Thomas Y. Crowell Company, 1955.

Emerson, Ralph Waldo. *Emerson's Essays*. New York: Thomas Y. Crowell Company, 1951.

Erlich, Viktor. *Russian Formalism: History, Doctrine*. The Hague: Mouton Publishers, 1980.

Flaubert, Gustave. *Letters of Gustave Flaubert 1830–1857*. Edited by Francis Steegmuller. Cambridge, Mass.: Harvard University Press, 1980.

————. *Letters of Gustave Flaubert 1857–1880*. Edited by Francis Steegmuller. Cambridge, Mass.: Harvard University Press, 1982.

————. *Madame Bovary*. Translated by Alan Russell. New York: Penguin Books, 1950.

————. *Three Tales*. Translated by A. J. Krailsheimer. New York: Oxford University Press, 1991.

Florensky, Pavel. *Iconostasis*. Crestwood, N.Y.: St. Vladimir's Seminary Press, 1996.

Foster, Elizabeth S. "Historical Note." In Herman Melville, *Mardi*. Evanston: Northwestern University Press and The Newberry Library, 1970.

Frank, Robert, and Henry Sayre, eds. *The Line in Postmodern Poetry*. Urbana: University of Illinois Press, 1988.

Freud, Sigmund. *The Standard Edition of the Complete Works of Sigmund Freud*, vol. 19, *The Ego and the Id*. Edited by James Strachey. London: Hogarth and the Institute of Psycho-Analysis, 1953.

Fried, Michael. *Realism, Writing, Disfiguration*. Chicago: University of Chicago Press, 1987.

Fuller, Margaret. "Summer on the Lakes, During 1843." In *The Portable Margaret Fuller*, edited by Mary Kelley. New York: Penguin Books, 1994.

Furst, Lilian R., and Peter N. Skrine. *Naturalism*. London: Methuen & Co., 1971.

Gallup, Donald. *The Flowers of Friendship: Letters Written to Gertrude Stein*. New York: Alfred A. Knopf, 1953.

Gavronsky, Serge. Introduction to Francis Ponge, *The Power of Language*. Berkeley: University of California Press, 1979.

Goethe, Johann Wolfgang von. *Goethe's Faust, Part One*. Translated by Randall Jarrell. New York: Farrar, Straus & Giroux, 1959.

Grant, Damian. *Realism*. London: Methuen & Co. Ltd., 1970.

Greenblatt, Stephen. *Marvelous Possessions*. Chicago: University of Chicago Press, 1991.

Grenier, Robert. *Cambridge M'ass*. Berkeley: Tuumba Press, 1982.

Grey, Zane. *Riders of the Purple Sage*. New York: Penguin Books, 1990.

Harryman, Carla. *Animal Instincts*. Berkeley: This Press, 1989.

———. *The Middle*. San Francisco: Gaz, 1983.

Heidegger, Martin. *On The Way to Language*. Translated by Peter D. Hertz. New York: Harper & Row, 1971.

Hejinian, Lyn. *A Border Comedy*. Forthcoming.

———. *The Cell*. Los Angeles: Sun & Moon Press, 1992.

———. *The Cold of Poetry*. Los Angeles: Sun & Moon Press, 1994.

———. *The Guard*. Berkeley: Tuumba Press, 1984; reprinted in *The Cold of Poetry*.

———. *Happily*. Sausalito: The Post-Apollo Press, 2000.

———. *The Hunt*. Tenerife, Canary Islands: Zasterle Press, 1991.

———. *My Life*. Los Angeles: Sun & Moon Press, 1987.

———. *Oxota: A Short Russian Novel*. Great Barrington, Mass.: The Figures, 1991.

———. *A Thought Is the Bride of What Thinking*. Willits, Calif.: Tuumba Press, 1976.

———. *Writing Is an Aid to Memory*. Berkeley: The Figures, 1978; reprinted Los Angeles: Sun & Moon Press, 1996.

Hejinian, Lyn, and Kit Robinson. *Individuals*. Tucson: Chax Press, 1988.

Hejinian, Lyn, and Leslie Scalapino. *Sight*. Washington, D.C.: Edge Books, 1998.

Hoover, Paul, ed. *Postmodern American Poetry: A Norton Anthology*. New York: W. W. Norton, 1994.

Irigaray, Luce. "This sex which is not one." Translated by Claudia Reeder. In *New French Feminisms*, edited by Elaine Marks and Isabelle de Courtivron. Amherst: University of Massachusetts Press, 1980.

Jakobson, Roman. *Language in Literature*. Cambridge, Mass.: Harvard University Press, Belknap Press, 1987.

James, William. *Essays in Radical Empiricism*. Cambridge, Mass.: Harvard University Press, 1976.

———. *A Pluralistic Universe*. Cambridge, Mass.: Harvard University Press, 1977.

———. *The Principles of Psychology*. Vol. I. Cambridge, Mass.: Harvard University Press, 1981.

———. *Psychology: Briefer Course*. Cambridge, Mass.: Harvard University Press, 1981.

Jameson, Fredric. *The Political Unconscious: Narrative as a Socially Symbolic Act*. Ithaca: Cornell University Press, 1981.

Jay, Martin. *Downcast Eyes: The Denigration of Vision in Twentieth-Century French Thought*. Berkeley: University of California Press, 1993.

Kolodny, Annette. *The Land Before Her*. Chapel Hill: University of North Carolina Press, 1984.

Kutik, Ilya. *Luk Odisseya*. Saint Petersburg, Russia: Sovietskii Pisatel, 1993.

Lee, Dorothy. *Freedom and Culture*. Englewood Cliffs, N.J.: Prentice-Hall, Inc., 1959.

Lefebvre, Henri. *Everyday Life in the Modern World*. Translated by Sacha Rabinovitch. New Burnswick, N.J.: Transaction Books, 1984.

Lemon, Lee T., and Marion J. Reis, trans. and eds. *Russian Formalist Criticism*. Lincoln: University of Nebraska Press, 1965.

Levin, David Michael, ed., *Modernity and the Hegemony of Vision*. Berkeley: University of California Press, 1994.

Lewis, Meriwether, and William Clark. *The History of the Lewis and*

Clark Expedition. 3 vols. Edited by Elliott Coues. New York: Dover Publications.

Lindsay, Jack. *Cézanne: His Life and Art.* London: Evelyn, Adams & Mackay, 1969.

London, Jack. *Martin Eden.* New York: Macmillan Publishing Co., 1978.

Lotman, Jurij. *The Structure of the Artistic Text.* Translated by Gail Lenhoff and Ronald Vroon. Ann Arbor: Michigan Slavic Contributions, 1977.

Lotman, Iurii M., Lidiia Ia. Ginsburg, and Boris A. Uspenskii. *The Semiotics of Russian Cultural History.* Edited by Alexander D. Nakhimovsky and Alice Stone Nakhimovsky. Ithaca, N.Y.: Cornell University Press, 1985.

Luhan, Mabel Dodge. *Intimate Memoirs.* Vol. 2, *European Experiences.* New York: Harcourt, Brace, 1935.

Lyotard, Jean-François. *The Differend.* Minneapolis: University of Minnesota Press, 1988.

Mack, Gerstle. *Paul Cézanne.* New York: Alfred A. Knopf, 1935.

Mackey, Nathaniel. "Other: From Noun to Verb." *Representations* 39 (Summer 1992).

Marks, Elaine. *Signs* 3, no. 4 (Summer 1978).

Marks, Elaine, and Isabelle de Courtivron, eds. *New French Feminisms.* Amherst: University of Massachusetts Press, 1980.

Marlowe, Christopher. *Doctor Faustus.* New York: Signet, 1969.

Matejka, Ladislav, and Krystyna Pomorska, eds. *Readings in Russian Poetics.* Ann Arbor: Michigan Slavic Contributions, 1978.

Mayer, Bernadette. *Midwinter Day.* Berkeley: Turtle Island, 1982.

Mead, George Herbert. *Philosophy of the Present.* Chicago: Open Court Publishing Company, 1932.

Merleau-Ponty, Maurice. *The Phenomenology of Perception.* Translated by Colin Smith. London: Routledge & Kegan Paul, 1962.

Messerli, Douglas, ed. *"Language" Poetries.* New York: New Directions, 1987.

Monk, Ray. *Ludwig Wittgenstein: The Duty of Genius*. New York: The Free Press, 1990.

Nadeau, Maurice. *The Greatness of Flaubert*. Translated by Barbara Bray. New York: The Library Press, 1972.

Nicholls, Peter. "Of Being Ethical: Reflections on George Oppen." *Journal of American Studies* 31 (1997).

Nielsen, Aldon Lynn. *Reading Race: White American Poets and the Racial Discourse in the Twentieth Century*. Athens: University of Georgia Press, 1988.

Nietzsche, Friedrich. *Philosophy in the Tragic Age of the Greeks*. Translated by Marianne Cowan. South Bend, Ind.: Gateway Editions, 1962.

Oppen, George. "The Anthropologist of Myself: A Selection from Working Papers." Edited by Rachel Blau DuPlessis. *Sulfur* 26 (Spring 1990).

———. *Collected Poems*. New York: New Directions, 1975.

———. *The Selected Letters of George Oppen*. Edited by Rachel Blau Du-Plessis. Durham, N.C.: Duke University Press, 1990.

Perelman, Bob. *Primer*. Berkeley: This Press, 1981.

———, ed. *Writing/Talks*. Carbondale: Southern Illinois University Press, 1985.

Perloff, Marjorie. *The Poetics of Indeterminacy: Rimbaud to Cage*. Princeton, N.J.: Princeton University Press, 1981.

Ponge, Francis. *The Power of Language*. Translated by Serge Gavronsky. Berkeley: University of California Press, 1979.

Pound, Ezra. *Literary Essays*. New York: New Directions, 1978.

Proust, Marcel. *Remembrance of Things Past*. Translated by C. K. Scott-Moncrieff and Terence Kilmartin. New York: Random House, 1981.

Rewald, John. *Cézanne and America: Dealers, Collectors, Artists and Critics 1891–1921*. Princeton: Princeton University Press, 1989.

Rimbaud, Arthur. *Arthur Rimbaud: Complete Works*. Translated by Paul Schmidt. New York: Harper & Row Publishers, 1976.

Robinson, Kit. *Ice Cubes*. New York: Roof Books, 1987.

Rosen, Charles, and Henri Zerner. *Romanticism and Realism: The Mythology of Nineteenth-Century Art.* New York: The Viking Press, 1984.

———. "What Is, and Is Not, Realism?" *New York Review of Books* (February 18, 1982, and March 4, 1982).

Rozanov, Vasily. *Solitaria*, quoted by Viktor Shklovsky in "Plotless Prose," *Poetics Journal* 1 (1982).

Russell, Bertrand. *Our Knowledge of the External World.* London: Allen & Unwin, 1926.

Safranski, Rüdiger. *Martin Heidegger: Between Good and Evil.* Translated by Ewald Osers. Cambridge, Mass.: Harvard University Press, 1998.

St. John de Crèvecoeur, J. Hector. *Letters from an American Farmer and Sketches of Eighteenth-Century America.* New York: Penguin Books, 1986.

Saussure, Ferdinand de. *Course in General Lingustics.* Edited by Charles Bally and Albert Sechehaye with Albert Reidlinger. Translated by Wade Baskin. London: Peter Owen, 1960.

Scalapino, Leslie. *Crowd and not evening or light.* Oakland: O Books; Los Angeles: Sun & Moon Press, 1992.

———. *Defoe.* Los Angeles: Sun & Moon Press, 1994.

———. *The Front Matter, Dead Souls.* Hanover, N.H.: Wesleyan University Press, 1996.

———. *Objects in the Terrifying Tense / Longing From Taking Place.* New York: Roof Books, 1993.

———. *The Return of Painting, The Pearl, and Orion.* San Francisco: Northpoint Press, 1991.

———. *The Weatherman Turns Himself In.* Tenerife, Canary Islands: Zasterle Press, 1995.

Seferis, George. *A Poet's Journal.* Translated by Athan Anagnostopoulos. Cambridge, Mass.: Harvard University Press, Belknap Press, 1974.

Shakespeare, William. *Shakespeare's Sonnets.* New Haven: Yale University Press, 1977.

Shklovsky, Viktor. "Art as Technique." In *Russian Formalist Criticism,* edited and translated by Lee T. Lemon and Marion J. Reis. Lincoln: University of Nebraska Press, 1965.

———. "Plotless Prose." Translated by Richard Sheldon, in *Poetics Journal* 1 (1982).

———. *Theory of Prose*. Translated by Benjamin Sher. Elmwood Park, Ill.: Dalkey Archive Press, 1990.

Silliman, Ron. *The New Sentence*. New York: Roof Books, 1987.

Spicer, Jack. *One Night Stand & Other Poems*. San Francisco: Grey Fox Press, 1980.

Sprat, Thomas. *The History of the Royal-Society of London, for the Improving of Natural Knowledge*. London: Royal Society, 1667.

Stafford, Barbara Maria. *Body Criticism: Imagining the Unseen in Enlightenment Art and Medicine*. Cambridge, Mass.: The MIT Press, 1991.

———. *Voyage into Substance: Art, Science, Nature, and the Illustrated Travel Account, 1760–1840*. Cambridge, Mass.: The MIT Press, 1984.

Stein, Gertrude. *As Fine as Melanctha*. New York: Books for Libraries Press, 1969.

———. *The Autobiography of Alice B. Toklas*. In *Gertrude Stein: Writings 1932–1946*, edited by Catharine R. Stimpson and Harriet Chessman. New York: Library of America, 1998.

———. *Everybody's Autobiography*. New York: Vintage Books, 1973.

———. *Four Saints in Three Acts*. In *Gertrude Stein: Writings 1903–1932*, edited by Catharine R. Stimpson and Harriet Chessman. New York: Library of America, 1998.

———. *The Geographical History of America*. In *Gertrude Stein: Writings 1932–1946*. edited by Catharine R. Stimpson and Harriet Chessman. New York: Library of America, 1998.

———. *Geography and Plays*. New York: Something Else Press, 1968.

———. *Gertrude Stein: Writings 1903–1932*. Edited by Catharine R. Stimpson and Harriet Chessman. New York: Library of America, 1998.

———. *Gertrude Stein: Writings 1932–1946*. Edited by Catharine R.

Stimpson and Harriet Chessman. New York: Library of America, 1998.

———. *How to Write.* Barton, Vt.: Something Else Press, 1973.

———. *How Writing Is Written.* Edited by Robert Bartlett Haas. Santa Barbara: Black Sparrow Press, 1977.

———. *Lectures in America.* In *Gertrude Stein: Writings 1932–1946*, edited by Catharine R. Stimpson and Harriet Chessman. New York: Library of America, 1998.

———. *Lucy Church Amiably.* Millerton, N.Y.: Something Else Press, 1972.

———. *Mrs. Reynolds and Five Earlier Novels.* New York: Books for Libraries, 1969.

———. *Painted Lace.* New York: Books for Libraries, 1969.

———. *A Primer for the Gradual Understanding of Gertrude Stein.* Edited by Robert Bartlett Haas. Santa Barbara, Calif.: Black Sparrow Press, 1971.

———. *Tender Buttons.* In *Gertrude Stein: Writings 1903–1932*, edited by Catharine R. Stimpson and Harriet Chessman. New York: Library of America, 1998.

———. *Three Lives.* In *Gertrude Stein: Writings 1903–1932*, edited by Catharine R. Stimpson and Harriet Chessman. New York: Library of America, 1998.

———. *Useful Knowledge.* Barrytown, N.Y.: Station Hill Press, 1988.

———. *What Are Masterpieces.* New York: Pitman Publishing Corporation, 1970.

Stein, Leo. *Appreciation: Painting, Poetry and Prose.* New York: Crown, 1947.

Stephens, John Lloyd. *Incidents of Travel in the Yucatan.* Norman: University of Oklahoma Press, 1962.

Sutherland, Donald. *Gertrude Stein: A Biography of Her Work.* New Haven: Yale University Press, 1951.

Taussig, Michael. *Mimesis and Alterity.* New York: Routledge, 1992.

Taylor, Joshua C. *America as Art.* Washington, D.C.: Smithsonian Institution Press, 1976.

Thompson, D'Arcy. *On Growth and Form.* Cambridge, England: Cambridge University Press, 1961.

Thoreau, Henry David. *The Maine Woods.* New York: Penguin Books, 1988.

Tynianov, Yurii. *The Problem of Verse Language.* Translated and edited by Michael Sosa and Brent Harvey. Ann Arbor, Mich.: Ardis, 1981.

———. "Rhythm as the Constructive Factor of Verse." In *Readings in Russian Poetics*, edited by Ladislav Matejka and Krystyna Pomorska. Ann Arbor: Michigan Slavic Contributions, 1978.

Valéry, Paul. *Analects.* Translated by Stuart Gilbert. Princeton, N.J.: Princeton University Press, 1970.

———. *The Art of Poetry.* Translated by Denise Folliot. New York: Bollingen Foundation and Pantheon Books, 1958.

Warner, Marina. *From the Beast to the Blonde: On Fairy Tales and Their Tellers.* London: Chatto & Windus, 1994.

———. "The Silence of Cordelia." In *Wordlessness*, edited by Mark Verminck and Bart Verschaffel. Dublin: The Lilliput Press, 1993.

Watten, Barrett. "The Bride of the Assembly Line: from Material Text to Cultural Poetics" *The Impercipient Lecture Series* 1.8 (October 1997).

———. "New Meaning and Poetic Vocabulary: From Coleridge to Jackson Mac Low," *Poetics Today* 18.2 (Summer 1997).

———. *Total Syntax.* Carbondale: University of Southern Illinois Press, 1985.

Weissmann, Gerald. *The Doctor with Two Heads.* New York: Vintage, 1991.

White, Gilbert. *The Natural History of Selborne.* New York: Penguin Books, 1977.

Whitman, Walt. "Leaves of Grass." In *The Complete Poems.* New York: Penguin Books, 1975.

Whorf, Benjamin Lee. *Language, Thought, and Reality.* Cambridge, Mass.: The MIT Press, 1956.

Wilson, Luke. "William Harvey's *Prelectiones:* The Performance of the Body in the Renaissance Theater of Anatomy." *Representations* 17 (Winter 1987).

Wittgenstein, Ludwig. *Philosophical Investigations.* Translated by G. E. M. Anscombe. New York: Macmillan, 1958.

Wordsworth, Jonathan, M. H. Abrams, and Stephen Gill, eds. *William Wordsworth: The Prelude 1799, 1805, 1850.* New York: W. W. Norton, 1979.

Wordsworth, William, "The Prelude." In *William Wordsworth: The Prelude 1799, 1805, 1850,* edited by Jonathan Wordsworth, M. H. Abrams, and Stephen Gill. New York: W. W. Norton, 1979.

Zola, Emile. "The Experimental Novel." In *Documents of Modern Literary Realism,* edited by George J. Becker. Princeton, N.J.: Princeton University Press, 1963.

Zukofsky, Louis. "An Objective." In *Prepositions.* London: Rapp & Carroll, 1967.

ACKNOWLEDGMENT OF PERMISSIONS

"Preface to *Writing Is an Aid to Memory*" was first published in *Writing Is an Aid to Memory* (Berkeley: The Figures, 1978); it appears here with the kind permission of Geoffrey Young and of Douglas Messerli, who published a new edition of the work after the first had gone out of print (Los Angeles: Sun & Moon Press, 1996).

"If Written Is Writing" appeared in L=A=N=G=U=A=G=E 1, no. 3 (June 1978) and was reprinted in *The L=A=N=G=U=A=G=E Book*, ed. Bruce Andrews and Charles Bernstein (Carbondale: Southern Illinois University Press, 1984); it is published here with permission from the editors and the publisher.

"Language and 'Paradise'" was initially published in *Line: A Journal of Contemporary Writing and Its Modernist Sources*, no. 6 (Fall 1985), edited by Roy Miki, and it appears here with the permission of the editor of that journal (retitled *West Coast Line*).

"Two Stein Talks" was first published in the late Lee Hickman's *Temblor* 3 (Spring 1986). The essay was reprinted in *Revista Canaria de Estudos Ingleses* 18 (April 1989), ed. Manuel Brito, and by Janet Rodney in *Two Stein Talks* (Santa Fe, N.M.: Weaselsleeves Press, 1995).

Permission to reprint "Line" is granted by Charles Bernstein and

Bruce Andrews, editors of "L=A=N=G=U=A=G=E Lines," in *The Line in Postmodern Poetry*, ed. Robert Frank and Henry Sayre (Urbana and Chicago: University of Illinois Press, 1988) and by the publisher.

"Comments for Manuel Brito" was included in *A Suite of Poetic Voices: Interviews with Contemporary American Poets*, ed. Manuel Brito (Santa Brigida, Spain: Kadle Books, 1992), and it is reprinted here with permission.

"The Quest for Knowledge in the Western Poem" first appeared in *Disembodied Poetics*, ed. Anne Waldman and Andrew Schelling (Albuquerque: University of New Mexico Press, 1995), and it is reprinted here with permission from the editors and the publisher.

"Three Lives," which is scheduled to be published as the Introduction to the forthcoming Green Integer edition of Gertrude Stein's *Three Lives*, appears here with the permission of Douglas Messerli; Green Integer © 2000.

Permission to include "Forms in Alterity: On Translation" is granted by the Nobel Foundation, publishers of the *Proceedings of Nobel Symposium 110: Translation of Poetry and Poetic Prose*, ed. Sture Allén (Singapore: World Scientific, 1999). Permission to quote passages of poetry by Charles Bernstein, Kit Robinson, and Ilya Kutik is granted by the authors. Further permission is granted by Douglas Messerli, publisher of Charles Bernstein's *The Nude Formalism* (Los Angeles: 20 Pages, 1989). and by James Sherry, publisher of Kit Robinson's *Ice Cubes* (New York: Roof Books, 1987).

"Reason" first appeared in *Shark* 1(1998); it is published here with the permission of the editors, Emilie Clark and Lytle Shaw.

"A Common Sense," which (under the title "Happily") will appear as part of the *Proceedings of the Conference on "Gertrude Stein at the Millennium,"* appears here with the permission of Steven Meyer, organizer of the conference and editor of the proceedings.

"Happily" was published as a small book (Sausalito: Post-Apollo Press, 2000); its publication here is possible thanks to the permission of Simone Fattal.

INDEX

Text: 10/15 Janson
Display: Janson
Composition: G & S Typesetters, Inc.
Printing and binding: Sheridan Books
Index: Andrew Joron

CPSIA information can be obtained
at www.ICGtesting.com
Printed in the USA
FSHW022117311019
63640FS